THE VIETNAM WAR

THE VIETNAM WAR

CHRISTOPHER CHANT

CHARTWELL
BOOKS, INC.

This edition published in 2010 by
CHARTWELL BOOKS, INC.
A division of BOOK SALES, INC.
276 Fifth Avenue Suite 206
New York, NY 10001
USA

**Copyright © 2010 Regency
House Publishing Limited**
The Red House
84 High Street
Buntingford
Herts
SG9 9AJ, UK

For all editorial enquiries please contact
Regency House Publishing Ltd.

ISBN-13: 978-0-7858-2704-7
ISBN-10: 0-7858-2704-8

Printed in China

All photographs supplied courtesy of
Cody Images, except for both images on
page 236 which were photographed by
Dean Sharp.

CONTENTS

CHAPTER ONE • A LONG LEGACY • 8

CHAPTER TWO • THE USA BECOMES EMBROILED • 32

CHAPTER THREE • THE GULF OF TONKIN INCIDENT • 48

CHAPTER FOUR • 'ROLLING THUNDER' • 66

CHAPTER FIVE • THE FATAL COMMITMENT • 94

CHAPTER SIX • THE BUILD-UP IN THE NORTH & SOUTH • 130

CHAPTER SEVEN • THE SIEGE OF KHE SANH • 170

CHAPTER EIGHT • THE TET OFFENSIVE • 194

CHAPTER NINE • EXCURSIONS & THE FALL OF SOUTH VIETNAM • 232

INDEX • 250

CHAPTER ONE
A LONG LEGACY

BELOW: *Vietnam 1949. The French position is overrun by the Vietnamese after a five-hour fight during the Battle of Pho Rang in north-eastern Vietnam.*

RIGHT: *French troops at the commencement of insurgent action in the Tonkin area in 1947.*

Also known as the Second Indo-China War and the US War in Vietnam, the Vietnam War lasted from 1965 to the Communist victory on 30 April 1975, but is sometimes dated to a start in 1959. Of the several other names associated with this conflict, the one most generally used is the Vietnam War. It is worth noting, however, that the appellation Second Indo-China War is useful in contextualizing the conflict in relation to the First Indo-China War that resulted in the departure of the French as the colonial power, and

linking the Vietnam War with the other conflicts being fought in South-East Asia at various times during this period: thus Vietnam, Laos and Cambodia can be seen as the theatres in which a larger Indo-Chinese conflict was fought, between the end of the Second World War in 1945 and the Communist victory in 1975.

The term Vietnam Conflict is used primarily in the USA to indicate that Congress never formally declared war on North Vietnam, and that in purely legal terms the president made use of his constitutionally mandated authority, on many occasions supplemented by resolutions in the Congress, to have the US forces fight what was described as a 'police action'.

The term Vietnam War is that which is most generally used in the English-speaking world, but falsely suggests that

it was fought wholly inside the two Vietnams, and so tacitly ignores the fact that the conflict spilled over into Cambodia and Laos.

Finally, the term most generally used in North Vietnam, and in the unified country until recent times, is the Resistance War against the Americans to Save the Nation. This is more a propaganda slogan than a real name, and in many ways mirrors the USSR's use of the term Great Patriotic War to describe its part in the Second World War.

On the final day of the war, the Communist forces under North Vietnamese leadership took Saigon, the capital of South Vietnam, even as the last US forces were being pulled out by air to vessels awaiting offshore, sealing the North Vietnamese military victory after more than 15 years of increasingly

ABOVE LEFT: British and French troops engaged in clearing the Saigon triangle in October 1945.

ABOVE: French armoured troops clearing countryside near Saigon in October 1945.

LEFT: French troops in 1952.

A LONG LEGACY

open warfare. The Vietnam War was the first major military defeat suffered by the United States of America, and as such was a very considerable psychological and emotional blow to a nation accustomed to success, but already socially and culturally riven by the anti-war movement, in the media as well as among major segments of the American population, which had played such a significant part in undermining the resolve of the American forces in South-East Asia.

Something in the order of 1.4 million military personnel, about one in 17 of them American, lost their lives in the war, and civilian deaths have been

estimated variously as between 2 and 5 million or slightly more for the two Vietnams, to which have to be added up to 700,000 Cambodian and 50,000 Laotian civilians. The war was fought between the Democratic Republic of Vietnam, generally known as North Vietnam, and the Republic of Vietnam, known as South Vietnam. The latter was supported by the USA and, at various times, by other allies, which supplied men and equipment in varying numbers and types. The Communist triumph led to South Vietnam's absorption by North Vietnam into the creation of a single Communist state.

The USA and other South Vietnamese allies sent large numbers of troops to South Vietnam between the end of the First Indo-China War in 1954 and 1973. US military advisers made their first appearance in Vietnam during 1950 to aid the French forces seeking to secure colonial rule in this part of Indo-China. They took over the complete task of training the Army of the Republic of

THE VIETNAM WAR

Vietnam, generally abbreviated as the ARVN, during 1956. From this time forward there was a steady increase in the attempts of Communist elements, under the control of the North Vietnamese, to subvert the pro-Western government and administration of South Vietnam, and this led to a steady escalation of the USA's support for South Vietnam. During his presidency, John F. Kennedy authorized the increase in US troop numbers in South Vietnam from 500 to 16,000, and this process was taken considerably further from 1965 by Kennedy's successor as president, Lyndon B. Johnson. The numbers of US troops were reduced steadily from the early 1960s as the USA attempted to 'Vietnamize' the anti-Communist effort, and nearly all of the US military personnel departed South Vietnam after

A Grumman F8F Bearcat ground crew lift bomb to wing.

A LONG LEGACY

the Paris Peace Accords of 1973, the last of them leaving on 30 April 1975 in Operation Frequent Wind, as the Communists moved into Saigon.

The war was extremely varied in its nature, as dictated by the course of events, the terrain over which the war was being fought, and the nature of the forces involved. The war therefore included small-scale fighting between minor units moving through the mountains and jungles, amphibious and airborne operations of different sizes, Communist guerrilla attacks on villages and urban areas, and major land battles of a conventional nature operating from land bases as well as aircraft carriers

manoeuvring off the east coast of Vietnam. Aircraft of the US Air Force and US Navy, complemented by machines of the US Army, undertook major air support of the forces fighting the 'in-country' war, and also launched huge bombing programmes directed at the industries, logistical systems (especially railway, road, river and canal networks), urban centres and ports of North Vietnam. Other aspects of the Vietnam War, which should not be ignored or belittled, are that Cambodia and Laos were also drawn into the conflict, and that the Americans sprayed very large quantities of chemicals onto the land from the air in an effort to reduce the amount of natural cover available to their foe. This use of defoliant agents marked the emergence of a new form of warfare, and has had a long-term effect on large parts of Vietnam and on the health of many Vietnamese.

For most of the period between 110 BC and AD 938, a large part of what is

THE VIETNAM WAR

now Vietnam was part of China. After gaining independence, Vietnam had to fight hard and long to retain this independence in the face of foreign aggression and internal conflict over many centuries between the Trinh and Nguyen lords. The latter ended only in 1802, when the Emperor Gia Long unified modern Vietnam under the Nguyen dynasty. Between 1859 and 1885, however, the French gained control of Indo-China (Cambodia, Laos and Vietnam) in the course of colonial wars. Indo-Chinese labourers were important to the French war effort in the First World War (1914–18), and at the Versailles Conference of 1919, which led to the Treaty of Versailles ending the war between Germany and the allies, Ho Chi Minh ('the Enlightener') requested

that a Vietnamese delegation be involved as an element of Vietnam's search for independence from French rule. Ho hoped it would catch the attention of the US president, Woodrow Wilson, who was a strong believer in the concept of national self-determination. Wilson refused to be drawn, but the Vietnamese cause was taken up by elements of the French left.

In the Second World War (1939–45), the authorities of Vichy France, the state which controlled that part of France left unoccupied by the Germans after the Franco-German armistice of June 1940, lacked the strength at home or abroad to resist the political and military pressure exerted by an expansionist Japanese empire, and came to co-operate with the Japanese forces which entered Indo-

China and established garrisons and bases there. Thus Vietnam came to be under the practical control of Japan, even though the latter was content to leave the French administration to run the colony.

It was during 1941 that a Communist-dominated national resistance group, the League for the Independence of Vietnam, more generally known as the Viet Minh, came into existence, quickly falling under the domination of Ho Chi Minh after his return to Vietnam. Ho had been a Comintern agent since the 1920s, but as the leader of an independent Vietnamese Communist party, he was now increasingly separating himself from Soviet influences and control while prudently maintaining good relations with the Soviets. Under Ho's leadership, the Viet Minh began to develop and refine a political and military strategy to seize control of the country at the end of the war, after the Japanese had been

LEFT: Japanese war criminals in Saigon after their arrival from Long Son.

BELOW: July 1950, when French troops became involved with the Communists in South Vietnam between Ba Ria and Cap St. Jacques. Here a Viet Minh (Communist) prisoner has been frisked by two French soldiers, one of whom is examining the flag bearing the hammer and sickle symbol found on the boy.

A LONG LEGACY

defeated by the allies, and appointed Vo Nguyen Giap as commander of the movement's clandestine military branch.

With a view to securing external aid for his movement, whose longer-term and real objectives remained veiled in secrecy, Ho used the guerrilla forces under Giap's supervision to make attacks on the Japanese. This persuaded the Americans, in the form of the Office of Strategic Services, which was the precursor of the Central Intelligence Agency, to provide funding and training. The Viet Minh guerrilla forces maintained a low-key campaign against the Japanese in Indo-China, and also aided other indigenous resistance groups. The Viet Minh effort was not all a blind, however, for it was able to provide the allies with important intelligence on Japanese troop movements, and also effected the recovery and succour of many of the crews of American warplanes that had been brought down in Indo-China. In overall terms, however, the USA believed the only correct strategy was to strike straight at the heart of the enemy's military and political strength, using the most direct course available. This suggested that the Americans saw the efforts of the Viet Minh in Indo-China as nothing more than a sideshow which might inconvenience the Japanese slightly, and should therefore be supported at only the most minimal level.

In 1944 the Japanese saw the possible advantage of a major change of tack in their grasp of Indo-China, and

ABOVE: Troops on Cap St. Jacques in September 1945.

RIGHT: The Bois Belleau *light aircraft carrier arrives in the Gulf of Tonkin in 1954.*

thus overthrew the Vichy French administration, while also subjecting its officials to humiliation in front of the Vietnamese population. Both aspects of the end of Vichy French rule had major repercussions within Indo-China, for they provided real proof that both the administration and personnel of a European power were just as vulnerable as they were themselves, and that independence, therefore, was not merely a pipe dream, but something they could work toward with a very real chance of success.

The Japanese also began to encourage the growth of nationalism, and made the shrewd political move of granting Vietnam independence, even though this was nominal rather than real. On 11 March 1945 the Emperor Bao Dai declared the independence of Vietnam within what the Japanese were pleased to call their Greater East Asia Co-Prosperity Sphere.

In the aftermath of the Japanese surrender in August 1945, various groupings within Vietnam, some nationalist, others Communist, and still others not overtly political in being aligned with neither of the major power blocs of the period, felt that they had every opportunity to seize control of Vietnam. In the event, the surrendering Japanese army transferred the reins of power to the Viet Minh, and the Emperor Bao Dai abdicated. On 2 September 1945 Ho declared Vietnamese independence from France in the so-called 'August Revolution'. It all seemed so clear-cut that US Army officers stood beside Ho on the platform, in front of a great audience in Hanoi, as the Viet Minh leader launched himself into a speech using the American Declaration

of Independence as one of its models: ' "All men are created equal. They are endowed by their Creator with certain inalienable rights; among these are Life, Liberty, and the pursuit of Happiness." This immortal statement was made in the Declaration of Independence of the United States of America in 1776… We…solemnly declare to the world that Vietnam has the right to be a free and independent country. The entire Vietnamese people are determined…to sacrifice their lives and property in order to safeguard their independence and liberty.'

In this manner Ho hoped to secure US approval for the assumption of power in Vietnam by an indigenous nationalist movement, despite the fact that it was of Communist ideology. Ho's hopes had been raised in this respect by a number of wartime speeches by President Franklin D. Roosevelt, opposing any return of European powers to their pre-war colonial empires. Ho also went as far as to tell a representative of the OSS that Vietnam would have 'a million American soldiers…but no French'. At this juncture, however, the anti-colonial feeling evident in the USA since its emergence as a nation in the War of American Independence (1775–83) succumbed to realpolitik. The American reasoning was simple: it was now clear that France could and should be a key player in US-led efforts to deter, and if necessary fight off the Soviet territorial ambitions in continental Europe, and that France's colonial ambitions were something that had to be factored into the equation.

The new Viet Minh government survived for only the briefest of periods.

European residents of Hanoi welcome French troops in March 1946.

At the Potsdam Conference, which ended on 2 August 1945, the allies had decided that Vietnam should be occupied, on a temporarily basis, by British and Chinese forces, which would accept the surrender of the Japanese troops in the country, disarm them, and begin the process of repatriating them to Japan. The first Chinese troops appeared in northern Vietnam only a few days after Ho's declaration of

more than 20,000 men of Major General D. Gracey's Indian 20th Infantry Division in to occupy Saigon. The first of the men reached the major city of southern Vietnam on 6 September, and the rest of the British-led Indian force arrived during the next few weeks, but were so overstretched that they had to rearm a number of Japanese prisoners-of-war to create the so-called Gremlin Force to aid them in less hard-pressed areas. The British began to withdraw from southern Vietnam during December 1945, but did not complete the bulk of this process until May 1946. The last British casualties in Vietnam were suffered in June 1946. Altogether 40 British and Indian troops were killed and over 100 were wounded. Vietnamese casualties were 600.

As the Anglo-Indian forces pulled out, the first elements of the returning French arrived, the French authorities immediately attempting to gain control

of the situation in the north as well as the south of Vietnam. The French negotiated with the Chinese nationalist forces of Generalissimo Chiang Kai-shek, agreeing to end French treaty concessions in China in exchange for Chinese authorization for a French return to northern Vietnam, so that they could start direct negotiation with the Viet Minh. Ho was just as enthusiastic about the possibilities attached to a Chinese withdrawal, and took advantage of the interregnum to kill as many as possible of the leaders and members of rival nationalist groupings.

Talks concerning the formation of a Vietnamese government within the new, all-embracing French Union ended in failure, and the French attempted to exert pressure with a bombardment of Haiphong, the major port lying close to Hanoi. In December 1946 the French occupied Hanoi, and the Americans studiously ignored a number of

ABOVE: Vietnam forces in Indo-China found that commando warfare in small bands was the most effective fighting method in wiping out the marauding and pillaging Viet Minh guerrilla bands infesting Tonkin. Here Indo-Chinese commandos are searching a fortified village in Tonkin. They must proceed with extreme caution because of the traps and hidden grenades that are planted everywhere.

RIGHT: Vietnamese Republican soldiers are seen entering a burning village in Indo-China during fighting with French forces.

independence, and the Viet Minh government thereupon went out of existence as a practical reality. The Chinese then seized control of the area of Vietnam north of the 16th parallel, the first British forces arriving in the area south of this *de facto* dividing line, where they began to take control from the dispirited Japanese, so restoring a measure of order in a region that had grown increasingly lawless. Admiral Lord Louis Mountbatten, the British commander-in-chief of the Allies' South-East Asia Command, moved

telegrams from Ho, asking for President Harry S. Truman's political support. In the short term, therefore, Ho decided that he and the surviving cadres of the Viet Minh would make a fall-back into the inhospitable mountains of north-western Vietnam to prepare and launch an armed insurgency.

This marked the beginning of the First Indo-China War (1946–54), which was to be both long and bloody, the military losses of the French and their allies, at 94,581 dead, 78,127 wounded and 40,000 taken prisoner, being greater than the USA would suffer during the Vietnam War. The Communist losses in the First Indo-China War would also be considerable, being in the order of more than 300,000 dead, more than 500,000 wounded, and about 100,000 taken prisoner.

It appears that the position of the USA vis-à-vis Indo-China was indecisive during this period. On the one hand the USA, convinced that colonialism was wrong, wished to convince France to reconsider its position in Indo-China but to leave the exact nature and timing of the process to France itself. During the Second World War, President Roosevelt had steadily stalled French demands for US help in reclaiming Indo-China, and after the end of the war the French agreed that decolonialization was probably the right long-term course and that, in accordance with the principles of the newly created United Nations Organization, a measure of autonomy should be offered to Indo-China, but only after France had managed to regain control of the region.

On the other hand, the USA had real concerns about Ho's allegiance, in world terms, following the Second World

War, when it was clear that the two major power blocs would be those led by the USA and the USSR. In the eyes of the power players in Washington, however, every element in the world admitting or claiming to be Communist had to be in thrall to the leadership of the USSR, therefore it was inevitable that the USA, when asked by Ho for recognition of the Viet Minh government of northern Vietnam, should perceive Ho, not as a neutral Communist but as a man concealing his control by the USSR. This was an American perception which played into

the hands of the French and, as US Secretary of State Dean Acheson wrote, '...the US came to the aid of the French...because we needed their support for our policies in regard to NATO...The French blackmailed us. At every meeting...they brought up Indochina...but refused to tell me what they hoped to accomplish or how. Perhaps they didn't know.'

The First Indo-China War, otherwise known as the French Indo-China War, Franco-Vietnamese War, Franco-Viet Minh War, Indo-China War and Dirty War in France, and as the French War in

French troops, still wearing US-supplied uniforms, depart from Marseilles to reinforce French forces in the Indo-Chinese conflict in September 1945.

A LONG LEGACY

Vietnam, lasted from 19 December 1946 to 1 August 1954, and was fought between the Far East Expeditionary Corps of the French Union, with the support of Bao Dai's Vietnamese National Army, and the Viet Minh led by Ho Chi Minh and Vo Nguyen Giap. Most of the fighting took place in the Tonkin region of northern Vietnam, although parts of the war spread to other parts of the country, as well as to the neighbouring protectorates of Laos and Cambodia within the French Indo-Chinese empire.

The war began as a rebellion launched by the Viet Minh against the French authorities controlling Indo-China. The first few years of the war took the form of a low-intensity rural insurgency against French authority, but once the Chinese Communist forces had advanced against the Chinese nationalist forces to the border of Vietnam and

ABOVE: Operation Artois, January 1953. An important clean-up operation began on the 16 January to the north-east and east of Thai Binh after serious combats at Lang Dong on the 20th and at An Trach and Lai Tri on the 21st and 22nd, in which 328 Viet Minh were killed and 183 prisoners and numerous armaments were taken by the French forces.

RIGHT: Communist troops move to take Haiphong.

THE VIETNAM WAR

essentially sound, and achieved very useful results in the Battle of Na San, a truly effective defence of French interests was impossible for lack of materials (especially concrete) with which to build the defences, of armoured fighting vehicles for lack of surface access, and of the air cover that would otherwise have exercised a dominant effect. Therefore the French were gradually being driven to a major and totally exhausting defeat, with significant losses among their most mobile troops.

General Philippe Leclerc de Hauteclocque had reached Saigon on 9 October 1945 in company with Colonel Jacques Émile Massu's Groupement de

LEFT: Vietnam 1953. A group of captured French officers after the fight for Nghia Lo. First on the left is the French area commander of Nghia Lo.

BELOW: A photograph of Ho Chi Minh goes up in Haiphong.

China during 1949, the scale and intensity of the conflict escalated sharply into conventional war between two armies equipped with modern weapons supplied by the two superpower blocs.

The forces of the French Union not only included troops from France's former colonies of Algeria, Cambodia, Laos, Morocco, Tunis and Vietnam, but also those from West and Central Africa, together with the professionals of the French Foreign Legion. The use of troops from metropolitan France was prohibited by the government in an effort to avoid unpopularity at home, but even so the level of antipathy to the war effort rose steadily, not only because of the cost, but also through the effort of left-wing elements, who called this the *sale guerre* (dirty war).

While the strategy of drawing the Viet Minh to attack well-defended bases in the remoter parts of the country at the extreme end of the Communist forces' logistical capability was

A LONG LEGACY

Marche. Leclerc's primary tasks were defined as the restoration of public order in southern Vietnam and the militarization of the Tonkin region of northern Vietnam, while his secondary tasks were the holding of the current position while awaiting the advent of more French forces with which to retake Chinese-occupied Hanoi, and then the undertaking of negotiations with the Viet Minh.

The war proper began in Haiphong after disagreement concerning the level of import duty on goods arriving at the port, and on 23 November 1946 French warships bombarded the city and, according to differing sources, in the process killed somewhere between 2,000 and more than 6,000 Vietnamese civilians in the single afternoon. The bombardment's positive effect, if that is the right way to describe it, was to persuade the Viet Minh to agree to a ceasefire and to depart from Haiphong. The Viet Minh saw this as a tactical reverse rather than a major defeat, however, and Vo Nguyen Giap soon brought up 30,000 men to attack Haiphong. The French were outnumbered but had better weapons and the advantages of heavy fire support from their warships, and this made it impossible for the Viet Minh to consider any form of frontal assault. By December, fighting had also erupted in Hanoi, and Ho was forced to leave the city and fall back into remote mountain areas relatively inaccessible to the French. This marked the stage at which guerrilla warfare became the standard way of waging the war, with the French in control of almost all apart from the most extremely remote of areas.

THE VIETNAM WAR

In 1946 Vo Nguyen Giap moved his headquarters to Tan Trao. The French tried to reach and attack his main centres of strength, but on every occasion Giap refused to be drawn into combat with superior strength and manoeuvred his forces out of the way: thus it became a standard Viet Minh tactic to disappear as the French approached. Late in 1947 the French undertook Operation Lea to take and destroy the Viet Minh communications nexus at Bac Kan, but failed to capture Giap and his senior subordinates, which had also been part of the operation's objectives. They nonetheless were able to kill 9,000 Viet Minh soldiers in the course of the campaign, which can be regarded only as a major defeat for the Viet Minh.

In 1948 France saw the sense of opposing the Viet Minh politically as well as militarily, and established an alternative government in Saigon. Here the French began negotiations with Bao Dai, the former Vietnamese emperor, to head an 'autonomous' government of the State of Vietnam within the French Union. Two years before, the French had refused Ho's similar suggestion, but with a number of restrictions on French power and a political evolution toward France's eventual withdrawal from Vietnam. Now the French were prepared to offer a similar 'deal' to Bao Dai as he had co-operated with the French in the past; lacking armed forces, Bao Dai was in no position to make any major objection, although he would be in possession of such forces in the near future.

In 1949 France officially recognized the State of Vietnam under Bao Dai as independent within the French Union. But this independence was only nominal, and then only within the

A LONG LEGACY

A French artillery position at Dien Bien Phu.

French Union, as France kept control of matters related to foreign and military affairs. The Viet Minh immediately denounced the State of Vietnam as a puppet of the French, demanding real independence. As a concession to the new state and as a means of increasing the number of troops available to it for service in Vietnam, France sanctioned the establishment of a Vietnamese National Army with Vietnamese officers. Once the VNA had been created, its units were employed to garrison quiet sectors, freeing the French forces for serious combat. (The private armies of the Cao Dai, Hoa Hao and Binh Xuyen criminal organizations were also used in the same manner.) In the same year, however, the Vietnamese Communists also began to receive outside aid, after

Mao's Communist forces gained total control of China by defeating Chiang's Kuomintang forces, which decamped to Formosa (Taiwan). Thus the Viet Minh gained a significant supporter and source of supplies in an area just across the border from its stronghold area.

It should be noted that, in the same year, France additionally recognized the independence, again within the context of the French Union, of Cambodia and Laos, the other two kingdoms constituting the French empire in Indo-China.

During 1950 the USA recognized the State of Vietnam but, even so, many other countries, even in the West, continued to regard it solely as a French creature. Part of the USA's new-found commitment to the region as its 'new

administration' took the form of weapons and military observers. On the other side of the 'front', however, the Chinese were supplying effectively unlimited quantities of Soviet matériel to the Viet Minh, so that Giap was in the position to reconstitute his guerrilla and other irregular forces into five conventional formations, namely the 304th, 308th, 312th, 316th and 320th Divisions. Strengthened and remodelled in this fashion, the Communist forces went over to the offensive, initially by attacking French bases effectively isolated along the Sino-Vietnamese border. In February 1950, Giap's forces overran the 150-strong French garrison at Lai Khe in the Tonkin region, just south of the border with China. Thereby encouraged, Giap next moved to Cao Bang, where on 25 May his forces attacked a garrison of 4,000 Vietnamese troops under French command but were repulsed. Giap again attacked Cao Bang, and also Dong Khe on 15 September. Dong Khe fell to the Communist forces on 18 September, and Cao Bang finally succumbed on 3 October. Giap moved immediately against Lang Son, which was held by 4,000 men of the French Foreign Legion. Falling back along Route 4, the legionnaires, and a relief force from That Khe, were ambushed along the length of their retreat by the Communist forces. The French dropped a paratroop battalion south of Dong Khe to draw off some of the Communist strength, but the battalion was cut off, surrounded and destroyed. On 17 October, and after seven days of Communist attacks, Lang Son fell. By the time the last elements of their defeated garrisons had entered the relative safety of the Red river delta, the

THE VIETNAM WAR

known as the De Lattre Line, between Hanoi and the Gulf of Tonkin via the Red river delta. De Lattre believed this line could be the fixed anvil against which his mobile force could shatter the Viet Minh, and initially his concept worked well.

The following 13 January saw Giap directing the 20,000 or more men of the 308th and 312th Divisions to attack Vinh Yen, which lies some 20 miles (32km) to the north-west of Hanoi, and which was held by the 6,000 men of the 9th Foreign Legion Brigade. The Viet Minh hurled themselves into a neatly conceived trap, when, caught in the open for the first time, the men of the Communist divisions were shot to pieces by concentrated French artillery and

LEFT: Members of the planning section at Viet Minh GHQ discuss future tactics.

BELOW LEFT: French prisoners taken after the Battle of Dien Bien Phu.

BELOW: Operation Castor in 1953.

French had lost 4,800 men dead, missing or taken prisoner, as well as 2,000 men wounded out of a garrison strength of more than 10,000. The French also lost 13 guns, 125 mortars, 450 trucks, 940 machine guns, 1,200 sub-machine guns and 8,000 rifles.

Thus China and the USSR recognized the Viet Minh as the legitimate administration of Vietnam,

and increased their flow of matériel and supplies.

In 1951 France began to detect a glimmer of distant light on the horizon when a new commander-in-chief, namely General Jean-Marie de Lattre de Tassigny, arrived to reconsider the problem of maintaining French rule. De Lattre ordered the construction of a fortified defence line, which became

along the coast. After losing 3,000 men dead and wounded, Giap ordered a withdrawal on 28 March.

The Communist military commander was nothing if not dedicated, however, and on 29 May committed his forces to yet another offensive, in which the 304th Division moved against Phu Ly, the 308th Division moved against Ninh Binh and, as the main effort, the 320th Division moved against Phat Diem, lying to the south of Hanoi. This co-ordinated trio of efforts suffered just as badly as had the earlier offensives, and the three divisions suffered heavy casualties.

This was the ideal moment for the French to strike, and de Lattre launched a counter-offensive against the Viet Minh, which had suffered something of a failure of morale over the last period of fighting and was now driven back

ABOVE: Franco-Vietnamese soldiers, supported by tanks, move forward under fire for a counter-attack on 23 March 1954 against the rebel Viet Minh forces around the besieged fortress of Dien Bien Phu. The action resulted in the obliteration of a complete Viet Minh company at a point south of the post.

RIGHT: Dien Bien Phu, 1954.

machine gun fire. By 16 January Giap was forced to admit defeat after losing more than 6,000 of his men killed, 8,000 wounded and 500 captured, and ordered a withdrawal. The Battle of Vinh Yen had been a disaster for the Communist cause in Vietnam, and the French now believed they possessed at least one tactical answer to the military problem of the Viet Minh.

On 23 March Giap made another move against the French, this time launching an attack against Mao Khe, lying some 20 miles (32km) north of Haiphong. The 11,000 troops of the 316th Division, with the partly rebuilt 308th and 312th Divisions in reserve, were held off and then repulsed in hand-to-hand fighting, the French defence effort supported by warplanes using napalm and rockets, and also by the guns of the French warships steaming

THE VIETNAM WAR

Giap's forces had risen almost catastrophically in this period, when the still comparatively lightly equipped Viet Minh faced high-quality French troops in prepared positions with an abundance of heavy weapons and air power at their disposal. The reverses even persuaded some leading Vietnamese figures, including some in the party, to question the leadership of the Communist government. But while the military balance in Vietnam had been tipped in favour of the French, the political and social balance in France was tipping in the other direction as opposition to the war increased. The financial cost to the French nation was high and increasing steadily, and while all of the French forces in Indo-China were professional soldiers rather than conscripts, there was great concern that officers were being

into the jungle, losing a number of outposts in the Red river delta by 18 June. The French counter-offensive cost the Viet Minh more than 10,000 more men killed.

Thus every one of Giap's attempts to break the De Lattre Line ended in defeat, and at the same time elicited a French counter-attack inflicting heavy losses on the Viet Minh. The losses of

expanded French position at Hoa Binh, forcing the French back to their original De Lattre Line positions by 22 February of the following year. The losses of more than 10,000, split equally between the two sides, clearly indicated that the war was still far from over.

In January 1952 de Latte was invalided back to France with cancer, and died shortly after reaching his homeland. He was replaced as French Commander-in-Chief in Indo-China by General Raoul Salan. Throughout 1952, and in most parts of northern Vietnam, the Viet Minh concentrated its efforts on severing the French lines of communication and supply, hoping to effect a serial erosion of the French forces' morale and resolve in the process. The Viet Minh launched an apparently never-ending sequence of raids, skirmishes and guerrilla attacks, but it was clear that this was not a decisive moment, and each side used the opportunity to prepare for larger operations.

On 17 October Giap committed a sizeable part of his strength to attacks on the French garrisons along the Nghia Lo, to the north-west of Hanoi, but broke off the attacks when the arrival of a French parachute battalion threatened his position. The Communist forces had control over most of the Tonkin region outside the De Lattre Line and Salan,

ABOVE: A Viet Minh leaflet advising French defenders of Dien Bien Phu to surrender.

RIGHT: French and Vietnamese forces launch a new attack against Viet Minh troops to the north of Dien Bien Phu on 1 and 2 February 1954.

killed at a rate greater than the training schools were generating replacements. The officer replacement factor was something which had to be resolved in France, but as far as the financial aspect was concerned, France turned to the USA for support.

On 14 November 1951 the French initiated an airborne operation to seize Hoa Binh, which lay some 25 miles (40km) west of the De Lattre Line, and were thus able to deepen their perimeter defences in this area. Inevitably, however, the Viet Minh counter-attacked the

THE VIETNAM WAR

US-supplied Douglas B-26 Invader attack warplanes, used in the Battle of Dien Bien Phu in March 1954.

perceiving this to be a critical moment, committed his forces in Operation Lorraine, along the Clear river, in an effort to compel Giap to lift the Communist pressure on the Nghia Lo outposts. This involved the greatest French effort in Indo-China up to that time, and began on 29 October as 30,000 French soldiers advanced from the De Lattre Line against the Communist supply dumps in the area of Phu Yen. The French took Phu Tho on 5 November, Phu Doan on 9 November, by means of an airborne operation, and

finally Phu Yen on 13 November. Giap did not react immediately to the French offensive, for he believed that it would be better to allow the more supply-dependent French to reach the end of their communication and supply capability before striking at these lines to cut the French off from their base area in the Red river delta. Salan was too astute to fall into this trap, however, and halted the operation on 14 November, taking his forces back toward the De Lattre Line. The only major fighting during the operation

came during the withdrawal, when the Viet Minh ambushed the French column at Chan Muong on 17 November. An Indo-Chinese *bataillon de marche* cleared the Viet Minh block with a bayonet charge, and the withdrawal continued. The operation was thus only partially successful, but while it revealed the fact that the French could strike out at targets beyond the De Lattre line, such efforts did not cause the Viet Minh to call off its own offensive, or inflict significant damage on the Communist logistical system,

A LONG LEGACY

RIGHT: Vietnamese refugees in a restaurant tent at La Pagoda wait for their 'passage to freedom' in September 1954.

BELOW: Members of the Vietnamese People's Army rejoicing after their victory at Dien Bien Phu in 1954.

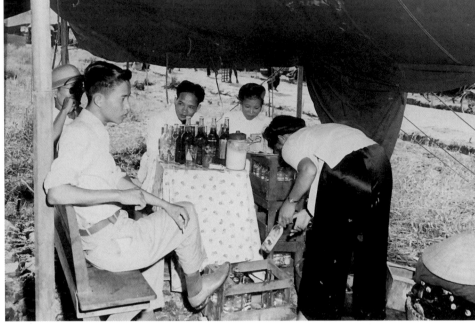

which was altogether more diffuse than that of the French, in that it was not wholly reliant on the road, rail and waterway systems of the area.

Giap used the winter of 1952–53 to reconsider his whole strategic approach to ousting the French from Indo-China. He now realized that direct attacks on an enemy enjoying the benefits offered by fixed positions and heavier weapons cost lives and equipment to no good effect, and decided to exert pressure on the French by opening another front. Thus on 9 April the Communist forces began to advance into Laos. During May, Salan was replaced as commander-in-chief of the French forces by General Henri Navarre, who signalled the French government that 'there is no possibility of winning the war in Indo-China', and that the best for which the French could hope was a stalemate. In the face of the Viet Minh's move into Laos, Navarre decided that the best course of action was the creation of centres of resistance, or 'hedgehogs', in locations which threatened the Viet Minh's lines of communication and freedom of movement: the Communist forces would

have to attack such hedgehogs, which could be supplied by air, and use their heavier weapons to inflict decisive defeats on the Viet Minh. Navarre selected Dien Bien Phu, which is about 10 miles (16km) north of the Laotian border with Vietnam and some 175 miles (280km) to the west of Hanoi, as the site of the hedgehog which would best block the Viet Minh from invading Laos.

Dien Bien Phu seemed to offer the French a number of positive features: it lay on the Viet Minh's line of communication into Laos along the Nam Yum river; it already possessed an airstrip, built in the late 1930s and improved by the Japanese to allow supplies to be delivered by air; and it lay in the hills where the Tai tribesmen, loyal to the French, were an active force with whom the Viet Minh would have to cope. Operation Castor was launched on 20 November 1953 as 1,800 men of the French 1st and 2nd Parachute Battalions dropped into the valley and swiftly eliminated the small Viet Minh garrison.

The French airborne force thus found itself in control of a valley 12 miles (19km) long and 8 miles (13 km) wide, surrounded by heavily-wooded hills. French and Tai units, operating from Lai Chau to the north, swept through the hills and encountered no Viet Minh opposition, leading the French to judge Castor a major tactical success. Giap appreciated that the French position had weaknesses, however, and began to shift a sizeable proportion of his strength from the De Lattre Line toward Dien Bien Phu. This move was achieved so rapidly that, by the middle of December, the French and Tai patrols in the hills around the small river-valley town were suffering losses so heavy in the course of Communist ambushes that the patrol effort was called off.

The 57-day battle for Dien Bien Phu was to become the longest and hardest-fought by France in its attempt to retain, or rather regain, control of Indo-China. The battle began on 13 March with a surprise assault from Communist forces supported, for the first time in the First Indo-China War, by heavy artillery as well as large concentrations of anti-aircraft artillery. The French plan had been conceived in ignorance of the Viet Minh's possession of such weapons, which soon severed the French lines of communication into the valley by land, as the heavy artillery was sited mostly on the reverse slopes of the flanking hills or otherwise in very carefully concealed positions on the forward slopes. It was soon also severed by air as the airstrip was destroyed, and transport aircraft proved hugely vulnerable to the massed anti-aircraft guns, as they attempted to operate from the remnants of the airfield and later to make parachute drops from altitudes low enough to avoid supplies drifting off into Communist-held areas. The French position quickly became untenable, particularly when the advent of the monsoons made the dropping of supplies and reinforcements considerably more difficult.

Facing imminent defeat at Dien Bien Phu, the French decided to fight on, despite high losses, and hold Dien Bien Phu as a bargaining counter in the peace conference scheduled to begin in Geneva on 26 April. The French made a final break-out of their shrinking perimeter on 4 May, which achieved no useful result. The Viet Minh then began to close on the exhausted French, whose ordeal was compounded by the arrival of yet another weapon new to the First Indo-China War, namely the Katyusha surface-to-surface artillery rocket, supplied by the Soviets via the Chinese. The Viet Minh's final defeat of the French outpost lasted for two days,

from 6–7 May, when the French were finally overrun by a frontal assault. General René Cogny, based in Hanoi and commanding the French forces in northern Vietnam, ordered General Christian de Castries, commanding at Dien Bien Phu, to surrender at 17:30, after destroying all matériel to prevent its later use by the Viet Minh. In one of the oddities with which military history

abounds, de Castries was also instructed not to use a white flag, so that the ending of hostilities could be treated not as a surrender but as a ceasefire.

The fighting died away on 7 May except in 'Isabelle', the isolated southern position of the French defence, where the battle ended at 01:00 on 8 May. At least 2,200 of the 20,000-strong French force had been killed or had died during

General J. Lawton Collins, US Army Chief of Staff (second from left) and General Jean de Lattre de Tassigny, High Commissioner of French Indo-China (with armband), accompanied by local officials en route to address citizens of Hanoi at a welcoming ceremony given in honour of General Collins in 1951.

A LONG LEGACY

RIGHT: French personnel stream into the huge belly of a USAF Douglas C-124 Globemaster at Orly airfield, France, for their 8,500-mile (13680-km) air journey to Indo-China. The airlift, the largest in aviation history, was directed by the USAF in Europe with aircraft flown from the United States of America.

BELOW RIGHT: A cameraman and other civilians crouch behind armoured vehicles in Saigon during the 1 November 1963 coup led by the military on the presidential palace. It resulted in the overthrow and subsequent death of Ngo Dinh Diem, the first president of South Vietnam. This picture was taken by an Associated Press staff photographer.

THE VIETNAM WAR

the battle, while the Communist forces of about 100,000 men suffered losses estimated at 8,000 killed and 15,000 wounded. The number of French prisoners taken at Dien Bien Phu was the largest so far achieved by the Viet Minh, totalling about one-third of all the men taken during the war.

Negotiations between France and the Viet Minh had begun in Geneva during April 1954. Pierre Mendès- France, who had been an opponent of the war since 1950, became prime minister on 17 June

on a manifesto of ending the war, with an armistice to be agreed within four months. In fact, agreement was reached on 21 July in the so-called Geneva Accords, which included, among other things, the recognition of the 17th parallel as a 'provisional military demarcation line', marking the temporary division of Vietnam into a Communist North Vietnam and pro-Western South Vietnam. The accords also called for free and universal elections during 1956, to select a government for

the whole of Vietnam, but the USA and the State of Vietnam refused to sign the document. The Emperor Bao Dai, who now lived in France, appointed Ngo Dinh Diem as the prime minister of South Vietnam and in 1955, with US support, Diem used a referendum to remove the emperor and declare himself president of the Republic of Vietnam.

When the elections were prevented by the USA and South Vietnam, Viet Minh cadres in South Vietnam were activated, beginning a campaign of terrorism against the government. North Vietnam invaded and occupied portions of Laos to facilitate their effort to supply the guerrilla and irregular forces of the National Liberation Front in South Vietnam, setting in motion the slide toward the Second Indo-China War.

ABOVE: Vietnamese commando troops patrol through swamp territory near Tonkin as they fight the Viet Minh Communist guerilla forces, using their own game of hit-and-run. French forces had also found commando groups more effective in this area. The man in the lead carries a rifle with an attachment for throwing grenades.

LEFT: The Viet Minh 'parade of victory' through the streets of Hanoi, it being the main force of troops to take up occupation in this capital and headquarters city. Approximately 5,000 troops marched or drove vehicles along the streets choked with thousands of Vietnamese civilians cheering them on. Many of the civilians rushed out to present flowers to the marching soldiers, while small children with peace flags waved them on poles above the crowds.

CHAPTER TWO
THE USA BECOMES EMBROILED

RIGHT: The helicopter became an
effective weapon of war in Vietnam.
These are Piasecki H-21 'Flying
Banana' twin-rotor helicopters, seen
early in the conflict as the USA began
to provide matériel aid to the South
Vietnamese.

BELOW: The Vietnam People's Army
(VPA), not to be confused with the Viet
Cong (NLF), was the official name of
the armed forces of the Socialist
Republic of Vietnam. During the
Vietnam War (1957–1975), the US
referred to it as the North Vietnamese
Army (NVA) or People's Army of
Vietnam (PAVN), terms commonly used
when speaking of the Vietnam War.

It is necessary to backtrack a little here, to explain the steadily increasing US involvement in the First Indo-China War, an effort which had included, by 1954, funding some 8 per cent of the French war effort. In 1950 the Democratic Republic of Vietnam and China had exchanged mutual recognition, and the USSR followed. President Truman responded by recognizing the government of Vietnam, despite the fact that it was merely a French puppet regime. This was tacit confirmation that the USA feared the Communist administration in Hanoi was just a tool of a China which was now ruled by the Communists, and by extension, therefore, a tool of the USSR. This was not in fact the case, and there remained strong historically based

antipathies between Vietnam and China; but even so, China was willing to provide large quantities of matériel and to support the Vietnamese Communists to the end of the war. Another significant factor in 1950, as far as the USA was concerned, was the start of the Korean War (1950–53), for it led to the general belief in US political circles that the First Indo-China War should no longer be seen only as a colonial war in Indo-China, but still another element in a programme of Communist expansionism controlled by the USSR.

Thus it was during 1950 that the US Military Assistance and Advisory Group (MAAG) arrived to check French

requests for equipment, provide advice on strategic matters, and help in the training of Vietnamese soldiers. By 1954 the USA had delivered some 300,000 small arms and had supported the French effort to the tune of US$1 billion.

For the French, their defeat at Dien Bien Phu marked the end of their attempt to regain control of Indo-China; at the Geneva Conference the French negotiated a ceasefire agreement, and granted independence to Cambodia, Laos and Vietnam. Together with the temporary partitioning of Vietnam along the 17th parallel, the Geneva Accords mandated the freedom of civilians to move between the two provisional states,

THE VIETNAM WAR

have signed the Geneva Accords, and without US support Diem refused to entertain the holding of the election. President Dwight D. Eisenhower later stated that in 1954 some 80 per cent of the population would have voted for the Communist Ho Chi Minh over Bao Dai, but this may not have been the case in the aftermath of the bloody and very unpopular land reform programme, and a peasant revolt which was quashed only with a major loss of life.

Despite its long-stated belief in the concept of democracy, the USA agreed with Diem that democratic elections could not be risked, its reasoning based on the current 'domino theory', which suggested that the loss of South Vietnam to Communism would trigger

as a result of which nearly a million people, most of them Roman Catholics, moved from the north to the south in fear of the new regime headed by Ho; at the same time it is believed that another two million were forcibly prevented from moving to the south. The Viet Minh established the Democratic Republic of Vietnam as a socialist state in the north and embarked on a programme of land reform in which very large numbers of 'class enemies' were put to death, an error for which Ho later apologized.

Meanwhile, a non-Communist state was established in the south, ruled by the Emperor Bao Dai with Ngo Dinh Diem as prime minister. As many as 90,000 Viet Minh fighters went north for 'regroupment', as agreed in the

Geneva Accords, but the Viet Minh, in direct contravention of the agreements, and having clearly appreciated the probable course of future events, left behind in South Vietnam some 5,000 to 10,000 cadres as the basis of later political and military operations to take control of South Vietnam.

As ordained by the Geneva Accords, the partition of Vietnam was designed as a temporary measure until the national elections scheduled for 20 July 1956 took place. The partition agreement had also stipulated the creation of a demilitarized zone (DMZ) along the 17th parallel to keep both North and South Vietnam separated and free from the threat of military action. As noted above, however, the USA was the only major power not to

Air America was the CIA's 'airline' in South-East Asia, and is here represented by a Curtiss C-46 Commando twin-engined transport.

a succession of losses ending with Communist domination of the whole of South-East Asia and, according to the wildest exponents of the theory, a further spread to the Hawaiian Islands and thence to the western seaboard of continental USA. According to the proponents of the domino theory, the spread of Communism had to be tackled sooner rather than later, and the best place to start this process was in South-East Asia rather than any part of the USA. Thus it was a powerful argument for the adoption of South Vietnam as a client state.

The USA's political and military thinking in this respect was based on the concept of containment and, on the basis of the North Atlantic Treaty Organization, a South-East Asia Treaty Organization (SEATO) was created to co-ordinate the defence of Europe and counter Communist expansion in the region.

Diem, the leader of South Vietnam as agreed by the USA, was a Roman Catholic, strongly anti-Communist and free of any connection with the French. However, in its ignorance of the reality of South-East Asian affairs, the USA failed to appreciate that Diem was also an autocrat, a believer in nepotism, and extremely narrow in his nationalism.

THE VIETNAM WAR

The Americans also made the major error of looking at the Vietnamese through American eyes, and therefore ascribed American motives to what were uniquely Vietnamese actions. Diem, in fact, warned the Americans of the fallaciousness of their concept and the futility of believing that a Vietnamese emulation of American methods, without thought or 'translation' into more appropriate local forms, would or even could solve Vietnamese problems.

Against US advice, Diem decided to simplify and consolidate his own position by removing opposition forces, as he perceived them, through the use of the military: operations were therefore undertaken between April and June 1955 against the Cao Dai religious sect, the Buddhists of the Hoa Hao, and the Binh

LEFT: A Viet Cong prisoner-of-war, captured by the Army of the Republic of Vietnam (ARVN).

BELOW: Council of a National Front for the Liberation of South Vietnam (NLF) or Viet Cong partisan unit in South Vietnam.

THE USA BECOMES EMBROILED

ABOVE: Entry of victorious Vietnamese People's Army troops into Ha Long (Hong Gai) in April 1955.

RIGHT: 'One of three North Vietnamese torpedo boats are shown in an attack on the destroyer USS Maddox*', reads the caption to this photograph, released by the US Defense Department shortly after the incident of 2 August 1964 took place in the Gulf of Tonkin.*

OPPOSITE: Ho Chi Minh, famous for leading the Viet Minh independence movement from 1941 onward. He established the Communist-governed Democratic Republic of Vietnam in 1945, defeating the French Union in 1954 at Dien Bien Phu. He led the North Vietnamese in the Vietnam War until his death in 1969, the war ending six years later with a North Vietnamese victory, with Vietnamese unification following on. Saigon, the former capital of South Vietnam, was renamed Ho Chi Minh City in his honour.

Xuyen criminal organization, this last being associated with elements of the secret police and some parts of the military establishment. The pretext used by Diem to justify these actions was that the targeted groups protected Communist agents. The ruthless nature of Diem's administration resulted in a broadening of the opposition to it, to which Diem responded by laying the blame on the Communists. From the summer of 1955 Diem initiated a 'denounce the Communists' campaign, paving the way for the arrest, imprisonment, torture and murder, not only of Communists but also of large segments of the opposition to his rule, the latter being classified as Viet Cong to remove all credibility from their claims to be nationalists.

The movement of refugees continued during this period, some 52,000 civilians moving from south to north, and up to 450,000 others, primarily Catholics, moving from north to south, most of them in French and US aircraft and ships.

Diem next called for a referendum on the future of the monarchy. This was controlled by Diem's brother, Ngo Dinh Nhu, in which it was claimed that 98.2 per cent of the vote had gone to Diem when, conscious that the referendum would be rigged, US advisers of the period had recommended that Diem should limit himself to a winning margin of 60 to 70 per cent. On 26 October 1955 Diem declared the new Republic of Vietnam, with himself as president, which reflected not only Diem's own ambitions but also the wish of the Eisenhower administration for the creation of a dedicated anti-Communist state within South-East Asia. What the USA ignored, wilfully or in ignorance, was that Diem was already widely distrusted in South Vietnam as a wealthy Catholic who 'must have had' a cosy relationship within the minority which aided the French to rule Vietnam, as a man opposed to the majority Buddhist beliefs of the region, and as one who was trampling on all manner of human rights.

In 1956 Le Duan, one of the leading Communists in the south, travelled to the north and recommended that a more determined stance be taken in the struggle to ensure that Vietnam was reunited under Communist rule. The problem for North Vietnam was that it was currently facing acute domestic problems because of its collapsed economy, and did not feel the time to be ripe for any large-scale military endeavour. North Vietnam feared US intervention at this stage, and also felt South Vietnamese conditions to be currently unsuitable for any 'people's

revolution'. The overall objective, nonetheless, remained the reunification of Vietnam under Communist rule, and in December 1956 Ho Chi Minh ordered the Viet Minh cadres in South Vietnam to begin a low-intensity insurgency. This 'armed propaganda', as it was termed, took the form mostly of kidnappings and terrorist attacks. Some 400 members of the South Vietnamese administration were murdered in 1957, and the pace of this low-level violence was steadily increased from local government officials to many elements of South Vietnamese society, such as teachers, health workers and agricultural officers: it is estimated that by 1958, 20 per cent of South Vietnam's village chiefs may have been murdered as part of this Communist effort, which was directed at the destabilization if not complete destruction of government control in South Vietnam's rural areas, so that a National Liberation Front shadow administration could be emplaced.

During January 1959, as a result of pressure from South Vietnamese cadres being increasingly targeted by the secret police, the Central Committee in North Vietnam promulgated to the cadres a secret resolution calling for the 'armed struggle' phase of the programme to take over South Vietnam. This phase was based on the launch of large-scale operations against the South Vietnamese military. Diem countered this with still stronger anti-Communist legislation, which was inadequate to prevent the increasing supply by North Vietnam of troops and supplies; the infiltration of still more men and weapons passed from North to South Vietnam via the many secret channels of the 'Ho Chi Minh Trail' through neutral Laos and

Cambodia, thereby bypassing the DMZ and avoiding the need, at this stage, to attempt major movements by sea where, with US support, South Vietnam was considerably stronger.

On 12 December 1960, the increasing level of South Vietnamese detestation of the corrupt Diem administration persuaded North Vietnam that the time was right for the creation of the National Front for the Liberation of South Vietnam (NLF), comprising nationalist and Communist groupings, although the latter had overall political control and steadily subsumed or eliminated the former. The task of the NLF was not overtly military, but covertly political, with the object of securing political control of South Vietnam by means of a popular rising. The key elements in the NLF's overall message, much boosted by a carefully orchestrated propaganda campaign, were patriotism, political and personal honesty, good government, the reunification of Vietnam, and the expulsion of US influences.

US administrations right through the period before and during the Vietnam War believed firmly but wrongly that North Vietnam exercised a monolithic control over the NLF, and thereby played down the extent to which the population of South Vietnam was being progressively alienated and angered by the repression and incompetence of Diem's paranoid administration. But it would be wrong to suggest that the NLF reflected an exclusively South Vietnamese reaction to Diem's rule, when, right from the start, North Vietnam had exploited any anti-Diem/anti-US feelings in South Vietnam for its own ends.

THE USA BECOMES EMBROILED

The bodies of Dang Van Bay and Phan Van Tro, killed by the Viet Cong at 19:30 on 13 October 1960, in Hoa Hiep Hamlet, Go Cong District.

During June 1961, only five months after his inauguration, President John F. Kennedy met Soviet premier Nikita Khrushchev in Vienna to discuss US/Soviet issues, but were unable to effect a significant rapport. In these circumstances, the US strategists and analysts of the period believed that South-East Asia would rapidly become the region in which Soviet forces would test the validity of the USA's policy of containment, which had been adopted somewhat tentatively in the course of the Truman administration, and had

become solidified, almost into dogma, as a result of the Korean War during the Eisenhower administration. The linchpin of the Kennedy administration's military policy was a US parity in long-range missile capability with the Soviets, but Kennedy was also a believer in the use of high-grade special forces, backed by the full extent of US technology and intelligence capabilities, to undertake successful operations in Third World countries to defeat the threat of Communist insurgencies. Kennedy believed that the tactics of low-intensity

warfare, employed by special forces such as the Green Berets, would be effective in a 'police action' campaign in Vietnam. Kennedy's beliefs, it should be noted, were based on the successful use of the tactics by the British to defeat the Communists in the Malayan Emergency (1948–60).

The year 1961 also saw the Kennedy administration faced with a trio of crises (the failure of the 'Bay of Pigs' invasion of Cuba, the construction of the Berlin Wall separating the Communist East Berlin from the three Western enclaves in the city's western part, and the settlement between the pro-Western government of Laos and the Communist Pathet Lao forces) and Kennedy himself came to believe that another US failure to check Communist expansion would seriously undermine the credibility of the USA with its allies. For these and other, sometimes personal reasons, Kennedy decided that Communism had to be checked in Vietnam. In May 1961 Vice-President Lyndon B. Johnson visited Saigon and told Diem that he could rely on more US aid to allow the development of a South Vietnamese military capability able to defeat the Communists. Throughout this apparently inexorable drift of the USA toward direct involvement in Vietnam, albeit only in an advisory capacity, Kennedy remained convinced that the solution had to be based on the defeat of the Communist irregular forces within South Vietnam by South Vietnamese forces, and initially refused to consider the deployment of US ground forces.

The trouble with this US perception, however, was that the South Vietnamese armed forces were qualitatively poor,

THE VIETNAM WAR

influential thinkers and analysts. By the middle of 1962, the original force of 700 military advisers in South Vietnam had swollen to a strength of 12,000.

By this time the Strategic Hamlet Program, schemed by South Vietnamese and US officials, had already begun. The object of this was to combat the Communist-led insurgency through the movement of populations which might otherwise fall under Communist influence or control. In 1961, therefore, US advisers launched a major effort to isolate peasant communities in the South Vietnamese countryside from contact with, and therefore influence by, the NLF. Together with its smaller-scale predecessor, the Rural Community

LEFT: Sgt Howard A. Stevens, an adviser from the 77th Ranger Detachment, conducting a class on the care and cleaning of the M-1 rifle in 1962.

BELOW: A helicopter of the US Marine Helicopter Squadron 92 passes over a lonely outpost in the guerrilla-infested mountain area of north-central Vietnam in 1963.

largely as a result of inadequate leadership by officers concerned with promoting their own interests rather than those of their men, corruption which robbed the men of their pay and the equipment they needed, and political interference which promoted Diem's adherents over all others. Thus the Army of the Republic of Vietnam (ARVN) was incapable of the tasks demanded of it, not only for the reasons listed above, but also as a result of the dismally poor morale stemming from the situation. In these circumstances the Communist irregular forces were able to raise the tempo of their attacks as the insurgency gathered momentum in the military vacuum provided by the ARVN's incapacity. American analysts suggested that some of the burden should be assumed by US troops, landed in South Vietnam in the guise of flood relief workers, and while Kennedy rejected the notion, he did authorize a further increase in military assistance, despite the warnings of several

Development Program, the Strategic Hamlet Program was of great significance in setting the course of South Vietnamese events in the late 1950s and early 1960s. The two programmes were akin to each other in seeking to ensure the separation of peasant communities from Communist irregular and insurgent forces through the establishment of fortified villages, and also by forcing the peasants to take an active role in what was, in effect, a civil war. The communities targeted in the Strategic Hamlet Program were of great importance to the Communist forces: together with tactics such as assassination, sabotage and sneak attacks on government troops, the irregular forces and guerrillas saw the obvious political as well as military advantages of winning the support of the peasant communities, which could thus supply recruits, shelter, food and, perhaps most importantly, current information. The adherence of South Vietnam's civil population, moreover, was in effect the touchstone of eventual success. Thus the Communists sought to win the rural communities over by propaganda, co-operation, and when these failed, coercion.

From 1954 or thereabouts, the South Vietnamese authorities had been coming down with an increasingly heavy hand on those whom it believed to be Communists or Communist sympathizers. All this achieved, in reality, was a further alienation of rural communities already disaffected by the greater wealth of urban communities, which they saw as the origins of all governmental evils. Soon after its formation in 1959, the NLF had built up what was, in effect, almost total control

THE VIETNAM WAR

over large sections of rural South Vietnam, at a time when there were only about 10,000 insurgents in the whole of South Vietnam. Diem and his brother recognized the threat that was being posed and launched the Rural Community Development Program (later 'Agroville') in the same year. Based in part on the success of a comparable effort by the British in Malaya, the Agroville concept attempted to isolate rural communities from contact with the Communist irregulars. Both incentive and force were employed in a 'carrot and stick' approach to uproot typical small rural communities for relocation into larger Agroville communities, with the result that some 23 of these, each with a population of several thousands, had been built by 1960.

This was, in effect, a forced migration, in that the obvious error had been made of separating the peasants from land which may have been in their families for many generations; when the peasant population demanded a reconsideration of the policy it was seen as playing right into the hands of the Communists. During 1961 the South Vietnamese government, with the aid of a number of US advisers, attempted to reshape the Agroville concept into what then became the Strategic Hamlet Program. This was based on smaller communities, each with fewer than 1,000 inhabitants, created on existing and also newly-developed settlements. Each of the hamlets was to be heavily fortified, relying for its defence on its own inhabitants supported by patrol forces as and when required. Each hamlet would have its own radio equipment for

THE USA BECOMES EMBROILED

despite the huge amounts of money being poured into the programme by the USA. As a result, the insurgents were finding it easier to sabotage and overrun these poorly defended communities, and so gained the access they required to the South Vietnamese peasantry. It is estimated that something in the order of 80 per cent of the hamlets in the heavily populated delta of the great Mekong river were under the control of the insurgents by the end of 1963.

The NLF, now increasingly known as the Viet Cong, capitalized on the general unpopularity of the Strategic Hamlets Program to launch its own programme of clever propaganda, which further exacerbated the peasant population's anger towards the South Vietnamese government. Few of the hamlet locations were both safe and possessed of good land; some peasants were forced to walk longer distances each day between their accommodation

ABOVE: Troops of a US 8th Airborne Battalion unload from a H-21 Shawnee helicopter to begin a mission. December 1962.

RIGHT: US adviser Captain Linton Beasley and Vietnamese 1st Lt Nguyen Tien inspect the weapons of a Vietnamese platoon during a training exercise. The US forces were in South Vietnam at that time as advisers and instructors, and to assist South Vietnam in matters of training, logistics, communications and transportation. They were under instructions not to fire unless fired upon. May 1962.

external communications, the arrangements for the hamlets also including supply lines, medical treatment and improved education facilities. In practice, few of these ever materialized.

South Vietnam was trying to accomplish too much too quickly when it began the Strategic Hamlet Program. In September 1962, the USA noted, 4.3 million people had been moved to 3,225 completed hamlets and another 2,000 or more were being developed; by July 1963 more than 8.5 million people had been settled in 7,205 hamlets. Thus in less than 12 months the number of completed hamlets and their populations had doubled, and this made it impossible for the South Vietnamese authorities either to support or protect the hamlets and their populations,

and the rice paddies, while others had been forced to leave the graves of their ancestors, or were compelled to work without payment to build the defences of their hamlets.

Coupled with the rising hatred for Diem, and his family, who controlled the programme and refused to listen to any complaint, the Strategic Hamlet Program was almost inevitably a failure, and in fact collapsed with the assassination of Diem late in 1963, the dissolution of the Committee for Strategic Hamlets occurring early in the following year.

One particular event early in January 1963 provided the USA with striking evidence that the Diem administration's earlier 'successes' against the Viet Cong were either illusory or the result of natural events rather than any real military capability by the South

Vietnamese army. Right at the beginning of 1963, South Vietnamese intelligence had discovered that a Viet Cong radio station was in operation close to the village of Ap Bac in the Plain of Reeds, estimating that the installation was being guarded only by a small force of irregulars. This seemed to be the opportunity for an easy victory, so the South Vietnamese command immediately dispatched a multi-battalion force composed of infantry, ranger (commando), helicopter and armoured units, supported by 51 US military advisers.

Almost everything that could go wrong did in fact go awry in the battle which followed on 2 January. Instead of encountering a company of irregulars, the South Vietnamese army force arrived at Ap Bac to face the Viet Cong 514th Battalion, a highly capable unit of some

400 regulars. Five US helicopters supporting the operation were destroyed within a few minutes: two succumbed to ground fire, one to an engine failure, and two after their pilots flew into the line of fire of the Viet Cong's weapons, in an attempt to rescue downed comrades who were, in fact, already safe behind friendly lines. As the fighting developed, the US advisers suggested the South Vietnamese, who had the benefit of a considerable superiority in numbers and firepower, should advance, but the South

ABOVE: US Army Sfc William D. Schultz (foreground left), assigned to the US Military Advisory Group, directs the loading of troops during a practice mission with the Vietnamese Airborne Brigade in 1962.

LEFT: A US Army adviser accompanies Vietnamese rangers in the Mekong river delta area in July 1962.

THE USA BECOMES EMBROILED

A base camp in the Vietnamese Highlands used by Communist irregular forces.

Vietnamese commanders (none of them above a captain, field-grade officers considering themselves too important to be risked in field service) were fully aware of Diem's feelings that casualties threatened his own position. The South Vietnamese officers procrastinated, one taking almost four hours to advance his armoured personnel carriers a mere 1,500 yards (1370m) in the face of Viet Cong small arms fire that was incapable of penetrating the vehicles' protection.

When the US advisers called for an airborne drop east of Ap Bac, to cut the Viet Cong's line of escape, the airborne troopers were in fact dropped to the west of the village and were therefore wholly wasted. When the US advisers called for a heavy artillery barrage, the South Vietnamese artillery responded with a mere four rounds per hour. The Viet Cong, therefore, were able to escape under cover of darkness, but not before a South Vietnamese air attack had

inadvertently struck a friendly unit, causing many casualties. Reliable sources report that besides the five helicopters destroyed, 11 more were damaged, and 65 South Vietnamese troops were killed, together with three US advisers. The wounded totalled about 100 South Vietnamese and six Americans.

American reporters knew nothing of the battle at the time of its start, but arrived shortly after it had ended and recorded the angry assessment of the US advisers concerning the performance of the South Vietnamese. One correspondent 'managed to overhear' a confidential briefing for General Paul D. Harkins, commanding the MACV, and other correspondents were in the area on 3 January when, in the course of mopping-up operations, South Vietnam artillery accidentally bombarded its own men. In these circumstances, therefore, the journalists had more than enough evidence to validate the most pessimistic estimations that they had already began to formulate.

The reports that appeared in US newspapers led to a considerable outcry against Diem within the USA. American commentators were able to show that the USA had spent US$400 million on South Vietnam and that 50 US service personnel had been killed while Diem steadfastly refuse to implement the programme of reform he had promised to make in exchange for US aid. Meanwhile, the Communist irregular forces were enjoying what was in effect a free run of South Vietnam's rural areas, and South Vietnamese officers were unwilling to commit their forces to combat even with the advantages of numbers and firepower. The only thing the USA could do in the circumstances,

THE VIETNAM WAR

unconvincing whitewash'. The Ap Bac episode further divided all levels of US representation in South Vietnam. So annoyed were they by the adverse press reports, that senior officials at the US Embassy limited their contacts with journalists to formal occasions, and set about putting the best face possible on the course of events on the ground. The converse of this approach, however, was that the US journalistic corps began to look at events in South Vietnam with increasingly jaundiced eyes, emphasizing and on occasion exaggerating everything they felt was wrong.

Of course, the South Vietnamese could have silenced the growing level of journalistic criticism by securing military success, or at least starting the programme of military reforms which

many commentators demanded, was to take full control of the war.

US officials in Washington and Saigon attempted to reassure Diem that they supported him despite the adverse press reports, but Diem still refused to implement the reforms that were manifestly required and had indeed been promised. The US attempt to shield and protect Diem only made matters worse. When representatives of the Department of State claimed that the South Vietnamese had fought with 'courage and determination' at Ap Bac, and both Harkins and Admiral Harry D. Felt, the commander-in-chief Pacific, stated that the battle had been a victory for the South Vietnamese, some US newspapers retorted that the situation in South Vietnam must indeed be critical if the US policy of loyalty to the Diem administration demanded the dissemination of 'such thin and

THE USA BECOMES EMBROILED

A South Vietnamese soldier questions a villager during an anti-Viet Cong patrol.

the USSR reached an agreement promising the neutrality of Laos.

By this time the US administration had become wholly exasperated with Diem, and it was the belief of some analysts that he might even be preparing to reach a political accommodation with Ho Chi Minh, being more concerned with preserving his own position than prosecuting the war. In the course of the summer of 1963, therefore, there was discussion concerning the possibility of 'regime change' in South Vietnam, but although the US Department of State was in favour of encouraging a coup against Diem, the Department of Defense and the Central Intelligence Agency each warned that this might be even more destabilizing than leaving Diem in place under increasing US pressure. Among the many suggestions as to the ways in which matters in South Vietnam might be improved was the removal of Diem's brother, Ngo Dinh Nhu, who headed the secret police and was widely perceived as the force behind the suppression of the Buddhists. But the USA appreciated the almost certain impossibility of persuading Diem to remove his brother, and this, in effect, sealed Diem's own fate.

The year was also marked by an altogether heavy-handed crackdown on Buddhist monks protesting about the Diem administration's discriminatory practices, and demanding their voice be heard in political circles. Diem's suppression of the protests by force triggered the 'Buddhist Revolt', in which several monks doused themselves in petrol before setting fire to themselves as they sat placidly on the road. Several of these self-immolations

the USA had demanded, but Diem attempted neither and allowed the course of events merely to drift.

At this stage of the conflict it was in the interests of all, including the Communists, that the conflict be limited to Vietnam, and on 23 July 1962 some 14 countries, including China, North Vietnam, South Vietnam, the USA and

were seen and recorded by the press for broadcast all over the world, leading to a wave of revulsion for the Diem administration. The Communist propaganda system exploited the situation for all it was worth, causing anti-Diem feelings to harden to destabilize South Vietnam's internal situation still further.

The CIA had already established links with South Vietnamese generals plotting the removal of Diem, and passed on the information that the USA would support any such move, even though the matter had not even been raised with the president. Diem was overthrown, and the two brothers were executed on 2 November 1963. The immediate consequence of the coup was total disorder in South Vietnam, a fact which North Vietnam immediately exploited to boost the level of support it was providing to the insurgents, who now had a freer hand as South Vietnam passed into a period of great political instability: military administrations followed each other in short order, and the approval of the South Vietnamese for their government fell steadily as the military came to be seen as little more than a puppet of the USA.

The rapid rise in the level and pace of the Communist insurgency persuaded Kennedy to authorize the despatch of still more advisers to South Vietnam, the ultimate figure being 16,300 to cope with rising guerrilla activity. These advisers were allocated to every level of the South Vietnamese military establishment, but whatever their competence at the purely military level, they lacked all but the most rudimentary appreciation, if even that, of the political situation, which was all-important in understanding the nature of the conflict being waged in South Vietnam. At the political level in the USA there was a greater understanding that the insurgency was a political power struggle, and the Kennedy administration was switching to a policy with its eyes on pacification and success in the 'hearts and minds' campaign intended to win the support of South Vietnam's population. But despite the warnings of the CIA, which highlighted the insurgency's control of much of South Vietnam's countryside, the Department of Defense remained convinced that the advisers should continue to be used only for training troops. By this time Kennedy had come to the conclusion that the USA's best course would be to extricate itself from South Vietnam, if only a way could be found to achieve this without the total disintegration of the USA's position and reputation as leader of the 'free world'.

Kennedy was assassinated on 22 November 1963 and was succeeded by his vice-president, Lyndon B. Johnson, who swiftly reaffirmed US support for South Vietnam. By the end of the year Saigon had received US$500 million in military aid, a large proportion of which was 'lost' in the mire of corruption endemic in the South Vietnamese administration. But Johnson allocated higher priority to his 'great society' and 'social progressive' programmes, and thus did not believe in the extreme urgency of the South Vietnamese situation as he took over from Kennedy. This tendency was exacerbated by the fact that Johnson was in essence a 'domestic' American and therefore had little understanding of the mindset of US foreign policy-

Captain Robert L. Webster, from Falls Church, Virginia, a pilot of one of the newly arrived UH-1B helicopters of the Utility Tactical Transport Helicopter Company, Saigon, examines MXL Emerson Squad 4 machine guns, mounted on his UH-1B, and operated by remote control by the co-pilot. December 1962.

makers, neither did he get on with McGeorge Bundy, the National Security adviser he had inherited from Kennedy. But on 24 November 1963 Johnson brought a small group together to talk with Henry Cabot Lodge, the US ambassador in South Vietnam, and was persuaded to offer his support in winning the Vietnam War. This was a promise hard to make but harder still to implement, even as the situation in South Vietnam was deteriorating

rapidly, especially in regions such as the Mekong delta, following the coup which had removed Diem.

The South Vietnamese Military Revolutionary Council, which now ruled the country, had 12 members and was led by Lieutenant General Duong Van Minh, tellingly described as 'a model of lethargy'. In the first month of 1964, however, Minh's administration was toppled by one led by Major General Nguyen Khanh.

CHAPTER THREE
THE GULF OF TONKIN INCIDENT

A Douglas A-1 aircraft of the USAF on active service in Vietnam, photographed from the cockpit of a US warplane. A North Vietnamese Mikoyan-Guryevich jet-powered fighter breaks away to port.

On 27 July 1964 the Johnson administration ordered the despatch to South Vietnam of another 5,000 military advisers, so raising the total to 21,000. Shortly after this there occurred the 'Gulf of Tonkin incident', which took the form of two 'attacks' by North Vietnamese naval forces on a pair of US Navy destroyers, the *Maddox* on 2 August and the *Turner Joy* two days later, steaming in international waters within the Gulf of Tonkin. Later findings, including a National Security Agency report, released in 2005, strongly suggests that the second attack did not in fact take place, as had long been believed, but also attempted to refute the equally long-standing belief that members of the Johnson administration had knowingly lied about the incident. At the time, the Gulf of Tonkin incident persuaded the US Congress to pass the South-East Asia Resolution ('Gulf of Tonkin Resolution') giving the president the authority to assist any country of South-East Asia threatened by 'Communist aggression'. The resolution also gave President Johnson the legal right to increase the US involvement in the Vietnam conflict, all of which took place less than a year after Johnson had become president. It was the preceding Kennedy administration which had begun to despatch military advisers to South Vietnam, and Kennedy himself had quite quickly begun to reconsider the suitability of this US move, largely as a result of his increasing perception of the Diem administration's corruption and abuse of civil rights, in combination with the South Vietnamese forces' revealed incompetence and steadfast refusal even to consider ways of redressing the situation. Just before his assassination, Kennedy had begun to reduce the number of US advisers, but Johnson believed that it was essential for the USA to challenge what was perceived to be the latest stage in Soviet expansionism, and therefore supported the growth of US involvement in Vietnam to prevent the domino effect from gaining momentum.

As far as the Gulf of Tonkin was concerned, this was the area in which a programme of clandestine attacks on North Vietnam had been initiated during 1961 as Operation 34A. The programme was initially supervised by

THE VIETNAM WAR

the CIA, but in 1964 was transferred to the Department of Defense, operated by the Studies and Operations Group of what was now the Military Assistance Command, Vietnam. The programme involved many elements, but for the naval part the USA had bought from Norway a number of Tjeld-class fast-attack craft and had shipped them to South Vietnam. The craft were manned by South Vietnamese crews, but their operational use was supervised directly by Admiral Ulysses S. Grant Sharp, commander-in-chief of the US Pacific Fleet, his headquarters being in Honolulu, Hawai.

Once the attacks on its coast had begun, North Vietnam protested to the International Control Commission, set up in 1954 to police the terms of the

LEFT: Camp Trai Trung Sup, in South Vietnam, the 3rd Corps Basic Training Centre for the Civilian Irregular Defense Group (CIDG), devised by the CIA in early 1961 to counter expanding Viet Cong influence in South Vietnam's Central Highlands, is commanded by the Vietnamese Special Forces (LLDB) and advised by Detachment A, 5th US Special Forces. Here, Sgt Alvin J. Rouly supervises CIDG trainees firing M-79 grenade-launchers.

BELOW LEFT: A member of a USAF Air Commando C-44 unit loads a battery of speakers onto the aircraft in preparation for a psychological warfare mission.

BELOW: Members of the 1st Special Forces and Vietnamese volunteers watch grenades exploding during a practice run atop Nui Ba Den in 1964.

THE GULF OF TONKIN INCIDENT

ABOVE: Forward air control aircraft (FACS) of the USAF.

RIGHT: Sgt Thomas G. Gallant, of Detachment A, 5th Special Forces Group, shows a Vietnamese soldier's wife the right way to care for his wounded foot, so that he can avoid making constant trips to the dispensary at Camp Bunard.

Geneva Accords, but the USA denied any involvement. Four years later, however, the Secretary of Defense, Robert S. McNamara, revealed to the Congress that US Navy destroyers had co-operated with the South Vietnamese FACs in their attacks on the North Vietnamese coast. Although her captain knew of the operations, the *Maddox* was not directly involved.

At the time of the Gulf of Tonkin incident, US-trained South Vietnamese commandos were active in the area: operating from Da Nang, just to the south of the DMZ, in the ex-Norwegian FACs, these commandos made attacks in the Gulf of Tonkin area on the nights of 31 July and 3 August. In the first of these undertakings, the commandos attacked a radio transmitter on the island of Hon Nieu, and in the second

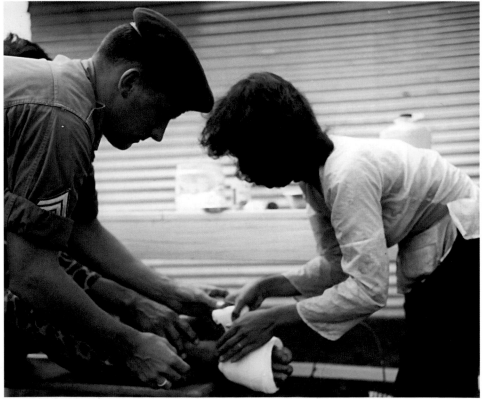

THE VIETNAM WAR

round, headed south toward South Vietnamese waters, and was there joined by the *Turner Joy*.

On 4 August another sortie into the waters off North Vietnam was begun by the two destroyers, under the command of Captain John J. Herrick, with orders to approach no closer than 11 miles (18 km) to the North Vietnamese coast. The destroyers detected radar and radio signals suggesting, it was believed, that the North Vietnamese navy was about to make another attack. For some two hours the ships fired on radar targets, manoeuvring within the context of electronic and visual reports of hostile craft, but shortly after this Herrick signalled that an attack might not have

LEFT: The US deployed planes on leaflet drop missions as the most efficient way of conveying information to the Vietnamese people.

BELOW: An American adviser and his South Vietnamese companions keep a sharp lookout for possible guerrilla attack as they cruise along a river near the Cambodian border. The troops were en route to a suspected Viet Cong encampment, where they burned buildings and destroyed cattle and food supplies. The menfolk were missing, but the community's women and children were evacuated from the area.

bombarded a radar site at Cape Vinh Son with a cannon on the FAC. The North Vietnamese responded by attacking warships in the area, of which the most evident was the *Maddox*, which was undertaking an electronic intelligence-gathering mission in the Gulf of Tonkin under the local command of Admiral George Stephen Morrison on the aircraft carrier *Bon Homme Richard*. On 2 August the *Maddox* was attacked by three North Vietnamese P-4-class torpedo boats some 28 miles (45 km) off the North Vietnamese coast in international waters. The *Maddox* evaded a torpedo attack and opened fire with her 127-mm (5in) guns, forcing the torpedo craft to withdraw. Warplanes from the carrier USS *Ticonderoga* then attacked the North Vietnamese craft as they pulled back, claiming to have sunk one of them and badly damaging another; in fact none of the craft was sunk. The *Maddox*, which had been hit by only one 14.5-mm (0.57-in) heavy machine gun

51

been attempted, and that there may actually have been no North Vietnamese vessels in the area. There followed an exchange of signals which failed to produce any reliable information, but the crew of the *Maddox* was sure that an attack had taken place, and the 'reality' of the attack also began to gain credence in Washington.

Thus warplanes were launched from the aircraft carriers *Ticonderoga* and *Constellation* to attack North Vietnamese torpedo boat bases and fuel facilities. These were ordered by Johnson, who was facing an election that year, and who addressed the nation on television that same day. Although the *Maddox* had been providing passive intelligence support for South Vietnamese attacks at Hon Me and Hon Ngu, McNamara denied to the Congress that the US Navy had actively supported South Vietnamese military operations in the Gulf of Tonkin. McNamara claimed, therefore, that the North Vietnamese attacks were 'unprovoked' as the ships had been in international waters. He also claimed that there was irrefutable proof that an unprovoked second attack had been made on the *Maddox*.

On 7 August the Congress passed the joint Gulf of Tonkin Resolution, giving Johnson the authority to conduct military operations in South-East Asia without any declaration of war, and granting him permission 'to take all necessary steps, including the use of armed force, to assist any member or protocol state of the Southeast Asia Collective Defense Treaty requesting assistance in defence of its freedom.'

The Gulf of Tonkin incident thus marked the beginning of major US

military intervention in the Vietnam War. At this stage of the conflict, it should be noted that the number of insurgents in South Vietnam was in the order of 100,000, a huge rise from the commonly accepted figure of 5,000–10,000 in 1959. Conventional military wisdom suggests that the efforts of ten conventional soldiers were required to defeat one insurgent, and the US was therefore committing itself to an effort needing more men that the US Army could ever hope to deploy to South Vietnam.

On the eve of his re-election as president during the first week of

OPPOSITE: South Vietnamese servicemen learn the intricacies of belt-fed machine guns on the outriggers of a Bell UH-1 Huey helicopter.

BELOW: Montagnard commandos prepare for a patrol into Viet Cong territory at a Commando Training Center (Special Forces) in 1963.

THE GULF OF TONKIN INCIDENT

feeling that a moment of decision was at hand was mirrored by the US public at large. By mid-November 1964 polls were now showing that the US population had the matter of Vietnam near to the top of the list of problems needing to be resolved. Yet the US seemed to have available to it little in the way of options, which were either to spur the South Vietnamese into effective reform and more capable military action, or itself assume the leadership of military affairs in South Vietnam.

Speculation about South Vietnam was increased when, on 27 November, Maxwell D. Taylor, the US ambassador in South Vietnam, arrived in the US for talks. The Department of State claimed that they were merely routine, but US journalists swiftly appreciated that something altogether more important was in the air, and suggested that Taylor

ABOVE: Australian soldiers on active duty in Vietnam.

RIGHT: Using a modern means of injection, a member of one of the 21 US military teams, under the Provincial Health Assistance Program (PHAP), inoculates an apprehensive Vietnamese woman against cholera. The PHAP programme was co-ordinated, and in many cases financed, by the Agency for International Development (US AID) and currently maintains 43 US and free-world medical teams in 43 provinces of South Vietnam.

November 1964, Johnson established an inter-agency working group to explore all the options available to the US in South Vietnam. Johnson did not wish to enlarge the war, either geographically or in the USA's overall commitment, but did appreciate that another approach was required to spur the South Vietnamese into greater and more effective action. The two main problems here were, of course, the fact that the South Vietnamese administration was beset by factional strife, and that the South Vietnamese army was achieving little if anything against the Viet Cong. Yet the situation was not so much static as deteriorating rapidly, and the rate of its deterioration would surely increase; it was believed, on the basis of MACV intelligence, that the Communists were moving men and matériel into South Vietnam at an increasing rate. Johnson's

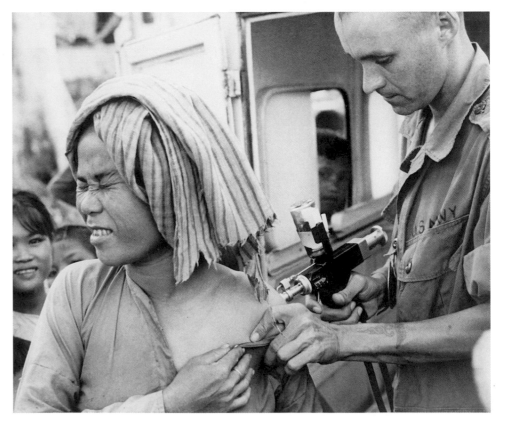

US soldiers surveying an area in Quang Tri province.

would recommend an escalation of the US commitment to the Vietnam War. To many, this seemed to be a course pregnant with the possibility of disaster, for if the course of events to date had provided absolute proof of anything, it was that it was impossible to rely on the South Vietnamese; but even to those who had a sense of impending doom,

there appeared to be no realistic alternative to an increased US commitment, as a withdrawal would have crippled the US's worldwide reputation for reliability and the support of its allies.

Taylor did suggest an increased US commitment, if only as a means of improving South Vietnamese morale.

But Johnson was firmly of the belief that the US should escalate its presence only if political stability in South Vietnam was improved, and Taylor recommended a compromise solution. The presidential working group had recommended a series of plans incorporating a carefully considered series of graduations in the

intensification of a US air campaign against the Communists, starting with attacks on Communist infiltration routes at the Laotian northern end of the Ho Chi Minh Trail and culminating in a limited but progressively more intense campaign of bombing against North Vietnamese targets. Taylor now suggested that the proposed plan for this air campaign closely mirrored the March North land campaign proposed by Khanh, and could therefore be recommended to the South Vietnamese as a pair of synergistic campaigns so long as the South Vietnamese were prepared to make a major effort commensurate with the US commitment. The US could thus inform the South Vietnamese that it was investigating the possibility of exerting military pressure directly on North Vietnam, offering to implement the plan if South Vietnam began the reforms which had been needed for so long. Taylor claimed that his suggested course of action would promote the stability long wanted by the US for South Vietnam, and would also convince the Communists that continued aggression against South Vietnam would in fact visit destruction on themselves.

Johnson accepted the concept, but at this stage authorized no more than its first elements. Although the Americans would intensify air attacks against infiltration routes in Laos, and support South Vietnamese covert naval operations along the coast of North Vietnam, it would go no further. Johnson also authorized Taylor to tell the South Vietnamese that there was the possibility of joint US and South Vietnamese air attacks on North Vietnam only as responses to

THE VIETNAM WAR

Communist attacks in South Vietnam, but also that he should lay emphasis on the fact that such attacks would start only when the US had evidence that the South Vietnamese had implemented the reforms which would allow them to cope with the almost inevitable escalation of the Communist effort in South Vietnam.

The level of operations authorized by Johnson were launched almost immediately after Taylor's return to South Vietnam, but neither the US air attacks on Laos nor the South Vietnamese naval operations along North Vietnam's coast had any appreciable effect. The naval programme

had barely been launched before the onset of the monsoon season caused its termination.

The escalation of the air war over Laos started on 14 December with the launch of Operation Barrel Roll, which also failed as Johnson had limited the effort to a pair of missions, each with only four aircraft, each week. Adding insult to injury, moreover, Barrel Roll was so limited that the North Vietnamese did not even know it existed, and believed the attacks were just another aspect of the armed reconnaissance flights American warplanes were already making. Just as

inevitably, the reforms to which Khanh had readily agreed were never implemented. Here the cause of the difficulty lay with the High National Council, a body established in the aftermath of the August 1964 crisis to draft a new constitution and pave the way to the establishment of a civilian government. Comprising of civilians of senior years, representing a broad cross-section of South Vietnamese society, the HNC met with universal indifference but nonetheless managed to get on the wrong side of Khanh, whose preoccupation was to ensure that a civilian government was little more than

THE GULF OF TONKIN INCIDENT

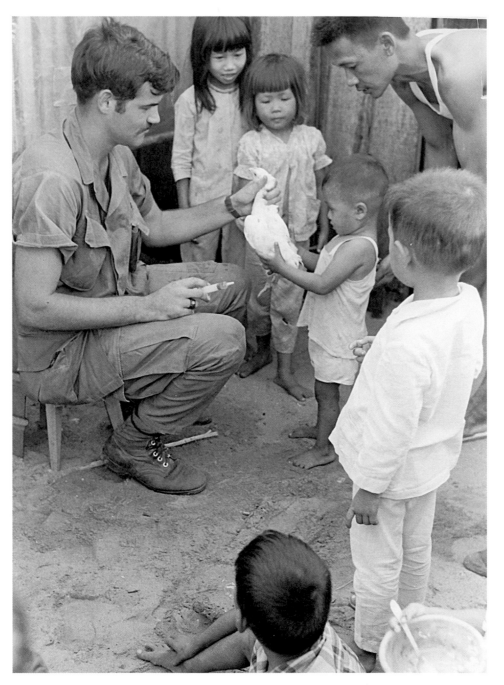

a respectable façade for continued military rule.

The HNC appointed an agricultural engineer of considerable years, Phan Khac Suu, as head of state, and Suu nominated a former schoolteacher and the current mayor of Saigon, Tran Van Huong, as prime minister. Progressing down the ladder of supposed power,

Huong selected technicians rather than politicians as tmembers of his cabinet, and in the process managed to alienate both the Buddhists and the Roman Catholics, each of whom demanded political power. Both religious groups were soon sponsoring street riots, but with Khanh's promise of military support, Huong declared martial law

and managed to suppress the rioters; this merely worsened matters, Khanh being in no real position to support Huong as he himself was in deep political trouble. The 'Young Turks', a group of young officers (so-called after the organization of young officers which dominated Turkish politics in 1908–18), had been among Huong's most important supporters, but were now becoming increasingly unhappy with Khanh. Air Vice Marshal Nguyen Cao Ky informed General William C. Westmoreland, Harkin's successor as head of the MACV, that the combination of military setbacks in rural areas, Khanh's compromises with the Buddhists, and his continued refusal to act decisively, had persuaded the Young Turks that there had to be a change of leadership.

Very soon after this, therefore, senior officers of the South Vietnamese armed forces established an Armed Forces Council to 'aid' Khanh in military matters. A showdown was clearly in the immediate offing, so Taylor and Westmoreland arranged an informal meeting of the opposing factions to warn that continued disorder would create a strongly adverse effect on the US's relationship with South Vietnam. Only political stability, the Americans insisted, would ensure an increase in US aid. The generals agreed to work together to promote this object but, as always in South Vietnamese politics, this was a mere fiction to buy time. In fact the time bought was very little, for on 19 December the Young Turks asked Khanh to remove the senior officers blocking the paths of their own promotions, by having the HNC mandate the retirement of all general officers with more than 25 years of service. Khanh agreed to do this, but the HNC refused and was thereupon dismissed, so triggering angry exchanges between Taylor, Khanh, and the Young Turks. Taylor saw that Khanh had effectively prevented any implementation of mutual military operations along the lines desired by the US administration's action, and severely chastised Ky and others of the Young Turks, on the grounds that irresponsible actions of the officer corps had ended the possibility of military planning reliant on South Vietnamese stability.

On the following day, Taylor met Khanh and suggested that the latter should retire and leave the country. Khanh responded on 22 December with an obvious attempt to unify the officer corps behind him by invoking national honour: it was better, Khanh promulgated in an order of the day, 'to live poor but proud as free citizens of an independent country than in ease and shame as slaves of the foreigners and Communists'. In an interview with a correspondent of the *New York Herald Tribune*, Khanh claimed that Taylor had undertaken activities 'beyond imagination as far as an ambassador is concerned'.

When Khanh's assertion appeared in print, the Department of State backed Taylor, confirming that the ambassador had acted with the full support of the US government. Secretary of State Dean Rusk began the process of checking the Young Turks by stating that the US would soon end some of its assistance to South Vietnam as the Khanh administration was clearly not prepared to use the aid properly.

In a terrorist attack of great audacity on 24 December, the Viet Cong bombed

A US adviser, working with children in Vietnam in August 1964.

the Brink Hotel in Saigon, where many US officers were billeted. The attack killed two Americans and injured 51 US and South Vietnamese citizens. This was the type of event which should have triggered joint US and South Vietnamese action but, against Taylor's advice, Johnson now refused to authorize air attacks on North Vietnam. In this refusal, Johnson was acting in the belief that without indisputable evidence of the Viet Cong's responsibility for the bombing, the US people might construe the attack as provocation engineered by

Khanh. Johnson also hoped that the Young Turks might draw the conclusion that the lack of retaliation was the result of their own performance in the periods just past, and so decide to eschew factionalism in favour of a united national resistance to Communism.

Johnson's thinking seems to have been right. Over the next ten days, the US embassy, Khanh and the Young Turks achieved a compromise which returned Huong and a civilian government to office, even though it did not restore the HNC. But the compromise had no effect

THE GULF OF TONKIN INCIDENT

on the task of restoring order in South Vietnam. The Buddhists were already sworn to oppose any regime headed by Huong and, on his return to office, began to look for a reason to remove him. Such a pretext arrived on 17 January 1965, when Huong decreed an enlargement of the national draft for the South Vietnamese forces. Buddhist agitators were almost immediately out on the streets preaching rebellion, civil unrest spread to every major urban centre in South Vietnam, the 8,000-book US Information Agency Library in Hue was destroyed, and a teenage girl burned herself to death in the first example of

self-immolation since the anti-Diem rioting more than 12 months earlier. On 27 January, the Young Turks, bent on action, launched a coup, declared that Huong was not capable of maintaining order, and demanded that Khanh form a new government.

Against the background of political turmoil in Saigon and South Vietnam's other major cities, fighting continued in the rural area around the capital, and here the Viet Cong inexorably gained the upper hand. During the last week of December 1964, for example, Communist forces occupied the village of Binh Gia (in Phuoc Tuy province), an

anti-Communist community of 6,000 people located on the coast near Saigon. The subsequent Battle of Binh Gia, which was only part of a larger Communist undertaking, was fought between 28 December 1964 and 1 January 1965; not only did it mark a signal defeat for the South Vietnamese army but it also provided striking evidence of the problem facing the USA as it struggled to find ways of propping up the South Vietnamese regime.

Toward the close of 1964, the fact that South Vietnam was facing political

THE VIETNAM WAR

In addition to normal combat operations while on a combined sweep operation in Binh Duong province in September 1965, approximately 20 miles (32km) north of Saigon, elements of the 173rd Airborne Brigade conduct civic action and psychological warfare activities. Sgt Arnold S. Jaudon, 172nd Missile Battalion, hands leaflets to be stored on the aircraft until drop time to 1st Lt James R. Paris, US Army Broadcast and Visual Activities, Pacific, who is on temporary duty to Military Assistance Command, Vietnam (MACV).

instability in the aftermath of the coup against Diem presented the Communists with the ideal opportunity to exploit the South Vietnamese government's adverse political and military situation, and at the same time pursue instructions from North Vietnam to start a programme of military offensives. Within this overall situation, the National Liberation Front seized the opportunity to commemorate the fourth anniversary of its establishment with a major military victory. The first operational formation of the Viet Cong, the 9th Viet Cong Division, was entrusted with the task, and in many respects far exceeded the hopes which had been placed on it. Thus the fighting in and around Binh Gia demonstrated that the Communist forces in South Vietnam had reached the level of military maturity at which they could commit themselves to combat with equanimity against the best South Vietnamese army formations.

On 11 October 1964 the senior political and military leadership in North Vietnam had ordered the NLF to carry out a series of offensives

THE GULF OF TONKIN INCIDENT

RIGHT & BELOW: A US Medical Civic Action Program (MEDCAP) team from the sub-sector, III Corps, MACV, treated 624 patients from the island village of Thai Hung, 9 miles (15km) north-west of Bien Hoa on the Saigon river. Pfc Marcelino Galvin (right), 25th Medical Battalion, 173rd Airborne Brigade Infantry Division, dispenses medicine to a villager who has been seen by the doctor. October 1966.

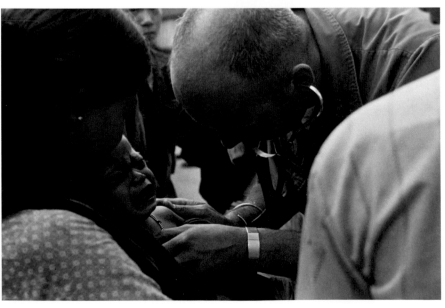

during the winter and spring of 1965. To help the southern insurgents carry out their offensive, General Nguyen Chi Thanh was nominated to supervise the full range of military operations in South Vietnam, while officers such as Major General Le Trong Tan were responsible for military preparations, which began during November. As part of the operation, the Nam Bo Regional Command identified its key areas of operations as the Baria-Long Khanh and the Binh Long-Phuoc Long regions. The 271st and 272nd Viet Cong Regiments were selected for the forthcoming operation and were placed under the command of the Forward Command Committee. Having completed their training, thay began to move in the direction of the Baria-Long Khanh region. With North Vietnamese assistance, the Viet Cong built up their stocks of weapons, ammunition and other vital matériel, and were instructed to destroy any South Vietnamese army units along Routes 2 and 15.

In the first days of November 1964, the 271st and 272nd Viet Cong Regiments, supported by the 80th Viet Cong Artillery Detachment, moved out of War Zone D, and by the end of the

THE VIETNAM WAR

month had reached their rendezvous location, where they were joined by the 500th and 800th Viet Cong Battalions from Military Region 7, the 186th Viet Cong Battalion from Military Region 6, and the 445th Viet Cong Company from the Hoai Duc district.

Before committing themselves to the main phase of the operation, the Viet Cong inflicted many casualties on South Vietnamese forces in five separate engagements, the South Vietnamese army losing two first-line and one reserve battalions. An entire company of South Vietnamese M113 Armored Personnel Carriers was also destroyed on 9 December, which

allowed the Viet Cong to overrun the Hoai Duc district and several strategic hamlets such as Dat Do, Long Thanh and Nhon Trach.

By a time early in January 1965 the Viet Cong had significantly enlarged its theatre of operations, and the Communists were planning more military operations against major South Vietnamese installations, with Binh Gia the next target. This village was surrounded by rubber and banana plantations, and was located about 42 miles (67km) from Saigon. Most of the inhabitants were Roman Catholics fleeing from North Vietnam as a result of Communist persecution, and the

local priest was the commander of the militia forces.

The 9th Viet Cong Division, with the 514th Viet Cong Battalion in the lead, began its assault during the early morning of 28 December, quickly overrunning several outposts and overwhelming the local militia forces without difficulty. Later in the morning of the same day, two South Vietnamese Ranger units attempted a counter-attack, but were unable to clear the Viet Cong from their positions, although they did briefly reach a point only 330 yards (300m) from Binh Gia village before a Viet Cong battalion drove them back. Reinforcements from the

American and allied soldiers during the defence of Saigon.

THE GULF OF TONKIN INCIDENT

A Soviet merchant ship transporting GAZ-53 cargo trucks in the Gulf of Tonkin, bound for North Vietnam. This photo was taken in January 1969.

One company of the 4th Marine Battalion was sent to the crash site to recover the bodies, but once again the South Vietnamese were ambushed and pinned down. On the morning of 31 December, the rest of 4th Marine Battalion was committed in an attempt to rescue the trapped company. At the site of the crash, the 4th Marine Battalion and its US advisers located fresh graves, which turned out to be a ploy for another ambush in which the Viet Cong launched strong attacks. Further South Vietnamese reinforcements, of the 29th, 30th and 33rd Ranger Battalions, were ambushed and took heavy losses. This latest stage of the battle led to the death of 35 South Vietnamese officers, 112 Marines and 71 wounded, bringing the total casualties to more than 300; six US advisers were also killed. On 1 January more South Vietnamese reinforcements arrived, but they were too late.

Despite the fact that it had been heavily defeated, the South Vietnamese army stubbornly asserted that it had won a victory, the Viet Cong being no longer in Binh Gia. The battle had nonetheless provided striking evidence of the Viet Cong's growing military strength, especially in the region of the Mekong river delta. This was the first occasion on which the National Liberation Front had undertaken a large-scale operation, holding its ground and fighting for four days against government troops supported by armour, artillery and helicopters. The Viet Cong had demonstrated that with the aid of weapons and supplies from North Vietnam it could fight and defeat the best units the South Vietnamese army possessed. In

30th and 33rd Rangers arrived on the following day but could not dislodge the Viet Cong, which was now well dug-in; after some heavy fighting the Ranger battalions were heavily damaged by Viet Cong machine gun fire. On the morning of 30 December, the South Vietnamese 4th Marine Battalion was delivered by helicopter, recapturing Binh Gia without difficulty as the Viet Cong had disappeared; but later on the same day a US Army gunship was shot down, and all four of the crew were killed.

THE VIETNAM WAR

recognition of the regiment's performance during the Binh Gia campaign, the NLF high command bestowed the honour title 'Binh Gia Regiment' on the 271st Viet Cong. After the campaign, all the Viet Cong units involved withdrew to War Zone D in order to plan the next offensive, which was to be directed against Dong Xoai.

This was an event of great significance, for it persuaded

Westmoreland that the Communist forces were trying out new tactics, possibly with a view to making the switch from irregular and small unit warfare to a more conventional conflict in which large units attacked to take and then hold ground. Westmoreland and Taylor agreed that in the hope of prompting a new sense of unity in the South Vietnamese, the US should respond in a fashion it had not yet tried, and therefore

recommended to Johnson that the bombing of North Vietnam should be commenced. Assistant Secretary of State William P. Bundy concurred with the suggestion of Westmoreland and Taylor, claiming that the Binh Gia setback indicated a new low in South Vietnam's already heavily compromised national morale. All that was required, everyone agreed, was for the North Vietnamese to provide the right kind of provocation.

CHAPTER FOUR
'ROLLING THUNDER'

The provocation for which the Johnson administration has been waiting was duly delivered on 7 February 1965, when the Viet Cong attacked the compound and associated airstrip of the US advisory team at Camp Holloway, near Pleiku in the Central Highlands, killing nine Americans and wounding more than 100. Following on almost immediately from the 'Tet Truce', an unofficial ceasefire by the Viet Cong from 1–6 February to mark the start of the Vietnamese New Year, the attack seemed to be a deliberate provocation, possibly designed to impress the Soviet premier, Alexei Kosygin, who was then in Hanoi on an official visit.

The leader of a US observation mission in Saigon at this time was McGeorge Bundy, the National Security adviser, who recommended an immediate retaliatory raid on North Vietnam. Johnson concurred, and on the very same day 49 warplanes of the US Navy attacked the Communist barracks at Dong Hoi just to the north of the DMZ, a target specifically selected so as to offer no threat to Kosygin. Delayed by inclement weather

until the following day, the South Vietnamese component of the attack struck another barracks at Vinh, in the same area.

Johnson told the USA: 'We have no choice now but to clear the decks, and make absolutely clear our continued determination to back South Vietnam in its fight to maintain its independence.' Soon after this, Taylor recommended to Johnson the beginning of a 'measured, controlled sequence of actions' against North Vietnam, a sentiment with which Bundy agreed.

THE VIETNAM WAR

The first series of air attacks following the Communist offensives on Pleiku and Qui Nhon were Operations Flaming Dart I and Faming Dart II. The attacks had originally been conceived as part of a three-phase 'program' that had begun with the Operation Barrel Roll air attacks on Communist targets inside Laos during December 1964, and had therefore already been planned. A total of 49 sorties was flown for Flaming Dart I on 7 February, and 99 sorties for Flaming Dart II on 11 February, the first targeting North Vietnamese army bases near Dong Hoi, and the second Viet Cong logistics and communications facilities near the DMZ.

The US reaction to the perceived Communist escalation was not limited to attacks on targets in North Vietnam. The Johnson administration also allowed the use of US warplanes to tackle

LEFT: The aircraft carrier CVAN-65 (USS Enterprise), equipped with Douglas A-4C Skyhawks, at sea off Vietnam.

BELOW: A Vought F-8 Crusader shot down in North Vietnam.

The Viet Cong struck again on 10 February, this time in Qui Nhon, destroying a hotel used as a billet for US enlisted personnel and killing 23 men as the building collapsed. Many other men were trapped and injured in the rubble. Johnson now authorized a second series of reprisals, and two days later announced that Operation Rolling Thunder would be launched as a 'measured and limited air action' against military targets in the regions of North Vietnam to the south of the 19th parallel.

'ROLLING THUNDER'

An F-8 Crusader on the aircraft carrier CVA-64 (USS Constellation).

Communist targets in South Vietnam. On 19 February Martin B-57 twin-jet bombers of the USAF undertook the first attacks flown by the US forces in jet-powered aircraft, rather than piston-engined machines such as the Douglas A-1 Skyraider and Douglas B-26 Invader, in support of South Vietnamese ground units. On 24 February jet-powered warplanes of the USAF were used again over South Vietnam, in this instance to destroy a Communist ambush in the Central Highlands by means of a massive series of tactical air sorties.

The first mission of the Rolling Thunder campaign was scheduled for 20 February but was cancelled, together with its immediate successors, after an attempted coup in Saigon, which caused the final overthrow of Khanh as Phan Huy Quat, a civilian, became the nominal prime minister as a front for continued military rule. Rolling Thunder was finally launched on 2 March, when US and South Vietnamese warplanes destroyed an ammunition depot and a naval base in North Vietnam. This was a week after the US administration made the first official announcement that US airmen were flying combat missions against the Viet Cong.

Rolling Thunder was planned as a graduated campaign in which any concessions by the Communists would result in a scaling-back of the air operation, but was a failure inasmuch as it appears to have had no significant material effect, and in fact probably hardened the resolve of the North Vietnamese and their South Vietnamese adherents to tightening the screw, Rolling Thunder having made little apparent impact by holding true to its overall plan. Part of this failure to make an immediate impact resulted from Johnson's refusal to allow more than two to four raids, by only modest numbers of warplanes, each week. Westmoreland believed, probably correctly, that this was a tactic which hardly suggested any real resolve in US planning, caused only insignificant damage, and at the same time added risk but not results to the US position vis-à-vis the Vietnam War. The North Vietnamese response was the exploitation of its links with the Chinese and Soviets to undertake, as a matter of great urgency, the construction of a comprehensive air-defence system of the Soviet pattern, with radar and observer sites feeding data to a central headquarters which exercised tight control of anti-aircraft artillery, surface-to-air missiles and fighters. Westmoreland had stated, quite prophetically, that Rolling Thunder would 'result in mounting casualties as the war goes on – perhaps more than we are willing or even able to sustain'.

Rolling Thunder was thus a sustained and graduated campaign by the US Air Force's 2nd Air Division (later the 7th Air Force), the US Navy, and South Vietnamese air forces against targets in North Vietnam to 1 November 1968. The operation's four objectives, which had not been fixed at the

THE VIETNAM WAR

benign of operating conditions, and within the context of a totally free military hand, but was in fact rendered difficult if not impossible by the political and military limitations imposed on the US and South Vietnamese air forces, and by the extensive nature of the military aid which North Vietnam received from the USSR and China.

The operation was the most intensive air campaign undertaken in the course of the 'Cold War' period, and also the most problematical undertaken by the US air forces since the US Army Air Force's daylight bombing campaign against Germany in the Second World War. With the aid of its Communist supporters in China and the USSR, the North Vietnamese were able to construct a complex and multi-layered air-defence system, using air-to-air as

LEFT: Three armed Vietnamese women. To resist the US Air Force bombing over North Vietnam between the 17th and 19th parallels, the inhabitants of the Quang Trach district in Quang Binh province constructed 60 miles (100km) of trenches, leading from each house to the centre of the village.

BELOW: Bombs from US aircraft strike their targets in North Vietnam. Operation Rolling Thunder was designed to inflict major damage on North Vietnam's physical infrastructure and convince the North Vietnamese of America's determination not to allow the defeat of South Vietnam. But the campaign was fought at too low a level and in too desultory a fashion to achieve its objectives.

beginning of the campaign and evolved during the period in which they were undertaken, were to bolster the morale and resolve of the South Vietnamese government; provide the North Vietnamese government with strong evidence of the futility of supporting Communist insurgency in South Vietnam; eliminate North Vietnam's transportation and communications networks, industrial base, and air-defence system; and to curtail if not halt the movement of men and matériel from North Vietnam to South Vietnam. The implementation of this entire scheme would have been difficult under the most

operations, which followed the Communist attacks on US personnel at Pleiku and Qui Nhon, to hit targets in the southern region of North Vietnam, where most of the North Vietnamese army and its supply dumps were located.

Then, after coming under considerable pressure from the Joint Chiefs-of-Staff as the Communist forces continued to gain success after success in South Vietnam, Johnson gave his approval to Rolling Thunder as a sustained bombing effort to be linked directly to any overt Communist activities. Rolling Thunder was initially to have been an eight-week campaign wholly consistent with the restrictions imposed by Johnson and McNamara, but if the Communist military operations in South Vietnam were pressed forward 'with DRV [Democratic

ABOVE: Pilots of Air Squadron 2 of the Vietnam People's Air Force, ready to take off in their Russian-made MiG-21s. 1968.

RIGHT: US airmen kit themselves up for a mission.

well as surface-to-air weapons, and this posed US airmen with some of the most difficult tactical problems they had ever encountered.

By the end of August of the previous year, in their follow-up to the Gulf of Tonkin Resolution, the Joint Chiefs-of-Staff had drawn up a list of 94 targets to be destroyed as part of a co-ordinated eight-week air campaign against North Vietnam's transportation network, and within this context bridges, railway marshalling yards, docks, barracks and supply dumps were to be attacked and destroyed. Johnson was concerned that the US campaign might spark a direct intervention by the Chinese or Soviets, which might escalate into a world war. With the support of McNamara, Johnson refused to authorize a bombing campaign that was so extensive in its targeting aims, and it was this which limited the scope of the Flaming Dart

THE VIETNAM WAR

LEFT: An F-4 Phantom fighter bomber refuelling from a KC-135 Stratotanker.

BELOW: After several unsuccessful attempts, a USAF F-4 Phantom, using laser-guided bombs, eventually destroys the Thanh Hoa Bridge spanning the Song Ma river in Thanh Hoa province.

Republic of Vietnam] support, strikes against the DRV would be extended with intensified efforts against targets north of the 19th parallel'. The Johnson administration believed that the combination of carefully controlled military and diplomatic pressure would persuade North Vietnam to call off its campaign in South Vietnam. The US military machine was not as optimistic, as the campaign as currently envisaged was limited to the region south of the 19th parallel, and even then the targets had to be approved on an individual basis by Johnson and McNamara.

On 2 March, the first mission of the Rolling Thunder campaign was flown against an ammunition storage dump in the area of Xom Bang, and on the same date South Vietnamese Skyraider warplanes attacked the naval base at Quang Khe. This first effort came as a

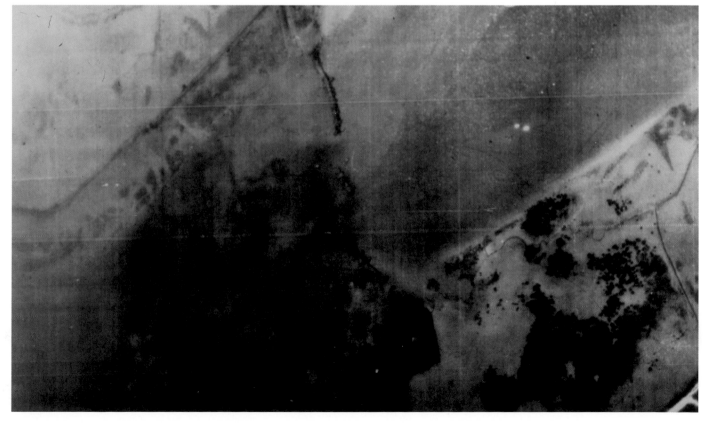

'ROLLING THUNDER'

important targets under constant threat by bombing those of lesser importance. From the very start of Rolling Thunder, these were decided by senior political and military figures in the USA, who set not only the targets to be attacked, but also even the tactical details, such as the time of the attack on the given day, the number and types of warplanes to be flown, the tonnages and types of ordnance to be used, and, on occasion, even the direction of the attack. Attacks were forbidden within 34.5 miles (55.5km) of Hanoi and 12.5 miles (20km) of Haiphong, and a buffer zone 34.5 miles (55.5km) wide extended along the North Vietnamese/Chinese frontier. Many have since demonstrated that the allocation of targets bore no relationship to the realities of the

military situation, and that the approval of targets was made on a random and even illogical basis. An obvious target type for initial attack, namely the airfields of North Vietnam, was also on the list of prohibited targets. These prohibitions were later interpreted more loosely or even removed, but the administration nonetheless exercised a very real control over the bombing on a day-to-day basis, with very adverse effects on the overall success of the campaign, as those in Washington could not be in full command of the situation in South-East Asia.

One of the campaign's primary objectives, as far as the military professionals were concerned, should have been Haiphong and other North Vietnamese ports, which could have been

ABOVE: A US pilot, captured by the North Vietnamese, has his injuries attended to by a Vietnamese woman.

RIGHT: Diving down on a military target in North Vietnam, the pilot of a USAF F-105 Thunderchief fires a volley of 70-mm (2.75-in) rockets. The Thunderchief is also equipped with 100-shot-per-second Vulcan automatic cannons for strafing.

very rude shock to the Americans, however, for they lost six aircraft shot down. Although five of the downed aircrew were rescued, it was clear from this very first stage that the US was not going to have it all its own way.

In accordance with the idea of graduated response, whereby the threat of next-step destruction was supposed to signal US determination more strongly than the destruction itself, it was deemed more beneficial to US intentions to hold

THE VIETNAM WAR

USAF personnel of the 435th Munitions Maintenance Squadron hurriedly pull the chocks away from an armed F-100 Super Sabre, ready for take-off from the Phan Rang airbase in South Vietnam.

mined to halt, or at least delay, the arrival of weapons and other matériel by sea from other Communist countries. Johnson felt this might be too great a provocation for the USSR and China to stomach, however, and it was only in 1972, when it was too late to affect the outcome of the war, that aerial mining of this type was finally permitted. There was almost no liaison between Johnson and his senior military officers in Washington with regard to the matter of selecting targets for Rolling Thunder:

even the chairman of the Joint Chiefs-of-Staff, General Earl G. Wheeler of the US Army, was not present for most of the critical discussions of 1965, and this was also true of the process in its later years.

Most of the Rolling Thunder attacks were launched from a quarter of Thai air bases, namely Korat, Takhli, Udon Thani and Ubon. After taking off and heading toward North Vietnam, the attacking warplanes generally refuelled in the air over Laos before entering

North Vietnamese air space. After attacking their targets, the process generally being a shallow dive-bombing manoeuvre, the warplanes then either returned directly to their Thai bases or departed over the relatively safe waters of the Gulf of Tonkin. Operational experience soon suggested that a system of routing was required to reduce the chances of air space conflict between USAF aircraft, arriving from the direction of Thailand, and US Navy/US Marine Corps aircraft making their

'ROLLING THUNDER'

entry from the Gulf of Tonkin, so the US planners divided North Vietnam into six target regions designated as 'route packages', and each of these was allocated to the USAF or US Navy/US Marine Corps, the aircraft of one service being strongly prohibited from entering any route package allocated to the other.

The attacks undertaken by aircraft of the US Navy and US Marine Corps were launched from the aircraft carriers of Task Force 77, cruising off the coast of North Vietnam on the so-called 'Yankee Station'. The naval and marine aircraft, which generally carried a lighter bomb load and had shorter range than their land-based counterparts of the USAF, were allocated the route packages that allowed them to approach their targets directly from seaward, and

ABOVE: Douglas B-66 Destroyer bombers prepared for action at Takhli Royal Thai Air Force Base in Thailand.

RIGHT: The Takhli airbase seen from the air.

THE VIETNAM WAR

and North Vietnam's other eastern ports. Their recommendation was therefore based, for the first time in the campaign, on the selection of targets on the basis of their military importance rather than their psychological significance as modified for political and diplomatic reasons.

Johnson and McNamara accepted the recommendation of the Joint Chiefs-of-Staff, and during the resulting four-week campaign 26 bridges and seven ferries were destroyed; other militarily important targets attacked during the same periods included North Vietnam's already large ground-based search and fire-control radar system, barracks, depots for ammunition, and other military supplies.

LEFT: December 1968: USAF F-105 Thunderchiefs on a Combat Sky Spot mission.

BELOW: The much criticized bombing raids in North Vietnam by US aircraft to smash the Communist supply routes nevertheless continued with stepped-up intensity, the initial spasmodic raids superseded by daily bombing sorties by multi-squadron formations. Apart from the raids hindering the supply of war materiél to the Communist troops, some observers believed it would place the US and its allies in a better bargaining position if a peace conference were to take place.

the very considerable majority of the attacks launched from aircraft carriers were therefore directed on targets in the coastal area of North Vietnam.

On 3 April the Joint Chiefs-of-Staff persuaded Johnson and McNamara that there was every reason to suppose that a sustained campaign, lasting four weeks, against North Vietnam's communications network, in the widest sense of that term, would yield a handsome operational dividend in isolating North Vietnam from the receipt of all but insignificant quantities of supplies from the USSR and China, and would also prevent the distribution of any supplies within North Vietnam and thence to the Communist forces in South Vietnam via the Ho Chi Minh Trail. The Joint Chiefs-of-Staff indicated that about 33 per cent of North Vietnam's imports arrived in the country along the north-east railway from China, and the other 67 per cent by sea through Haiphong

'ROLLING THUNDER'

A bridge in North Vietnam, extensively damaged by USAF bombers.

Throughout the period, it was the panhandle southern region of North Vietnam which was still the primary focus of the air attacks, and the number of sorties flown over the region increased from a figure of 3,600 in April to 4,000 in May. Also of note during this period, moreover, was a slow switch from attacks on fixed targets to operations deemed to be of the 'armed reconnaissance' type. In this latter, small groups of warplanes overflew roads, railways, rivers and canals, constantly on the look-out for targets of opportunity. Sorties of this type had grown from two to 200 per week by the end of 1965, and the continuing nature of this effort, which yielded very useful

results, meant that late in the Rolling Thunder campaign armed reconnaissance sorties amounted to some 75 per cent of the bombing effort. The growth of the armed reconnaissance mission in part reflected its success, and in part the growing realization that tight control from Washington was a process of extreme complication and inflexibility when attacks on fixed targets had to be requested, selected and finally authorized.

Rolling Thunder was conceived as the means to indicate to North Vietnam the determination of the USA to prevent a Communist takeover of South Vietnam, but signally failed in this objective, for North Vietnam persevered

in its sponsorship and involvement in the war in South Vietnam. When the US suggested peace talks to North Vietnam on 8 April, the latter's government replied that it would only consider such an undertaking after the US bombing attacks had been called off, the US had removed all its forces from South Vietnam, the South Vietnamese administration recognized the demands of the NLF, and there was general agreement that all matters pertaining to the reunification of the two Vietnams be negotiated by the Vietnamese themselves, without representation by any external power. This counter to the US suggestion was nothing less than a robust rejection of the US's overture, and came a mere five days after the North Vietnamese air force was first encountered by American warplanes in the skies over North Vietnam. During this first aerial encounter, US aircraft came under attack by Mikoyan-Guryevich MiG-15 fighters, which were jet-powered machines supplied by the USSR. These were technically obsolescent warplanes, as quickly appreciated by the Americans, but were being flown with increasing levels of tactical skill and would in time pave the way for the introduction of more capable aircraft.

The entire nature of the US commitment to South Vietnam changed radically and irrevocably on 8 March 1965, the date on which some 3,500 men of the US Marine Corps landed on the beach at Da Nang, on the northern coast of South Vietnam. It was claimed at the time that the arrival of this force was designed to provide protection for the South Vietnamese airfields involved in the Rolling Thunder campaign, but

THE VIETNAM WAR

the task of the newly-arrived force very soon changed from a defensive to an offensive nature as the Marines extended their patrol activities and began to search for Communist forces to tackle in combat. From this time onward the air campaign, which had been seen as the key to persuading North Vietnam to call off it efforts in South Vietnam, steadily became secondary to a growing land campaign in which the USA used the US Marine Corps and US Army in an attempt to secure military victory over the Communist forces operating in South Vietnam. US ground troops were pouring into South Vietnam in ever-increasing numbers, and both the extent and intensity of the ground war was escalating rapidly.

Into the third week of April, the supposedly strategic air attacks of the Rolling Thunder campaign over

North Vietnam had at least achieved parity with the tactical air operations flown over South Vietnam, but from this time onward the tactical air operations had the greater priority, and attacks on North Vietnamese targets, which interfered with the tactical air war over South Vietnam, were curtailed or even cancelled.

By 24 December 1965, the balance of success and failure in Rolling Thunder was based on the loss of 180 US aircraft (85, 94 and one, by the USAF, US Navy and US Marine Corps respectively), while the North Vietnamese air force had lost eight fighters. The men of the USAF had flown 25,971 sorties and dropped 32,063 tons of bombs, while US Navy and US Marine Corps crews had made 28,168 sorties and dropped

ABOVE: A USAF Douglas A-1 Skyraider over South Vietnam in 1966.

LEFT: Preparing to add further red stars to the 8th Tactical Fighter Wing MiG-kill scoreboard is Colonel Robin Olds (right), the first triple MiG-killer of the Vietnam conflict. Other victors in a 20 May 67 encounter with MiG-17s, 40 miles (65km) north-east of Hanoi, are (left to right) Major Philip P. Combies, 1st Lt Daniel L. Lafferty, Major John R. Pardo, 1st Lt Stempen B. Croker and 1st Lt Stephen A. Wayne (front centre), Major Combies and Lt Wayne having been credited with two MiGs each. Colonel Olds later went on to become the only quadruple MiG-killer of the Vietnam conflict.

'ROLLING THUNDER'

USAF Boeing B-52 Stratofortress heavy bombers over Vietnam in 1966.

11,144 tons of bombs; the South Vietnamese air force, meanwhile, had flown 682 missions to deliver an unrecorded tonnage of bombs.

The planners and commanders of the America's air forces also became highly concerned after 5 April 1966, when the interpretation of photographs taken by US reconnaissance aircraft indicated that the North Vietnamese were building the types of sites associated only with the basing of surface-to-air missile batteries. The USAF and US Navy then approached the authorities in Washington jointly, for authorization to attack and destroy these sites before the missiles for which they were intended could reach operational status, but were turned down on the basis that the majority of the sites in question lay near to if not actually inside the urban areas which political considerations had placed off-limits for US air attack. Thus it was no great surprise to the US military when a Republic F-105 Thunderchief attack warplane was brought down by an SA-2 'Guideline' missile on 24 July. This event at least served to focus the minds of those in Washington on a major shift in the balance of the air war, and three days later permission was granted, albeit on a one-time basis, for an attack on the

to power its industries than the Americans had been prepared to concede and, in combination with draught animal and human power, the currently available POL stocks were adequate to the task.

The Rolling Thunder campaign also revealed many problems with the US forces involved, and had an adverse effect on its other forces. A major difficulty, and one which found no solution until 1968, was command and control of the air effort in the whole of South-East Asia. While the USAF's 2nd

LEFT: This Hanoi hospital was the target of B-52 bombers in 1973.

BELOW: B-52 bombers strike the Ai Mo warehouse complex early in the Linebacker II operations (18 December 1972), destroying the facility and its stockpiles of supplies.

two missile sites believed to have been involved in the episode. Adding insult to injury, the US attack then flew into a North Vietnamese trap, the two 'missile sites' being dummy installations; while trying to tackle them the American pilots had been flying their warplanes into a concealed nest of radar-directed anti-aircraft guns around the sites, as a result of which six US aircraft were shot down, with two pilots killed, one declared missing, two captured and one taken captive.

On 29 June 1966, Johnson authorized attacks on North Vietnam's petroleum, oil and lubricant storage areas. This was the type of operational-level target which the military had wanted to attack right from the start of the campaign, on the grounds that the loss of all its POL facilities would strike at the very heart of North Vietnam's ability to sustain the Communist forces in South Vietnam. The first attacks on

these newly-authorized targets seemed to indicate a major success as they destroyed the facilities near Hanoi and Haiphong, the CIA then estimating that North Vietnam had lost 70 per cent of its POL facilities, although the US had also suffered heavily in the form of 43 aircraft which failed to return. North Vietnam, however, was not as reliant on oil products as the US believed, and had also appreciated the fact that the US might attack its major facilities. The North Vietnamese government had therefore arranged the dispersion, right across the country and in large numbers of individually small caches, of most of the country's POL stocks in drums. The US attacks on North Vietnam's POL facilities were terminated on 4 September after US intelligence resources admitted the attacks had had little if any effect on North Vietnam's ability to sustain its war effort. North Vietnam was making greater use of coal

'ROLLING THUNDER'

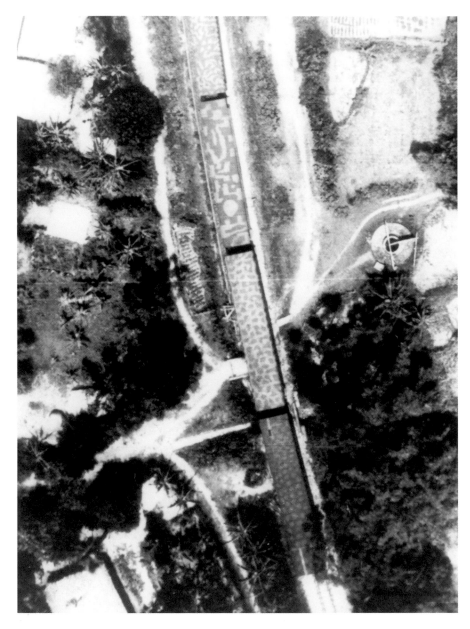

Air Division, which was succeeded by the 7th Air Force on 1 April 1966, was nominally responsible for air operations over North and South Vietnam, it was actually the Air Component Command of the Military Assistance Command Vietnam, and it was the belief of Westmoreland, the MACV's commander, that the war would have to be won inside South Vietnam. The 7th/13th Air Force, based in Thailand and thus the origin of most of the

USAF's heavier attacks on North Vietnam, had twin command structures, reporting to the 7th Air Force on operational matters and to the 13th Air Force, headquartered in the Philippine Islands, on logists and administration. This complex command and control factor became still more difficult after the division of the air campaign into four competing operational areas in South Vietnam, North Vietnam, and Laos (north and south). The US Navy's

Task Force 77 received its instructions via 7th Fleet from the commander-in-chief Pacific, a naval officer based in the Hawaiian Islands, via one of his subordinates, the USAF commander of the Pacific Air Forces.

Inter-service rivalries were also an interference, to a certain extent at least, in the smooth planning and conduct of air operations. The US Navy was not readily prepared to see the full integration of its air activities over

THE VIETNAM WAR

having a single officer manage any air campaign, with sole responsibility within his terms of reference for the control and co-ordination of all air operations within a given theatre of war. Thus it is hardly surprising that operational and tactical flexibility, and the ability to react swiftly and appropriately to a situation which could change dramatically in as little as an hour, were virtually impossible: when the 2nd Air Division in South Vietnam and Task Force 77 off the coast of Vietnam believed that a particular attack was necessary and appropriate, they were obliged to ask for authorization via PACAF and hence CINCPAC, who in turn passed the request on to the Joint Chiefs-of-Staff, who then solicited the

LEFT: Flying an A-7 Corsair from the aircraft carrier USS Midway *(CVA41), Lt J.G. Robert Noll destroyed the south span of the Phu Ly railroad bridge and caused heavy damage to another of its spans when he dropped six bombs on this rail link with Hanoi, located some 31 miles (50km) south-south-east of that city on 7 October 1966. According to his flight leader, 'Bob put all six bombs right on the bridge. When the black smoke cleared the span wasn't there.'*

BELOW: On 11 August 1966, bombs dropped by aircraft flying from the decks of the carrier USS Constellation *(CVA-64) almost levelled the newly-built thermal power plant at Uong Bi.*

North Vietnam with those of the USAF. General William Momyer, commanding the 7th Air Force, had the impression that CINCPAC and PACAF wanted to keep the warplanes based in Thailand away from his operational influence and, by extension, that of Westmoreland and the MACV, whom they felt to be more concerned with operations in and over South Vietnam than over North Vietnam.

Further complicating a process that was already approaching Byzantine complexity, Graham Martin and William H. Sutherland, the US ambassadors to Thailand and Laos, were able to exert a certain level of political influence over operational and command arrangements. This overlapping and often ill-defined complexity, with political and supposed diplomatic factors often as important as overtly military aspects, was wholly contrary to the USAF's doctrine of

ABOVE: Surrounded by undamaged farmlands and homes, the ruins of a Communist North Vietnamese supply depot smoulder after it was destroyed on 30 April 1965 by aircraft flying from the carrier USS Midway. *Forty tons of conventional ordnance were dropped with pinpoint accuracy on the depot, which contained military supplies used against the South Vietnamese. Seventy US Navy jet- and propeller-driven aircraft, striking at low altitudes, encountered only light ground fire over the target, which was photographed by a photo-reconnaissance aircraft once the clouds of black smoke had dissipated.*

RIGHT: A collapsed bridge near Duong Phuong Thuong, bombed by aircraft from the attack aircraft carrier USS Hancock *(CVA-19).*

comments of the Department of State and the CIA before passing the request to the White House, where decisions concerning matters of this type were made only on a weekly basis. Approval was frequently not given but even when it was, the go-ahead still had to pass back down the military chain-of-command to the local commanders before it could be implemented. This meant that any air operation schemed as a response to events on the ground or within North Vietnam was often well over a week old before approval was granted or refused, and might then be irrelevant to the situation on the ground.

The main weight of Rolling Thunder, in terms of tonnages dropped if not in sorties flown, rested on the USAF, and it quickly became clear that this branch of the US armed forces was not well-prepared for the tasks demanded of it. This resulted not so much from any actions, or even inactions, by the USAF

itself, but from the overriding importance which, since the late 1940s, had been placed on the US forces to plan and prepare for a 'third world war', with the use of nuclear weapons a likelihood rather than a possibility to protect the West against the threat of Soviet aggression. The USAF was therefore optimized for largely strategic nuclear warfare in a high-intensity, high-technology environment within countries similar to the USA in climatic conditions, and was now faced with demands to

undertake a comparatively low-intensity and wholly conventional air campaign in a decidedly low-technology environment with tactical and occasionally operational level objectives, and in a region of temperatures and humidities far greater than those for which the warplanes had been designed.

The air campaign over the two Vietnams also revealed that the USAF had for too long neglected the science and practice of conventional tactics, both of these being failings which were

compounded by reliance on warplanes whose overall performance, flight and armament were only poorly suited to the task. The USAF's lack of preparedness was also highlighted by the fact that the US Navy and US Marine Corps were altogether better prepared, and when based on an aircraft carrier also had superior conditions for aircraft maintenance and repair.

In the Grumman A-6 Intruder, the two maritime services operated the only all-weather medium-attack warplane in the US arsenal, with a pinpoint attack accuracy as a result of its advanced suite of navigation and attack electronics, and were also in the process of introducing a magnificent new warplane in the form of the McDonnell F-4 Phantom II as successor to the Vought F-8 Crusader. Though classified as a fleet defence fighter, and optimized for the carriage of missile armament and therefore not fitted, for the first time in any US fighter, with inbuilt gun armament, the Phantom II had been created from an attack fighter concept, which greatly aided the type's rapid development as a true multi-role warplane. So superior was the Phantom II to anything it had in its current inventory or under final development, that the USAF had no realistic alternative but to place large orders for it in a version only little altered from its carrierborne counterpart, except for the later incorporation of a fixed gun armament in the form of a six-barrel 20-mm (0.78-in) cannon. Thus the Phantom II emerged as the single most important warplane fielded by the US forces during the course of the Vietnam War.

Once air-to-air combat had begun to occur over North Vietnam, the USAF again found itself at something of a

disadvantage in terms of air-to-air armament. In this arena, and with European operations at the heart of its thinking, the USAF had long concentrated its development effort on the AIM-4 Falcon. Designed for use at medium ranges against largely non-manoeuvring targets, such as bombers, the missile had a seeker unit which could be cooled to operational status only in a time as long as six seconds to secure a lock onto the target, and carried only a comparatively small and impact-fused warhead. This was effectively useless against small, manoeuvring targets such as the Mikoyan-Guryevich fighters supplied to the North Vietnamese by the Soviets, and once again the USAF had to turn to the US Navy, this time for its AIM-9 Sidewinder short-range and AIM-7 Sparrow medium-range missiles.

The USAF also opposed a major adaptation to the demands of the Vietnam War, which it saw largely as a short-term and atypical interruption, as this would have distracted the service from its 'proper' task of preparing for a US/Soviet war. Among other things, this suggests that the USAF's higher command echelons had no conception that the Vietnam War might last for nearly 10 years.

In the Boeing B-52 Stratofortress eight-engined strategic bomber, the USAF possessed a warplane with an all-weather flight, navigation and bombing capability, with a truly awesome bomb-carrying capacity. Believing that its use might be seen as too great an escalation of the air war, however, the Johnson administration initially refused to consider the use of this great 'bomb truck', whose control remained vested throughout in the Strategic Air

Command, against any target more than a short distance north of the DMZ. In this the administration was supported by the USAF chief-of-staff, General John P. McConnell, who opposed the commitment of his major strategic weapon in the increasingly intense air-defence environment which North Vietnam had by now become. The operations of the B-52 force were therefore limited during the Rolling Thunder period to Route Package One close behind the DMZ.

As if this were not enough in itself, the Department of Defense created another problem by instituting a one-year rotation policy for the personnel posted to South-East Asia. Although the first aircrews to reach the theatre were well-experienced, the accelerating tempo of operations and arrivals in-country combined with the lengthening nature of the war to create an ever greater number of personnel, and this compounded the difficulty already being experienced in a growing inadequacy of aircrews which were both trained and experienced. Here the USAF itself intervened to worsen the problem by demanding a universal pilot-training regime and at the same time refusing to post anyone but volunteers for a second tour of combat duty. The effect of this policy was to commit rotating personnel to different aircraft types. The US Navy, on the other hand, had a policy of keeping aircrew within the same basic 'community' (particular types of aircraft) for the entirety of their flying careers. This ensured continuity and the retention of skills in a particular flying niche, but had a downside in the greater losses suffered by experienced crews in the course of several tours of combat flying.

The nuclear-powered attack aircraft carrier USS Enterprise *(CVAN-65) comes alongside the fast-combat support ship USS* Sacramento *(AOE-1) in the Gulf of Tonkin for underway replenishment. The* Sacramento *functioned as an oiler, ammunition, and refrigerated stores ship, all rolled into one.*

already supplemented by a few MiG-19 Farmer marginally supersonic twin-engined fighters, were further reinforced with more modern Soviet-built fighters in the form of the MiG-21 Fishbed, which possessed Mach 2 performance as well as considerable agility in the air, and could thus fight on a more equal footing with the US aircraft. By 1967, the North Vietnamese air force had a fighter arm averaging about 100 aircraft, many of which were based at airfields on the Chinese side of the Vietnamese-Chinese frontier, thereby facing no threat from American air attack while they were being maintained and their pilots resting.

Despite the successes of their air-defence arm, both artillery and fighters, the North Vietnamese rightly appreciated that their industrial capability and other key elements of their national economy were nonetheless vulnerable to US air attack, and therefore embarked on a programme of industrial and economic decentralization. As part of this effort, the larger factories, most of which were located in the delta of the Red river, were disassembled and their elements transported to naturally protected or inconspicuous locations, such as caves and apparently innocent rural villages all over the northern part of North Vietnam.

In the southern part of the country, just to the north of the DMZ, and where the main effort of the US bombing campaign was concentrated,

damaged they were quickly repaired, or when destroyed replaced by the large-scale diversion of traffic onto unpaved roads, making river crossings by means of fords, ferries and a combination of underwater and pontoon bridges. This was a monumental effort but, as events later proved, it was all worthwhile, being durable and easily repaired, and which bombing was mostly ineffective in closing down.

The key component in this effort was the North Vietnamese population, working with enormous dedication under the most adverse of conditions. It is believed that in 1965 some 97,000 North Vietnamese volunteered for a full-time commitment to repair the damage caused by the bombing, and that between 370,000 and 500,000 more volunteered for a part-time commitment

LEFT: Lt J.G. Charles Hartman and Lt Cdr Edwin Greathouse show RADM William F. Bringle how they shot down a MIG-17 during a mission over North Vietnam.

BELOW: Gulf of Tonkin. A catapult crewman aboard the attack aircraft carrier USS America (CVA-66) watches as two bomb-laden A-7A Corsair II attack aircraft head out to sea following their launch from the flight deck.

huge tunnel complexes were built deep underground, into which the populations of a great number of villages disappeared for the rest of the war. These and other measures helped the North Vietnamese to survive the worst effects of the US bombing and to maintain their war effort, but what cannot be denied is that there was an acute shortage of food, especially in urban areas, as the North Vietnamese transport network lost a major part of its capacity, what was left being dominated by movement in support of the military effort. The problem was made worse by the fact that rice farmers were among those who volunteered or were drafted into military service, or as part of the growing organization required to repair the damage caused by US bombing. There was also a major effort to diversify the North Vietnamese transport system, and when bridges were

to the same task. When the North Vietnamese transport network was attacked, a number of emergency measures had been prepared for implementation in this eventuality: supplies and other matériel being moved by rail were divided into smaller loads, which were transported by rail and road convoys of small size only at night and which to air reconnaissance were of apparently little military significance. This primary logistic effort was bolstered by the delivery of other supplies and equipment by sampan, cart, wheelbarrow and even human porterage.

When the North Vietnamese air-defence system started to introduce SAMs to supplement its already formidable array of anti-aircraft artillery, US pilots were faced with a difficult tactical problem: if they remained at lower altitudes they were relatively immune to the SAMs but vulnerable to the AA artillery, while opting for higher altitudes meant that they faced the reverse of the low-altitude situation, becoming easier prey to the SAMs. There was no perfect answer to this tactical conundrum, but the growing US employment of electronic and other countermeasures did in fact seriously degrade the capabilities of the North Vietnamese air-defence system over time: here, one of the primary weaknesses which the US forces found in the North Vietnam system was its reliance on centralized control on the basis of radar and observer information. The use of electronic countermeasures interfered severely with the performance and overall capability of the ground radars, while the use of electronic and infra-red countermeasures gradually

provided a steady reduction in the ability of SAMs to hit their targets. Thus the success rate for North Vietnamese SAMs, which was in fact never very high, declined steadily from a typical figure of one kill for every 30 missiles launched in the early stages of the campaign, to one success for every 50 missiles launched later on. Even though each missile had only a low probability of success, the US bombing effort paid particular attention to the missile sites and all ground elements associated with them, but the North Vietnamese never ran short of missiles.

The US bombing effort had been designed to persuade the North Vietnamese government of the determination of the USA to prevent the fall of South Vietnam into the hands of the Communists, and the gradual nature of its development was intended to show that the Americans could, and indeed would, increase the weight of their effort until they achieved the result they wanted. In this it failed, and at the same time provided North Vietnam with the opportunity and the time, in the early, and less fraught stages of the campaign, to come to grips with the situation.

It is believed that by 1967 North Vietnam had 25 SAM battalions, each with six missile-launchers, and that these battalions were kept on the move between about 150 sites to make it more difficult to target them. The USSR also supplied the equipment and technical knowledge to allow the rapid creation of the associated radar network, which was an integrated and centralized system with more than 200 sites. This provided radar coverage of the whole of North Vietnam as well as the northern

part of South Vietnam and the eastern parts of Laos and north-eastern Cambodia, allowing the central command system to track raids as they approached and entered North Vietnamese air space, providing ample time for fighter, SAM and AA artillery units to be warned and prepared for the responses which had been decided. The North Vietnamese system may have been monolithic and cumbersome, but it did prove effective: in 1967, for example, the USA lost 248 aircraft (145 USAF, 102 US Navy, and one US Marine Corps) over North Vietnam.

While the numbers of US aircraft committed to attacks on North Vietnam rose, so too did US losses. This demanded that the USA create and implement new and more effective tactics as a matter of urgency. Large-scale attacks, which were known to the USAF as 'force packages' and to the US Navy as 'alpha strikes', were centred on the warplanes tasked with the relevant offensive action, but came to include a swelling number of support aircraft to protect the fighter-bombers and thereby allow them to complete their missions.

To pave the way for other aircraft, the target area was first entered by aircraft optimized for the 'Iron Hand' defence-suppression role. These were F-105 hunter/killer teams of the 'Wild Weasel' type, carrying advanced electronic systems to detect and fix the location of the radars associated with SAM guidance and control, and also electronic countermeasures for self-protection. The aircraft controlled attacks to suppress AA artillery and carried AGM-45 Shrike anti-radiation missiles, another weapon type created for the US Navy to home in on SAM radar systems. The SA-2 SAM possessed greater range than the Shrike, but if the Shrike was launched and the radar remained active to guide the missile, the Shrike homed in on the signal and destroyed its source. The development of the Iron Hand concept then led to the emergence of a see-saw development race of increasing technical sophistication between the North Vietnamese radar operators and the crews of the Wild Weasel aircraft. While the Iron Hand role was particular to the USAF, the US Navy proceeded along an analogous path without the creation of specialized units.

With the North Vietnamese ground-based defence system either destroyed or forced to shut down for fear of obliteration, the target area was then deemed safe enough to be entered by the attack aircraft with their loads of different bombs, although their vulnerability in the bomb-laden stage was reflected in their support by fighters operating in the CAP (combat air patrol) or MiGCAP role, and other aircraft carrying the electronic jamming gear to ensure further degradation of the North Vietnamese radar capability. Throughout the Vietnam War, new ECM systems were being designed and built in the USA in an almost endless stream of equipments and upgrades to existing equipments, and rushed to South Vietnam and Thailand as soon as they were deemed sufficiently combat-capable. It was in matters such as this that the US was able to exploit its great technological capabilities and industrial ability to get systems into production very rapidly: the problem was that large numbers of these equipments were technologically successful in boosting

the protection of attack packages, but technically incapable of surviving the humidity and poor servicing facilities of South-East Asia for all but the shortest of times.

Other elements of the US concept of missions penetrating North Vietnamese air space were Boeing KC-135 Stratotanker inflight-refuelling facilities, a steadily improving progression of combat search-and-rescue helicopters (with increasing amounts of armour and guns) to find and rescue downed airmen, and aircraft to protect the SAR helicopters. This last fixed-wing type was usually the A-1 Skyraider, piston-engined and with performance that did not exceed that of its charges by any great degree, being of long endurance and with the capability of carrying the large and diverse weapons to tackle Communist forces trying to reach downed men before the arrival of the helicopter, and then suppressing any fire which the opposition might loft in an attempt to down the SAR helicopter and capture or kill the downed men. This combat SAR capability was of great significance to the US forces, not only for recovering downed men but also in raising the morale of airmen, who could be confident that they would no longer be left to the mercies of the Communist ground forces.

Despite the fact that Rolling Thunder was manifestly failing to achieve the result it had been created to produce, between mid-1966 and the final stages of 1967 Johnson and McNamara continued to authorize attacks on new and important targets only on a one-by-one basis, at the same time using this tactic as evidence to opponents of the war in the US Congress, and indeed

inside the administration, that they had only limited objectives which they were tackling with strictly limited resources. This palliative effort also included the occasional scaling-back of the bombing, together with a number of low-key attempts to lure the North Vietnamese into peace talks.

Despite the USA's introduction of technical aids, better weapons and tactics, and the combat SAR force, the very fact that it had to overfly North Vietnam to attack targets, which then had to be attacked again on a frequent basis, began to have an adverse effect on the morale of aircrews. After a fact-finding visit to South Vietnam during September 1966, Admiral David McDonald, the Chief of Naval Operations, informed the other members of the Joint Chiefs-of-Staff committee that the men involved in Rolling Thunder were angered by the nature of the target-selection process, and felt that the entire operation had been wrongly conceived in establishing 'guidelines requiring repetitive air programs that seemed more than anything else to benefit enemy gunners'. In 1967, which was the second complete year of Rolling Thunder, the USA lost 362 aircraft (208 USAF, 142 US Navy and 12 US Marine Corps) over North Vietnam.

The years 1967 and 1968 saw Rolling Thunder attain its final form, in which the object of the entire operation, especially in the higher-numbered route packages on North Vietnam's northern regions, became the interdiction of the quantities of supplies and matériel flowing into North Vietnam for local purposes as well as for further dissemination to the Communist forces operating in South Vietnam, and the

'ROLLING THUNDER'

Aircraft of the attack carrier Air Wing
Nine *(CVW-9) in the Gulf of Tonkin
wait on the after flight deck of the
attack aircraft carrier USS*
Constellation *(CV-64) to be launched on
air strikes in the Haiphong area of
North Vietnam.*

not only because of the greater combat
experience now possessed by their North
Vietnamese pilots but also because US
radar coverage of North Vietnam did
not include the Red river delta, a
primary target area for the Americans
and one in which the North Vietnamese
could get their fighters into the air in
good time to 'bounce' unsuspecting US
warplanes. The problem was
compounded by the fact that the radar
of US airborne early-warning aircraft
was not picking out these small fighters
at low altitude in the clutter of ground
returns, and the North Vietnamese
fighters were also hard to spot visually
because of their small size.

It was not all one-way traffic in air
combat, however, and it should be noted
that F-105 pilots achieved 27 air combat
'kills', giving North Vietnamese and US
successes nearly equal parity. In January
1967 the Americans did manage to catch
the MiG fighters completely off balance
and score a useful success in the course
of Operation Bolo. In this, F-4 Phantom
multi-role fighters used the same radio
call signs, as well as the approach vector,
altitude and speed, as a typical flight of
fully loaded F-105 fighter-bombers, so
luring the North Vietnamese fighters
into an attack on what was an altogether
more formidable group of warplanes:
during a 12-minute engagement, the
Phantoms shot down seven MiG fighters
without loss to themselves.

The US air forces began what was as
yet their most intensive and sustained
effort late in 1967, in the hope of forcing
North Vietnam into peace negotiations.
By this stage of Rolling Thunder, almost
every target authorized to the Joint
Chiefs-of-Staff had come under air
attack, the targets including airfields

comprehensive destruction of North
Vietnam's industrial and economic
infrastructure relevant to the military
effort. In this period the majority of US
warplane losses resulted from AA
artillery fire, but SAMs and North

Vietnamese fighters also became an
increasing threat to workhorses of the
bombing effort, such as the USAF's F-
105 Thunderchief and US Navy's
Douglas A-4 Skyhawk. The MiG-19 and
MiG-21 became an increasing problem,

THE VIETNAM WAR

which had earlier been on the prohibited list. Only central Hanoi, Haiphong, and the North Vietnamese-Chinese border were declared inviolable in this latest stage of the offensive, in which the core of the US plan was the isolation of North Vietnam's cities and major towns by the destruction of bridges and the severing of communications networks. Other targets included the Thai Nguyen steel manufacturing complex, electricity-generating facilities, ship and railway repair workshops, and warehouse complexes. The gravity of the offensive was such that the North Vietnamese fighters were committed in large numbers to the defence of Hanoi, the kill ratio falling to one US warplane for every two MiG fighters.

During 1968, the North Vietnamese fighters were responsible for shooting down 22 per cent of the 139 US warplanes (75 USAF, 59 US Navy and five US Marine Corps) lost over the north. This was the main reason why US attacks were finally authorized on the last North Vietnamese airfields, whose bombing had previously been banned. Despite the commitment which the USA poured into Rolling Thunder, and the devastation caused in North Vietnam, the Communist forces in South Vietnam were still very potent, as indicated on 30 January 1968, when they started their largest land offensive yet, lashing out at targets throughout South Vietnam during the lunar New Year holiday. This Tet Offensive saw some of the war's most bitter fighting, but ended as a major operational and tactical defeat for the North Vietnamese and their South Vietnamese Communist allies; at the same time it was a major strategic and psychological victory for the

Communists as the American people, long assured that the war would soon end in a major victory for the US and South Vietnamese forces, now saw that the task was in fact still very much in the balance, with much time and many casualties to be endured in the future if victory was indeed to be won. The anti-war movement in the USA grew ever more strident and began to spread ever wider, and indeed psychologically deeper, into the US population at large. This had obvious ramifications for the politicians in Washington, where the determination of the administration and legislature alike was severely weakened.

Fortunately for North Vietnam, many of the believers in the US bombing policy were convinced it would be unwise to risk its primary strategic bomber, the B-52, over North Vietnam, even though this was the one available warplane with the capacity to deliver huge tonnages of bombs with great accuracy under all weather conditions by day and by night. Without the commitment of the B-52 there was no way in which the US air forces could escalate their air effort in response to the Tet Offensive, for the seasonal bad weather made it impossible to undertake any but small-scale tactical warplane operations until the advent of better conditions in April.

By the spring of 1967, McNamara and other civilian leaders of the Johnson administration were now gloomily sure that Rolling Thunder and the ground war in South Vietnam were failing. The bombing campaign had clearly failed either to force North Vietnam to its knees militarily or economically, or persuade the Communist administration to come to the negotiating table. There

was a distinct feeling of war-weariness in Washington, and many of those who felt that way were in a position to oppose the recommendations of the Joint Chiefs-of-Staff, both to increase the pace and weight of the air war against North Vietnam and to loosen the restrictions imposed on the military with regard to target selection. In this respect the military leadership now found itself in an impossible situation of its own making: the generals and admirals had long stated they were winning the war over North Vietnam, but were now asking for a relaxation of the targeting policy precisely so that the air campaign

Military target area 12 in Operation Linebacker was the Hanoi/Bac Mai airfield.

'ROLLING THUNDER'

Guided under radar control by a B-66 Destroyer, USAF F-4C Phantom crews return to drop bombs on Communist military targets after the longest lull in the Vietnam air war.

would in fact now succeed. To any but the wilfully blind, it was now altogether clear that there was a total incompatibility between the restriction to limited goals resulting from US foreign policy and the objective of total victory now espoused by the military leadership. What no one could answer, of course, was the thorny problem of now to defeat the Communist forces in South Vietnam, sponsored by North Vietnam, without wholly defeating North Vietnam itself.

On 9 August 1967 the Armed Services Committee of the US Senate opened hearings on the bombing

campaign, largely as a result of the complaints received by a number of senators from members of the armed forces. The members of the Joint Chiefs-of-Staff testified before the committee, making critical comments about the graduated nature of the air war and the restrictions imposed on the conduct of purely military matters by civilians reacting to political and diplomatic events. What they wanted, the military advised, was to be set a task by the administration, and then to be freed to secure the attainment of the stated objective by the best means available to them. It was clear that McNamara, as

the only civilian subpoenaed and the last to be asked to testify, was to be the scapegoat. McNamara was too astute a wheeler and dealer to be caught in this fashion, however, and neatly stated his objections to an unlimited air war while also rebutting the claims of the military. There was an almost prophetic ring to McNamara's admission that there was 'no basis to believe that any bombing campaign...would by itself force Ho Chi Minh's regime into submission, short, that is, of the virtual annihilation of North Vietnam and its people'. It was now obvious to Johnson, though, that McNamara was now a major liability to his administration, and in February 1968 McNamara resigned and was replaced by Clark Clifford, a personal friend of Johnson and a long-standing opponent of McNamara's recommendations that US troop numbers in South Vietnam be stabilized and Rolling Thunder terminated.

Adding to the administration's problems, however, was the fact that McNamara's position was almost immediately adopted by Dean Rusk, the Secretary of State, and up to now a strong believer in Rolling Thunder. Rusk proposed limiting the campaign to the panhandle of North Vietnam just above the DMZ, without preconditions, and awaiting North Vietnam's response. But within just a few months, Clifford also changed tack and adopted McNamara's position, in the process slowly but steadily becoming a proponent of the concept that the USA had to withdraw from its open-ended commitment to South Vietnam.

Disappointed by political defeats at home and hoping that North Vietnam would enter into negotiations, on 31

THE VIETNAM WAR

March 1968 Johnson announced the end of all bombing north of the 19th parallel. Thus the US air forces now concentrated all the offensive effort which had previously been spread over the whole of North Vietnam into the smaller region between the 17th and 19th parallels. The USAF increased the number of sorties sent into Route Package One by 100 per cent, which entailed more than 6,000 sorties now being flown against movement 'chokepoints', the destruction of roads, and the hunting and destroying of truck traffic. The North Vietnamese response was a doubling of the number of AA artillery batteries in the panhandle region of North Vietnam, though most of the SAM battalions were left in position around Hanoi and Haiphong.

Despite its earlier ultimatum that it would not enter negotiations while the bombing continued, North Vietnam finally agreed to a meeting with a US delegation in Paris for preliminary talks. Johnson then announced that there would be a complete halt to the Rolling Thunder bombing of North Vietnam from 1 November 1968, a date just before the US presidential election. This bombing halt was linked with the achievement of progress in the peace talks, but the Joint Chiefs-of-Staff believed that the administration would not order a resumption of the bombing campaign under any circumstances and, as events were to prove, they were right.

In the period of Rolling Thunder between March 1965 and November 1968, USAF warplanes flew 153,784 sorties against North Vietnam, and the US Navy and US Marine Corps added 152,399 more. On 31 December 1967, the Department of Defense announced that, at 864,000 tons, the weight of bombs dropped on North Vietnam during Rolling Thunder was greater than that dropped in the entire Korean War, and greater still than in the Pacific campaign of the Second World War. On 1 January 1968 the CIA revealed an estimate suggesting that US$370 million of damage had been inflicted on North Vietnam in terms of the physical destruction caused by the bombing, this figure including US$164 million of damage to fixed assets, such as factories, bridges and electricity-generating stations. The report also estimated North Vietnamese casualties of 1,000 per week, which added up to some 90,000, including 72,000 civilians, for the 44-month duration of the campaign.

Combat and operational losses suffered by the US air forces totalled 526 USAF, 397 US Navy and 19 US Marine Corps aircraft over or near North Vietnam. Some 745 men had been downed with these aircraft, and of these USAF recorded 145 rescued, 255 killed, 222 captured (of whom 23 died in captivity), and 123 missing. Equivalent US Navy and US Marine Corps figures are more problematical, but during the 44 months of the operation 454 naval aviators were killed, captured, or posted missing during operations over North Vietnam and Laos.

Rolling Thunder had been an undertaking designed to exert psychological and physical pressure, but had rapidly become a tactical and operational campaign of interdiction. It failed for two main reasons, both of them linked directly to the civilian and military policy-makers in the USA: firstly, neither ever conceived that North Vietnam would or indeed could survive under the weight of bombs which was to be dropped on it, and the civilian element also lacked the understanding of air power to comprehend that its policies were nugatory in terms of effective use of air power; secondly, the US military leadership signally failed, right from the start, to propose, develop and later press for the adoption of strategy apposite to the situation in Vietnam.

It should also be recorded that Rolling Thunder suffered from the same deadening 'managerial' attitude to decision-making as did the rest of the US military effort in South-East Asia. Thus it was the number of sorties generated which became the measure by which the campaign was judged, regardless of the fact that the number of sorties made and the tonnages of bombs dropped might have been useful in judging levels of efficiency, but were certainly not useful in estimating progress toward a stated aim. Throughout this time, North Vietnam remained a formidable enemy as a result of its own strengths and determination, aided by the physical and diplomatic support of China and the USSR.

CHAPTER FIVE
THE FATAL COMMITMENT

RIGHT: Three North American T-28s escort a Lockheed Hercules transporting munitions over Vietnam.

BELOW: Sfc Willie C. Smith, 1st Special Forces Group, Nui Ba Den, is shown teaching grenade practice to Vietnamese volunteers.

Even as Rolling Thunder was being fought in the skies over North Vietnam, the military situation on the ground in South Vietnam was deteriorating steadily and, it seemed, inevitably. At a time early in March 1965, the MACV forecast was that if the current trends persisted, South Vietnamese strength would soon be confined to district and provincial capitals, which would be essentially unmanageable because of the huge numbers of refugees which would overwhelm local services and administrative capabilities. In his capacity as head of the MACV, Westmoreland believed and said that South Vietnam could be wholly in Communist hands within 12 months.

Early in 1965, therefore, the only hope of bringing the Communists to a halt, if not actually defeating them, seemed to lie not with the South Vietnamese ground forces, with limited US technical and logistical support, but with US air power striking deep into North Vietnam in Rolling Thunder, in the misconceived hope of persuading the North Vietnamese to negotiate, and of severing the lines of communication (in particular the portion of the Ho Chi Minh Trail in eastern Laos) by which the North Vietnamese were able to nourish and bolster the Communist ground effort in South Vietnam. In the light of the Communist attacks on the bases at Pleiku and Qui Nhon, however,

Westmoreland had very little confidence in the ability of the South Vietnamese army to provide an effective defence of the airfields on which US aircraft were based for the support of the selfsame South Vietnamese army. Westmoreland's intelligence staff estimated that no fewer than 12 Communist battalions, with 6,000 men, lay within striking distance of the air base at Da Nang, a large and crucially important facility containing large matériel dumps but protected by only a comparatively small and badly-trained South Vietnamese force, which was low in morale and unwilling to undertake all but the most limited patrol work. Da Nang was a base from which many of the Rolling Thunder attacks

were launched, and could thus only be a magnet for Communist attack. The only realistic solution, if many millions of dollars-worth of aircraft and other matériel were not to be lost, was the replacement of the South Vietnamese troops around Da Nang and other vital bases by US combat troops, and it was the arrival of these troops which effectively signalled the start of the USA's involvement, on an escalating basis, in the ground war in South Vietnam.

The USA had already begun to strengthen the defence of Da Nang early in February, when a US Marine Corps air-defence battalion arrived with its complement of HAWK surface-to-air missiles, launchers, and associated equipment. Late in the same month, Westmoreland's deputy, Lieutenant General John Throckmorton, visited Da Nang and soon reported the tactical situation to be so dangerous that a

complete Marine expeditionary brigade (three infantry battalions with artillery and logistical support) was required as a matter of urgency. Westmoreland trimmed the recommendation from three to two battalions, and recommended such a deployment.

Maxwell Taylor was concerned that the deployment would open the conceptual floodgates to an ever-increasing flow of US combat troops to South Vietnam, and a parallel South Vietnamese abandonment of as much combat as possible to the Americans, but nonetheless felt that Westmoreland was right and added his support to the request sent to Washington, which gained further recommendation from Admiral Ulysses S. Grant Sharp, the

ABOVE: A Viet Cong prisoner, recently taken captive.

LEFT: An officer examines the entrance to a NLF bunker complex. The Communist forces were notably adept at constructing and using such complexes in many parts of South Vietnam.

since 1962. Even so, the advent of the 9th Marine Expeditionary Brigade was a momentous step in the development of the Vietnam War.

As the 9th Marine Expeditionary Brigade, which was soon redesignated as the III Marine Amphibious Force, began to arrive, Westmoreland perceived the South Vietnamese military situation as

critical, as noted above. He believed that the situation in six months, unless there was a momentous change, would become one in which the South Vietnamese would hold only 'a series of islands of strength clustered around district and province capitals', the South Vietnamese administration crippled by internal dissent between various factions

ABOVE: Four of seven prisoners captured in a Viet Cong tunnel complex in the Thanh Dien Forest during Operation Cedar Falls. During the course of the campaign, US infantrymen discovered and destroyed a massive tunnel complex in the Iron Triangle, used as the headquarters for guerrilla raids and terrorist attacks on Saigon.

RIGHT: A US Marine outside a burning Vietnamese house.

commander-in-chief Pacific. President Johnson authorized such a deployment on 26 February, and on 8 March Brigadier General Frederick J. Karsh's 9th Marine Expeditionary Brigade landed on the beach at Da Nang. These were not in fact the first men of the US Marine Corps to see service in South Vietnam, this honour going to Marine advisers who had served with the Vietnamese Marines since 1954, and the Marines' 'Shu-Fly' helicopter task unit which had been operational at Da Nang

advocating different levels of accord with the Communists. Westmoreland's gloomy prognostication was based on the current situation, but further gravity was added by the fact that the MACV commander knew that a division of the North Vietnamese army had infiltrated its way into secure positions in the mountains and jungles of South Vietnam's Central Highlands. This was clearly only the vanguard of larger North Vietnamese army forces committed to operations in South Vietnam, but Westmoreland had no idea how large a force the North Vietnamese intended to deploy into South Vietnam. In fact, the North Vietnamese intended to commit very sizeable forces to implement a 1964 decision of the North Vietnamese administration to force a military decision in South Vietnam before US forces could be committed in large numbers. Even with the limited intelligence information available to him early in 1965, Westmoreland knew that the North Vietnamese deployment into the Central Highlands marked the beginning of the change from an internal war of insurgency in South Vietnam, with North Vietnamese support, to a conventional war based in increasing measure on the commitment of significant North Vietnamese regular forces.

It would need something in the order of a year, even if the necessary change of attitude and commitment could be imposed on the South Vietnamese, to raise their army to the level of capability at which it could handle the increasing activity of the Viet Cong insurgents, and the presence of North Vietnamese regular forces was not factored into this assessment. Even if US bombing led the

North Vietnamese to the negotiating table, which he believed to be a forlorn hope, Westmoreland believed that it would happen only at the end of a six-month aerial effort, by which time the South Vietnamese defence might well have dissolved.

Westmoreland believed the optimum solution to the problem, as it now existed, was the creation of an international force of about five divisions. This would be delivered by sea to points along the DMZ and by air and land across the Laotian panhandle, which was the region of Laos through

which the Ho Chi Minh Trail extended to the west and south of Vietnam above and below the DMZ. Such a force would offer significant military strength in its own right, and by its very creation serve to advise the North Vietnamese that the Western world would not tolerate Communist aggression against South Vietnam. Even if Johnson had approved the idea, which he did not, it would still have taken several months to create and deploy such a force. In the circumstances, therefore, Westmoreland had no option but to call for the deployment of more US combat rather

Corporal Lindy R. Hall of 3rd Platoon, K Company, 3rd Battalion, 3rd Marines, sets fire to a Vietnamese hut during Operation Prairie III in 1967.

THE FATAL COMMITMENT

than support troops to hold the Communist forces in check until such time as the South Vietnamese army had been turned into an effective force.

The North Vietnamese division's deployment into the Central Highlands suggested that the Communist plan was to sever South Vietnam though its narrowest point, before striking north to take the northern portion of the divided country. It made sense to Westmoreland, therefore, to deploy a US division into this high-threat area, and to receive two more US Marine Corps battalions to guard the air bases in the threatened northern provinces, so that they could continue to function effectively within the context of the Rolling Thunder campaign.

The proposals were recommended to Johnson when Taylor visited Washington late in March, but the US ambassador immediately discovered that the president was still vacillating about the advisability of an enlarged US commitment to South Vietnam. Johnson therefore approved the deployment only of two US Marine Corps battalions for the air base protection task. Even so, Taylor was able to convince Johnson to agree to a so-called 'enclave strategy', which seemed to Westmoreland to be wrong. This strategy was based on the creation of defensive enclaves centred on air bases and ports in a process that was economical in terms of troop requirements, but nonetheless confirmed the USA's determination to support South Vietnam. In another significant change to the 'rules of engagement' pertinent to South Vietnam, Johnson conceded that the US could abandon the previously mandated defensive posture and patrol to a radius of 50 miles

(80 km) from any enclave, with the object of disrupting any Communist build-up and preparations for an attack on the enclave in question.

The trouble with Johnson's decisions was that while the number of men who might have to be deployed was kept to the minimum, they offered protection only to US interests, and at the same time revealed a diplomatically significant indecision of longer-term strategic purpose. This became all the more evident when Johnson summoned a conference of senior figures of the administration and the military. Those involved, apart from Johnson himself, included McNamara, Taylor, Westmoreland and General Earle G. Wheeler, chairman of the Joint Chiefs-of-Staff, the conference assembling at Honolulu on 20 April. Here there was not a single expression of confidence in the successful outcome of the Rolling Thunder campaign without a parallel improvement of the situation on the ground in South Vietnam. All agreed that the only way in which this improvement could be secured was the commitment of a further nine battalions of US troops, so raising the total in South Vietnam to 13 battalions, and at the same time beginning the start of an undertaking to create an international force, as first suggested in recent times by Westmoreland, from other South-East Asian, East Asian and Australasian countries, most especially Australia, New Zealand and South Korea.

The decision to solicit the support of other countries, otherwise the 'More Flags' policy, in fact had its origins in 1961, when a number of administration officials had recommended the creation and deployment of a 25,000-man force

taken from the members of the SEATO alliance, including the USA, UK, Australia, France, New Zealand, the Philippines, Thailand and, at that time, Pakistan. It was recommended that such a force be deployed either on the border between Laos and South Vietnam or in the Central Highlands. The UK, France and Pakistan expressed themselves unwilling to contribute, the first to respond positively being Australia, which sent 30 jungle warfare experts to reinforce the US advisory teams in the northern provinces of South Vietnam during August 1962. By 1969, more than 7,000 Australians were serving in Vietnam, along with about 550 New Zealand troops, as the manpower of three combat battalions and five air squadrons (one bomber, one helicopter and three transport). Another element of Australian support was the Royal Australian Navy's destroyer *Perth*, later relieved by her sister, *Hobart*, which operated with elements of the US Navy.

Eventually five other nations provided troops for the anti-Communist effort in South Vietnam. Other than Australia and New Zealand, these were the Philippines, South Korea and Thailand, and there were miniscule parties of less than 30 men each from Spain and Taiwan. The non-US contribution to the war effort in South Vietnam reached its peak in 1969, as 68,900 combat troops and 34 other countries provided support of a non-combatant nature. The arrival of these other 'foreign' troops presented a problem of command: while the US population would never have stood for the commitment of US troops under South Vietnamese command, the South Vietnamese were unwilling to commit themselves, for reasons of obvious national pride, to service under US command. While a unified command structure would have offered the standard military advantages, Westmoreland did not want to press for such an arrangement for political and diplomatic reasons: the commitment of South Vietnamese troops under US command would have played into the hands of the North Vietnamese, who claimed that the South Vietnamese were already 'puppets' of the Americans, and might also have set back the US efforts to persuade the South Vietnamese to play a more effective and self-reliant role in the war by reforming their armed forces. In this respect Westmoreland was fully in accord with the USA's perception that the war in South Vietnam could be won, at the military as well as the political level, only by the South Vietnamese, with the Americans providing support.

Westmoreland therefore opted for a dual-command system, more fully integrated, it was hoped, by close co-ordination at all command levels. Within this overall command concept, the 'foreign' forces also maintained their own identities, but were also involved in the programme of close co-ordination. It was a flexible system which could have paved the way for the emergence of inter-allied rivalries, but in South Vietnam the arrangement appears to have worked with little problem.

Within the US chain of command, Westmoreland's headquarters remained in essentially the same position that the MACV had occupied since its creation in February 1962. The MACV was thus a joint command, including elements of all four US forces, but with the US

Army predominant, and was subordinate to the commander-in-chief Pacific, Admiral Sharp, headquartered in the Hawaiian Islands with responsibility for the entire Pacific region. Westmoreland had responsibility for all operations inside South Vietnam and also for tactical air attacks in Laos and the southern part of North Vietnam just above the DMZ, while Sharp exercised responsibility for air operations over the rest of North Vietnam. Also under Sharp's overall command was the 7th Fleet, although Westmoreland was able to call on this for tactical air attacks on targets in South Vietnam by carrier-borne warplanes. At a later stage, after the use of the B-52 Stratofortress heavy bomber over Vietnam had been authorized, overall command was exercised from the USA by the commander-in-chief Strategic Air Command, although the headquarters of the MACV was responsible for the recommendation of targets for approval in Washington. Though not formally required, it gradually developed that all signals between Westmoreland and Sharp were copied to the Joint Chiefs-of-Staff.

With the growth of the US military strength in South Vietnam, it became necessary to establish subordinate commands for the US Army, USAF and US Navy/US Marine Corps components as the US Army, Vietnam as an administrative and logistical command, the 7th Air Force, and the Naval Force, Vietnam. By this time the South Vietnamese had already divided their nation into four 'corps tactical zones', and in three of these the US created parallel American commands along the lines of a corps headquarters. The I

Corps zone covered the northern provinces, and in this the US headquarters was the III Marine Amphibious Force. The II Corps zone covered the central provinces, and in this the US headquarters was the I Field Force. And the III Corps zone comprised the provinces centred on Saigon, and in this the US headquarters was the II Field Force. The last South Vietnamese corps tactical zone was the IV Corps area, comprising the provinces of the Mekong river delta and here, where large US forces were to be committed, command of the US forces was allocated to the senior US adviser to the commander of the South Vietnamese IV Corps. The senior adviser role in the other corps zones fell to the commanders of the I Field Force, II Field Force and III Marine Amphibious Force.

As the nine battalions approved by the administration began to reach South Vietnam in May and June 1975, Johnson tacitly forgot the 'enclave strategy' when he permitted Westmoreland to engage in 'counter-insurgency combat operations'. The administration was worried that the US public would perceive these changes as an enlargement of the US commitment to South Vietnam, however, and therefore did not publicly reveal the widening of Westmoreland's remit. Thus there began to emerge the administration's 'head in the sand' perception that the US public could readily be fooled, for US journalists in South Vietnam rapidly appreciated and also reported that US forces were not merely holding defensive positions around key bases and the like, but starting to take the war actively to the Communist forces. Despite this, the

THE FATAL COMMITMENT

The move of new US units and formations into South Vietnam was comparatively slow, and had to be followed by a period of acclimatization in both the climatic and tactical senses. So it was some time before the new forces could start to play any major role in the conduct of the ground war in South Vietnam. The Communists did not waste the opportunity presented to them, and the Viet Cong thus stepped up the tempo of its recruitment efforts and increased the number and strength of its attacks. Operating at up to regimental strength, the Communist forces captured some district capitals, ambushed and destroyed one South Vietnamese battalion, and besieged an outpost in the Central Highlands. Events of this type and nature themselves suggested the imminence of a major crisis, but the South Vietnamese position was saved, at least temporarily, by the unexpectedly lethargic performance of the North

Vietnamese division in the Central Highlands.

This presented Johnson with the opportunity to implement a number of other measures, including the despatch of several US Coast Guard vessels to support the fledgling South Vietnamese navy in its immensely difficult task of seeking to halt the flow of Communist reinforcements into South Vietnam by sea. Johnson issued permission for the 7th Fleet to provide air and gunfire support for US Marine Corps operating in the northern provinces. But perhaps of the greatest importance of all, Johnson responded favourably to a request from Westmoreland for the use of B-52 heavy bombers, initially from the US bases on Guam in the Marianas Islands group but later from bases in Thailand, in attacks on the Communist forces' bases in jungle and mountain regions too remote for any land attack to be practical. These bases were so well dug-in and protected that attacks

ABOVE: US Army personnel in the Rung Sat Special Zone.

RIGHT: Viet Cong suspects by the Mekong river.

administration continued to maintain that there had been no change in the US forces' 'defensive mission': thus was created the credibility gap between the Johnson administration and the media, and by extension between the administration and the public, which was destined to play a significant part in the conduct and thus the outcome of the Vietnam War.

THE VIETNAM WAR

A South Vietnamese army interpreter questions a Viet Cong prisoner before passing his answers on to Capt. Dennis K. Anderson in September 1967, during Operation Cook. This was a search-and-destroy mission being conducted in the mountains of Quang Ngai province, approximately 320 miles (515km) north-east of Saigon, by elements of the 2nd Battalion, 502nd Infantry, 101st Airborne Brigade.

by tactical warplanes had provided no success worthy of the name, but the B-52 bombers, operating at very high altitude where they could be neither heard nor seen from the ground, were able to bomb accurately and devastate the whole of a base area with a massive weight of free-fall ordnance. With total destruction visited on them by aircraft they did not even know to be in the area, the Communist forces came to dread the B-52 more than any other single weapon used in the Vietnam War.

These moves were individually useful, but could not check, let alone reverse, a military situation which was becoming ever more parlous. The crisis in the land war perhaps inevitably resulted in another change in the government of South Vietnam. There had been a weak attempt at a coup d'état in May, and in its aftermath Quat attempted to revise his cabinet. He failed in this attempt, resigned, and handed the government over to the military, which was, of course, already

the de facto ruler of the country. With the South Vietnamese air force to the fore, the military established a ten-man Committee for the Direction of the State with General Nguyen Cao Ky as prime minister and General Nguyen Van Thieu as head of state. Given the nature of South Vietnamese politics up to this time, there was every reason to suppose that the new administration would not last long, but the doubters were, in fact, to be proved wrong.

THE FATAL COMMITMENT

An M48 tank in action in 1969. Some of these were assigned to US Marine Corps units, arriving in Vietnam in 1965, while others went to three US Army battalions, the 1/77th Armor near the DMZ, the 1/69th Armor in the Central Highlands, and the 2/34th Armor near the Mekong delta.

Given the apparently volatile nature of the South Vietnamese administration and the effective disintegration of the South Vietnamese Army, which was losing battalions more rapidly than replacement units could be raised and trained, the collapse of South Vietnam seemed imminent. Westmoreland came to the inevitable conclusion that the situation could be stabilized only by a major injection of new US combat troops. At this time, it had become clear,

the Communists' major units had adopted the tactics of decoying South Vietnamese units deep into sparsely populated areas for destruction or such decimation that they ceased to be effective. This left the more heavily populated areas with little or no defence, which were then easy prey to the local Communist guerrilla forces in the areas around cities and towns, and for the political cadres within the cities and towns. This two-handed approach was

therefore destroying the South Vietnamese army and leaving the urban areas prey to terrorism, intimidation and the assassination of professional men, such as doctors, teachers, lawyers and administrators. The only solution was to deploy more US combat troops to assume the main burden of fighting the Communists' larger units, so leaving the South Vietnamese army free to protect the population of the urban areas.

So Westmoreland requested the forces to boost the US presence in South Vietnam to 34 battalions, with ten from other countries: this was, admittedly, not a force large enough to win the war, but just enough to prevent a South Vietnamese defeat. Westmoreland's request provoked considerable controversy in Washington and, as the arguments continued, Johnson gave Westmoreland the authorization to make use of US troops in any situation in which Westmoreland thought it necessary 'to strengthen the relative position' of the South Vietnamese. The wording was clearly ambiguous, but Westmoreland took it as permission to justify the launch of the first large-scale US operation of the war, namely a raid into War Zone D, a long-established Communist sanctuary to the north-west of Saigon and in the area which also included the US air base at Bien Hoa.

Centred on the US 173rd Airborne Brigade, a force of US, Australian/New Zealand and South Vietnamese troops, totalling eight battalions, force struck into the sanctuary on 27 June. There were several sharp clashes but, like most raids, the operation was inconclusive, although there are some indications that it threw the Communist forces

THE VIETNAM WAR

to return in this position as Taylor's successor, at its head. Westmoreland told McNamara that it would need about 175,000 US troops merely to stabilize the position in South Vietnam, with another 100,000 following to ensure that the situation was kept under control and then turned to advantage. Westmoreland added that he could 'halt the losing trend' with this troop strength by the end of 1965, undertake a long offensive in 1966 and, in the aftermath of that successful first effort, defeat or capture the surviving Communist forces over a period of 12 to 18 months.

When the fact-finding team reported back to Washington, there was still determined opposition from officials who saw the dangers inherent in an open-ended commitment of this size to

LEFT: Marines from the USMC Combined Action Platoon Oscar-3, entering Tum Piang Ville.

BELOW: A USAF H-34 helicopter operating in Vietnam.

temporarily off balance, thus preventing a planned attack on Bien Hoa. The Australian troops were of the 1st Battalion, Royal Australian Regiment, and were part of a 1,400-strong Australian force which had arrived in South Vietnam only recently. The force was limited by its current Australian remit to 'local security operations' within a radius of 22 miles (35km) from Bien Hoa; in fact the Australian soldiers were undertaking search-and-destroy patrols in conjunction with US forces within days of their arrival. A New Zealand artillery unit, arriving at the same time as the main Australian force, was committed equally quickly.

Still uncertain about his response to Westmoreland's request for additional US troops, Johnson sent a 'fact-finding mission' to Saigon with McNamara and Henry Cabot Lodge, earlier the US ambassador to South Vietnam and soon

THE FATAL COMMITMENT

any larger-scale US involvement in South Vietnam. But both McNamara and the Joint Chiefs-of-Staff supported Westmoreland, and Johnson acceded to the request. On 28 July the president appeared on national television to state: 'I have today ordered to Vietnam the Airmobile Division [1st Cavalry Division (Airmobile), only recently formed] and certain other forces which will raise our fighting strength from 75,000 to 125,000 men almost immediately. Additional forces will be needed later, and they will be sent as requested.'

This announcement marked a turning point in the Vietnam War, as the USA had thereby committed itself to a war which was to prove altogether more bloody, costly, difficult and lengthy than anyone in the USA had yet conceived. It would be only after seven years, and with the war still not concluded, that a morally divided USA would be able to extricate itself after suffering extremely high losses.

As he received news of Johnson's authorization for the despatch of the forces he needed, Westmoreland saw the situation in South Vietnam as akin to a building (the South Vietnamese state and people) whose foundations were being eaten away and weakened by termites (Communist cadres and irregular forces), so that when the foundations had been sufficiently weakened the building could be toppled by the advent of other destructive elements (the major units of the Communist forces lurking in the jungles and mountains). Westmoreland felt that the first step in defeating this infestation was to destroy the major units, or at least to harass them so severely that they would be incapable of attacking the building, thereby providing

the breathing time in which the irregular forces and cadres could be destroyed systematically and the building repaired.

Thus Westmoreland decided right from the start to use his US combat forces to fight the Communists' major units, leaving the protection of the South Vietnamese population, the defeat of the irregulars, and the elimination of the cadres to the South Vietnamese army; the all-important task of improving the civil population's way of life would be left to the South Vietnamese administration with the support of US civilian agencies. This broad concept fell into three phases. The first involved the use of American troops to protect the development of the logistical bases which were essential, given South Vietnam's underdeveloped infrastructure and lack of vital military facilities, such as airfields, ports, storage facilities and communications networks. Westmoreland envisaged, nonetheless, that even during this essentially preparatory stage and an immediate threat by Communist major forces, some units could be diverted to check them. The second phase involved a drive into South Vietnam's sparsely populated hinterlands to reach and destroy the Communist bases, a process which would bring the Communist forces to battle in fighting favourable to the US forces' superior firepower on land and in the air. The third phase was based on the implementation of sustained offensive operations against the Communists' major units, with the object of destroying or crippling them sufficiently for the strengthened South Vietnamese army to complete the process of their elimination with only limited US support.

The primary reasons for Westmoreland's decision to rely on US rather than South Vietnamese troops to take on the Communist enemy's major units was first their possession of greater firepower and mobility, second their ability to bring that firepower to bear usefully in remote regions, thus reducing the probability of catastrophic casualties and physical damage in more densely populated regions, and third the probability that South Vietnamese troops would not fight with any notable dedication against members of the same ethnic group when dealing with their own people. Despite the second reason above, Westmoreland had decided that whenever they were not needed in the remoter areas, US troops would be deployed for operations against less capable Communist units in the more densely populated parts of South Vietnam.

As suggested above, it had been the US intention right from the start that military operations would be only one part of the overall US effort, whose other aspect was a series of civic action programmes to improve the everyday lives of the people of South Vietnam. This was not a wholly altruistic factor but an intrinsic element of a 'hearts and mind' undertaking designed to boost the South Vietnamese population's adherence to its government. Westmoreland appreciated that once they had discovered the basic tenets of the US effort, they might attempt to keep the major US forces engaged in remoter areas and therefore not in any position to aid the South Vietnamese civil population, but felt that the greater mobility of his forces would make it all but impossible for the Communists'

THE VIETNAM WAR

major forces to keep the US forces committed in remoter areas for any extended period. Even if the Communists did succeed in this, moreover, this too would serve a purpose inasmuch as the Communist forces could not then become involved in attacks on the main centres of urban population.

Another factor Westmoreland was forced to contend with was the security of South Vietnam's 900-mile (1450-km) frontier. It was clearly impossible to seal the full length of this tightly enough to prevent infiltration, and the only alternative was reliance on fixed frontier posts around which the infiltrators would have to pass, patrols and aerial reconnaissance to find and locate the forces which were infiltrating through gaps between the frontier posts and, finally, artillery, air attack and mobile ground forces to fix and destroy any groups discovered.

The key to protecting the frontier positions was to employ men from the ethnic minority populations, aided by advisers from the US Army's special forces, for the men of these remoter regions knew their own territory intimately, often had little love for the Vietnamese, and were skilful and fearsome fighters. As far as the notoriously porous DMZ was concerned, Westmoreland still hoped that an international 'peacekeeping' force might be made available to seal this sector of the frontier.

The most difficult problem facing the US and South Vietnamese forces, however, was the network of extemporized roads, tracks and paths collectively known as the Ho Chi Minh Trail. Passing from North Vietnam into

neutral Laos and Cambodia, it offered the Communists a veritable mass of avenues along which to pass men, matériel and supplies that were virtually undetectable, except in miniscule portions, was impossible to sever, being possessed of so many tentacles, and lay largely in neutral countries. Westmoreland did hope eventually to sever and close the Ho Chi Minh Trail through Laos and northern Cambodia, but did not initially request authority to enter Laos as he felt that the forces on hand were too small to allow any diversion of strength for the task.

What it all amounted to was, in effect, a war of attrition, because there was no single enemy formation against which Westmoreland could direct the US strength for a decisive campaign of the type forming the heart of the US military philosophy. He was faced with political restrictions denying him the right to undertake military operations outside South Vietnam, and the prospect of a force sufficient to hold only portions of South Vietnam in any strength, so Westmoreland could envisage no alternative.

This meant the Vietnam War would inevitably be long, as are all wars of attrition, but there was the longer-term prospect that an American success and a revitalized South Vietnam would create a security situation in which the Viet Cong would be unable to recruit or impress sufficient South Vietnamese to maintain their struggle. This would leave the North Vietnamese with regular units with which to continue the war on their own against strengthening anti-Communist forces, that would ultimately result in insupportable losses.

The general scheme was that US divisions and brigades should be located at semi-permanent base camps and operate from these into the surrounding region that would constitute the division's or brigade's area of tactical responsibility; there was also provision for the division or brigade to be moved, on a temporary basis, to tackle major Communist formations and units in other parts of South Vietnam. In such an eventuality, the division or brigade would detach a small security force which would be left to garrison the base camp. The rest of the division or brigade would move out into the required area and there construct a temporary base camp shielded, at a distance, by fire-support bases prepared for all-round defence and operating as artillery firing positions and patrol bases. Depending on intelligence assessments of the opposition's strength, components of the division or brigade, up to a strength of several battalions, would be launched on sweeps of the region around the fire-support bases, bringing the Communist forces to combat in conditions where the US firepower superiority, especially in artillery, would be dominant. In overall terms, this was the system known as 'search-and-destroy'.

Even though US firepower was to be concentrated in the remoter regions of South Vietnam, it was conceded that damage to villages was inevitable. On occasions, the Communist forces might be so deeply entrenched within villages and among the civilian population that relocation of the civilians would have to be undertaken and their original settlement destroyed to create 'free-fire zones' in which the Communist forces

THE FATAL COMMITMENT

could be found, fixed and destroyed, opening the possibility that the original inhabitants might be able to return at a later date. Neither of the only alternatives to this tactical scheme, either to enter combat with the civil population still present, or to abandon the area to the Communists, was acceptable for fear of causing high civilian casualties and because, if left to their own devices, the Communists would be able to extend the area and depth of their control over the region and civil population.

The first major offensive operation involving only US troops took place in August 1965, when US Marines,

protecting an airfield on the north-central coast at Chu Lai, located a Viet Cong regiment on the Van Tuong peninsula. Since the Viet Cong force was a mere 15 miles (24km) distant, and was therefore a tactical threat to Chu Lai, the commander of the III Marine Amphibious Force, Lieutenant General Lewis W. Walt, inaugurated Operation Starlite. This was launched on the basis of intelligence information provided by Major General Nguyen Chanh Thi, the commander of the South Vietnamese forces in I Corps area in northern South Vietnam.

The operation was undertaken as a combined arms undertaking, involving

ground, air and naval units, the core of the effort being the deployment of men of the US Marine Corps by helicopter into the designated landing zone, while more men of the same corps were delivered by amphibious landing. The operation began on 17 August 1965, and involved 5,500 men of the 9th Marine Amphibious Brigade. The brigade comprised the 2nd Battalion 4th Marines (2/4), 3rd Battalion 3rd Marines (3/3), 3rd Battalion 7th Marines (3/7) and 3rd Battalion 7th Marines (3/7) from the Special Landing Force (originally a reserve component). Also involved were the US Navy's cruiser *Galveston* and dock landing ship *Cabildo* for naval gunfire support, the 3rd Battalion 12th Marines being the artillery unit in direct support. The tank landing ship *Vernon County* carried elements of the 3rd Battalion 3rd Marines at Chu Lai, and steamed south along the coast to An Thuong, where the men were landed.

The Viet Cong forces, totalling some 1,500 men, comprised the 1st Viet Cong Regiment, made up of the 60th and 80th Viet Cong Battalions, the 52nd Viet Cong Company, and one company of the 45th Viet Cong Weapons Battalion.

'Mike' Company of 3/3 was to be the blocking force for deployment on 17 August, using tracked landing vehicles to reach its landing area; after coming ashore the men were to move 4 miles (6.4 km) to establish the required block. The 3rd Battalion 3rd Marines was then to make its amphibious landing and begin to drive the Viet Cong towards 2/4, which was to be lifted by helicopter into three landing zones west of Van Tuong. Secrecy was paramount, and no South Vietnamese army commander

LEFT: The Chinook helicopter played an important part in the movement of equipment and troops.

BELOW: A CH-47A Chinook brings the main body of 3rd Brigade troops down on to the mountain ridge of secured Landing Zone 5.

ambushed west of its position. Recoilless rifle fire from the Viet Cong positions hit five tracked landing vehicles and three flamethrower tanks, and the men of the US Marine Corps had to mount a rescue, suffering five dead and 17 wounded after they were hit by heavy mortar and rifle fire. The Marines called in artillery and air support to suppress the mortar and automatic fire.

The evolving nature of the engagement required the deployment of 'Lima' Company, 3/7, from the helicopter assault carrier *Iwo Jima* to join 'India' Company in providing assistance to the ambushed supply column. Toward nightfall, the Marines

or units were to be informed of the forthcoming operation.

The men of the US Marine Corps met only light resistance as they moved in to the attack. 'Echo' Company, 2/4, spotted Viet Cong in the open and called in artillery fire from the 3rd Battalion 12th Marines, a barrage which is said to have killed 90 Viet Cong soldiers. 'Hotel' Company, 2/4, then assaulted the 60th Viet Cong Battalion, which resisted strongly. One prisoner was taken and 40 weapons were captured. 'India' Company, 3/3, attacked An Cuong after taking heavy fire from the hamlet and losing its company commander in the engagement.

'India' Company was ordered to join 'Kilo' and 'Hotel' Companies and clean up any opposition, but was caught in a crossfire from Nam Yen Dan Hill 30. 'Hotel' Company established a defensive perimeter and was then instructed to wait for reinforcements, but this additional strength was diverted to assist the supply column which had been

US soldiers with a Viet Cong prisoner.

James M. Gavin and Colonel (later Lieutenant General) John J. Tolson started to investigate the helicopter as the means of bypassing the USAF's concerns about the US Army's use of large fixed-wing aircraft while still providing the US Army with the reconnaissance capability it so clearly needed. Gavin and his staff thereupon proposed a new US Cavalry, but in this instance carrying out its task on 'flying horses'. Gavin sent Tolson to Fort Benning as head of the Airborne School to work out a doctrine for the efficient use of helicopters and, in parallel, Brigadier General Carl I. Hutton and Colonel Jay D. Vanderpool were proceeding along the same line at the Army Aviation School at nearby Fort Rucker, Alabama. Vanderpool managed to obtain the use of some helicopters, armed them with locally improved weapon systems, and by 1957 was testing his 'Sky-Cavalry' platoon as a precursor to future divisions built round this radical concept.

The various aviation research projects by the Ordnance, Transportation and Signal Corps were co-ordinated at Fort Rucker to some extent, and in 1959 the US Army gave the US aviation industry guidelines to develop a 'light observation, manned

the Howze Board, led by the US Army's first director of aviation, presented McNamara with a 3,500-page report recommending five new divisions, each with an organic strength of 459 helicopters. The Huey would undertake the tactical deployment of troops, the new Boeing CH-47 Chinook twin-rotor medium-lift helicopter would carry the division's artillery of Honest John rockets and 105-mm (4.13-in) howitzers, the intelligence branch would have some fixed-wing aircraft with cameras or radar, and a new, and currently non-existent attack helicopter gunship would complete the requirements for the 'air assault division' by suppressing enemy fire on and around the landing zone (LZ) for the Huey machines, before providing the landed troops with light fire support.

LEFT: A USAF A-1E Skyraider releases 500-lb bombs over a Viet Cong target in South Vietnam in April 1965.

BELOW: A bomb explosion in a US Army vehicle in Saigon on Christmas Eve 1964.

surveillance, and tactical transport aircraft'. In fact the Bell company was already well-advanced in the development of a turbine-powered utility helicopter, the Model 204, which later became the UH-1 Iroquois, or 'Huey', helicopter workhorse of the Vietnam War. By this stage in the proceedings, many US Army officers looked on army aviation development in very positive terms, and the Rogers Board urged that each division be allocated helicopters with a tactical radius at least as great as the farthest reach of that divisional artillery. Nevertheless, the helicopter development programme was very slow until a time early in 1962, when Secretary of Defense Robert McNamara pronounced the whole effort to date to have been 'dangerously conservative'. The US Army aviators leapt at the challenge and, within 90 days of its establishment,

THE FATAL COMMITMENT

ABOVE: The M42A1 Duster was an improvement on the old M19 twin 40-mm anti-aircraft tank of the Second World War, and was engaged in much action throughout the Vietnam conflict.

ABOVE RIGHT: A US Navy Patrol Air Cushion Vehicle (PACV) hovercraft picking up Viet Cong personnel.

RIGHT: Members of the US 1st Cavalry Division begin patrol duty from a helicopter landing base in 1965.

THE VIETNAM WAR

LEFT: Members of the 4th Battalion, 503rd Regiment of the 101st Airborne Division board an American Airlines Astrojet at Fort Campbell, Kentucky, for the first leg of their flight to Vietnam in June 1966.

PAGE 115: Christmas 1965: the comedian Bob Hope boosts morale onboard the USS New Jersey.

McNamara agreed with the concept, and the 11th Air Assault Division was formed at Fort Benning in January 1963. By a time late in 1964 it was common to see flights of Huey helicopters progressing at 115mph (185km/h) just a few feet above the trees. Five Huey gunships first broke over the planned LZ, raking it and the surrounding area with sustained rocket and machine gun fire. After another pass, the Huey gunships climbed to circle as seven other Huey helicopters, echeloned vertically, dropped into the LZ, disgorged their troops, and rapidly lifted off as the landed men raced to their rallying points off the LZ. As the first troopships rose in a swirl of dust, more arrived until an infantry company or more was on the ground, concentrated, and moving

toward its objective. The commander overhead in his command and control machine had brought a substantial force from miles away to be 'injected' deep into enemy territory with total surprise, and all in fewer than 15 minutes. This air-mobility concept clearly worked, and would prove as necessary a development for the Vietnam War as airborne doctrine had been for the Second World War.

By the spring of 1965 Lieutenant General Charles Rich had finished his tests for the Howze Board, and had been so impressed by the efforts of the 11th Air Assault Division that he wished to keep it in existence as an operational formation. The Department of Defense concurred, and with the approval of General Creighton W. Abrahams, the

Vice Chief-of-Staff, the 11th Air Assault Division was reconstituted as a cavalry formation – the 1st Cavalry Division (Airmobile).

In South Vietnam, meanwhile, the US was seeking to persuade the South Vietnamese military and civil administration, based on the urban elite, to take a greater interest in the 'hearts and minds' of the rural population in a countryside increasingly dominated by the Viet Cong and its sympathizers. The USA also pushed forward the Cheu Hoi scheme to rehabilitate co-operative Viet Cong and North Vietnamese army prisoners and deserters, and sought to promote the creation of an urban bourgeoisie which would identify its new-found prosperity with the South Vietnamese government and therefore support it. It was an impossible task, for the corruption and nepotism of the South Vietnamese administration, whoever was running it, was a national cancer that persuaded everyone to look after himself. For the South Vietnamese in general it was a case of seeking survival and advantage wherever this could be obtained, and to many this meant collaboration with both the South Vietnamese administration and the Communist insurgency. America put enormous effort and huge resources into its effort to reform and stabilize South Vietnamese society, but the Viet Cong was quietly rampant in rural areas. The South Vietnamese army undertook countless patrol operations, but the Viet Cong faded from sight whenever threatened, only to re-emerge as soon as the coast was clear. Thus the Viet Cong and North Vietnamese army continued to run their now well-established shadow governments and effectively control the rural population.

The Communist political and military machine had the benefit of an excellent intelligence apparatus, which was so pervasive that most South Vietnamese operations were known, at least in part, before they began. Unless they were fortunate, most South Vietnamese patrols returned to their compounds empty-handed and with a number of dead and wounded from ambush, or perhaps a few 'suspects', the latter generally seized arbitrarily from the rural population, whose sense of alienation from the government was thereby strengthened.

As part of the US assistance scheme, General Taylor had as early as 1961 recommended there be greater use of US air assets. Advisers soon saw, in the resulting delivery of Vertol (Piasecki) H-

21 Shawnee twin-rotor helicopters, the opportunity to gain a tactical advantage over the Viet Cong and so win back the element of surprise. US training and equipment had improved both the skills and, to a lesser extent, the morale of the South Vietnamese army, and the US advisers saw in the newly arrived helicopters the possibility of trapping Communist forces and preventing their escape, so forcing them to fight on terms advantageous to the matériel-richer South Vietnamese forces. On 24 December 1961 1,000 South Vietnamese troops were helicoptered into a suspected Viet Cong stronghold near Saigon, where they routed a small Viet Cong detachment.

The US advisers saw this as heralding a new dawn, but there were only a few helicopters available and the great majority of South Vietnamese soldiers still moved on foot along the often-mined paddyfield dykes and roads between booby-trapped tree lines. By 1965 the South Vietnamese army had still not been able to devise and implement any means of pinning down and destroying sizeable Communist forces, and the US therefore decided to commit its airborne forces to tip the scale.

In May 1965 the 173rd Airborne Brigade from Okinawa landed in Vietnam. The brigade, commanded by Brigadier General Ellis W. Williamson, knew of the air-mobility developments at Fort Benning, and with the helicopters available to him started to train his men in the new air-mobility tactics At first, the paratroopers were unconvinced of these new tactical concepts, but confidence and co-ordination improved. When the 173rd Airborne Brigade was joined by the 1st Battalion Royal

Australian Regiment and a battery of gunners from the Royal New Zealand Artillery, plus two more airborne battalions from Tolson's parent unit, the 503rd Parachute Infantry Regiment, its men started to mount successful air-mobile operations. One of the first of these, near the Dong Nai river, resulted in the deaths of 56 Communist soldiers, the capture of 28 more men, and the seizure of hundreds of tons of rice and documents.

The North Vietnamese army was at the same time preparing its offensive to cut South Vietnam in two with an eastward offensive from the mountains to the sea. Commanding the Western Highlands Field Front, General Chu Nuy Man planned a major thrust from Cambodia and the traditional Communist lurking grounds in west-central Vietnam along the Ia Drang river straight through four provinces to the sea. Intelligence suggested that this effort would start during the summer or autumn of 1965, at a time when Rich had finished testing his air assault division. Thus the new 1st Cavalry Division (Airmobile) was available and was sent by sea to deploy its 16,000 men, 1,600 vehicles and some 400 aircraft in the central part of South Vietnam.

The division's move in eight weeks presupposed an administrative landing, but its component units were then advised that they might have to fight their way ashore with their mothballed helicopters left on the decks of the transport vessels. Fortunately, elements of the 101st Airborne Division had also been alerted for deployment to South Vietnam, and arrived in time to secure the landing place for the 1st Cavalry Division (Airmobile). US airborne units had already led the way into South Vietnam, and proved the worth of the new air-mobile tactics in cordon and search operations Now the 1st Cavalry Division (Airmobile) was to head west from An Khe to test air-mobility in action against a large and militarily sophisticated force.

On 19 October 1965 the Communist forces kicked off the Tau Nguyen campaign by hitting the Plei Me Special Forces camp about 19 miles (30km) to the south of the provincial capital, Pleiku. Westmoreland ordered Major General H.W.O Kinnard to take his 1st Cavalry Division (Airmobile) to help in the South Vietnamese army's operation to relieve the camp and pursue the Communist attack force, but when the division's 1st Brigade arrived, the Communist forces had, as usual, melted away. Kinnard and his intelligence staff felt the Communists had probably fallen back to their base area and despatched the division's Air Cavalry Squadron to locate them.

Operating at low level in an area of forests and ravines, the Hughes OH-6 light observation helicopters gained contact 6 miles (10km) west of the camp, which led to the capture of a North Vietnamese army field hospital. In the fighting for the hospital and in their sweeps, the relatively inexperienced US soldiers learned that the units of the North Vietnamese army were well-equipped – also skilled and determined. Wherever the US forces established a perimeter, the North Vietnamese crawled so close that defending fire was rendered ineffective; they also sniped and otherwise harassed the US soldiers at distances of 10 yards (9m) or less. The men of the 1st Cavalry Division learned

Members of the 2nd Battalion, 3rd US Marine Division vacating helicopters during an operation to penetrate Viet Cong territory outside the dense perimeter of Da Nang airbase in South Vietnam.

swiftly, however, and in the hospital fight killed 78 North Vietnamese soldiers, taking 57 prisoners at the loss of five of their own men killed and 17 wounded.

By this stage of the Communist offensive, both South Vietnamese and US intelligence were now sure that the Communist main body was moving west through the Ia Drang valley toward the Chu Pong mountains on the South

Vietnamese side of the border, a region that had been a safe staging area for the North Vietnamese over a considerable time. On 2 November 1965 the 1st Squadron, 9th Cavalry Regiment flew into a small clearing, designated LZ 'Mary', setting up an ambush on the side of the hills running down from the Chu Pong massif toward the Ia Drang river. This was the division's first

attempt at a night air-mobile ambush, and was supported by a company of infantry also brought at night. The ambush led to the Communist loss of 150 North Vietnamese killed, and to US losses of four killed and 25 wounded. The inescapable conclusion was that the Communist main body was located in this area, and having laid the groundwork, the air cavalry turned

THE VIETNAM WAR

With the arrival of the 173rd Airborne Brigade from Okinawa on 5 May 1965, SP4 Archie L. Gaffee plots a fire mission for the 81-mm mortar squads.

over the completion of the task to the infantry.

By 9 November Chu Nuy Man's forces were located in two major staging areas, with the 32nd North Vietnamese Regiment on the northern bank of the Ia Drang and quite close to the South Vietnamese/Cambodian frontier, with the high-quality 66th North Vietnamese Regiment and the less capable 33rd between the river and the eastern slope of the Chu Pong massif. The 33rd North Vietnamese Regiment had lost about one third of its original strength of 2,200 men in the fighting for Plei Me, and was now revised as a composite

battalion, albeit still of nearly regimental size. The division's 120-mm (4.72-in) mortars and 14.5-mm (0.57-in) twin-barrel anti-aircraft machine guns were still on the Ho Chi Minh Trail in Cambodia, but Chu was happy with his formation's security on the rocky and wooded slopes of the area and prepared another attack on Plei Me.

The search for the North Vietnamese position was entrusted to Colonel T.W. Brown's 3rd Brigade and the 1st Cavalry Division. The 3rd Brigade included, among its manoeuvre battalions, two from the famous 7th US Cavalry. Much of the brigade had trained together in

the 11th Air Assault Division experiments and had excellent morale. The brigade began to search the valley by setting-down squads and platoons in a process of so-called saturation patrolling, but the search area near the massif appeared so promising that Lieutenant Colonel H.G. Moore, commanding the 1st Battalion, 7th Cavalry, decided to look for an LZ where he could set-down the whole of his battalion. On the morning of 14 November Moore reconnoitred the area from the air in an apparently casual manner, and in the process evaluated three possible LZs before opting for the largest of these, which had the size to accommodate eight to ten helicopters simultaneously. From the air the LZ appeared to be moderately open, with tall, brown elephant grass beneath scrub trees of up to 100ft (30m) high, even though the terrain undulated and was dotted with anthills about 8ft (2.4m) high. The woods grew denser toward Chu Pong, and a dry stream-bed extended along the western edge of what would become LZ 'X-Ray'.

On returning to his base camp, Moore despatched an OH-6 helicopter to check the area once again. When the helicopter's crew reported seeing communications wire in the area of LZ X-Ray, Moore ordered his battalion to mount up. At 10:17 two 105-mm (4.13-in) howitzer batteries of the 1st Battalion, 21st Artillery, located some 5.5 miles (8.8 km) east of LZ X-Ray, began a 20-minute barrage of preparatory fire onto LZ X-Ray and, for purposes of deception, the two other possible LZs. The aerial rocket artillery of the 2nd Battalion, 20th Artillery, lifted off and the second the last artillery projectile detonated, the helicopters swept in and over a period of some 30 seconds expended half their loads on LZ X-Ray before climbing and waiting near the LZ ready for any call for more support. The escorting gunships of 'A' Company, 229th Aviation Battalion, raked the area before 'B' Company landed with Moore in personal command. By 10:48 the helicopters were returning to collect and deliver A Company, and at much the same time Moore's operations officer, artillery liaison officer, and USAF forward air controller arrived overhead to call in artillery and tactical air attacks as

necessary, and to relay radio communications if required.

Once he was on the ground, the commander of 'B' Company detached small parties off to check the tree line, while holding the bulk of his company in a thicket on the LZ to react to any sign of Communist activity. At 11:20, a North Vietnamese army deserter was brought in and told Moore that the US company was faced by at least three fully-prepared North Vietnamese army battalions. Chu had, in fact, already started his movement toward Plei Me when the landings were reported, and immediately positioned his 33rd and 66th North Vietnamese Regiments to the west of Chu Pong and along its base in a totally silent, very rapid movement in less than one hour. B Company continued searching to the north-east of the LZ along a spur extending from the mountain, with two platoons abreast and the third platoon in reserve behind the left-hand platoon. As the left-hand platoon came off the spur and crossed a dry stream-bed, it moved slightly ahead of the right-hand platoon and was suddenly taken under heavy and accurate small arms fire from an estimated North Vietnamese platoon hidden in the grass. Both flanks of the US platoons were exposed, and the commander of B Company responded by ordering the reserve to press forward, sending the right-hand platoon over to the right flank of the pinned platoon.

As soon as the right-hand platoon received the order, a skirmish line was formed with a 7.62-mm (0.3-in) M60 machine gun on each flank, and started to work its way toward the firing. As the platoon advanced, its reserve squad, in the rear, saw about 20 North Vietnamese

soldiers disappear behind anthills on its left flank, between the place where it was and the location at which it hoped to find the left-hand platoon. The reserve squad's grenadier immediately fired a series of 40-mm grenades from his M79 launcher into the anthills, but was then cut down by a burst of fire from his right. This signalled a major firefight and the right-hand platoon now found itself in difficulty. The platoon leader despatched his two machine gun crews to cover the reserve squad, the rest of the platoon forming a tight perimeter which was taken under North Vietnamese mortar and rocket fire. Soon the reserve squad and one of the machine gun crews ran into the comparative safety of the perimeter carrying the dead grenadier's launcher. The other four-man machine gun team did not make it and the North Vietnamese soon brought the captured gun to bear on the platoon.

As the weight of fire increased, the commander of B Company attempted to report the situation to Moore, with emphasis on the situation to his front, but the trees, tall grass and smoke severely curtailed his ability to discern what was happening. As he reported, Moore and his radio operator themselves came under fire, and one North Vietnamese soldier got to within 15 yards (14m) before the commander of B Company stopped him with grenade and rifle fire. The company commander was now sure that his left-hand platoon, which had been the original object for rescue, had now to become the rescuer after the reserve platoon had joined it. Meanwhile, Moore set up his command post at the LZ and was bringing in A Company to the left to protect B

THE VIETNAM WAR

As members of the 2nd Battalion, 503rd Infantry, 173rd Airborne Brigade launch a large-scale operation against the Viet Cong, 7.5 miles (12km) north of Bien Hoa airfield, artillery troops prepare to fire 81-mm mortars in support of advancing troops during an assault on an area heavily infested with Viet Cong.

Company's flank, imagining that the two left-hand platoons of B Company would be exposed as they turned to assist the isolated platoon. It was now about 13:30 and the first men of 'C' Company were landing. Moore sent them to cover A Company by taking positions just off the LZ to the south and south-west. The rear of Moore's position was not covered, and mortar fire was falling on the LZ, but he could do little else. Meanwhile, the rest of C Company and

the whole of 'D' Company had not yet landed.

Second Lieutenant Walter J. Marm of A Company landed and quickly moved his platoon off the LZ in a skirmish line toward the sound of firing. He almost immediately took two prisoners, and soon linked up with B Company's reserve platoon. With it Marm planned to make for the trapped platoon, but then his command and the reserve platoon came under heavy fire.

The same North Vietnamese unit which had tried to cut off the right-hand B Company was now apparently moving to surround the whole of B Company and also Marm's A Company platoon. As they returned fire, Marm tried to evacuate his wounded, but the sergeant detailed for the mission reported that he could not get through. The North Vietnamese force then broke off and moved down into the dry stream-bed in an effort to circle behind Marm, but in

THE FATAL COMMITMENT

C and D Companies was reducing the amount of North Vietnamese fire sweeping the LZ, and as fast as he could personally guided in the last three loads of C Company, the Scout (reconnaissance) platoon, a Pathfinder team, and the executive officer and first D Company. Up on the line A and B Companies had pulled back to co-ordinate, while C and D Companies held the perimeter with the aid of artillery fire on trajectories at right angles to the air attacks. The North Vietnamese lay only yards away from the isolated platoon, so close that the men could not raise their arms to dig for cover. The platoon leader and platoon sergeant were among the eight men who had been killed. The next senior, Sergeant Savage, and his medic displayed great leadership in rallying the seven unwounded and 12 wounded, many of the latter remaining on the line.

Because the 7th Cavalry was air-mobile, and could therefore carry more per man, it was policy for every man to carry more than 300 rounds for his 5.56-mm (0.22-in) M16 rifle, at least two fragmentation grenades, two canteens of water, and one ration packet. Each grenadier carried about 30 grenades and each machine gunner had at least 800 rounds for his M60. Most men carried more than this, so unless they were overrun by superior numbers, the isolated platoon stood every chance of holding on.

Moore issued a preparatory order to A and B Companies to attack and bring in the platoon. At 16:20 the two companies moved forward from the stream-bed after artillery and air artillery preparation had been brought in as close as 275 yards (250m) to B Company's front. It made little difference. The North Vietnamese had quietly moved up almost to the tops of the stream-bank. Hiding in anthills and trees, they were fully ready when the two companies moved out. The ensuing fight was terrible for the Americans: Marm's platoon was stopped by a machine gun just 30 yards (27m) to its front but concealed in the grass. Marm raised himself out of cover in an effort to pinpoint its location, and when his sergeant's grenade fell short, Marm raced out, scooped it up and hurled it into the machine gun nest, dispatching the remaining crew with his rifle. However, the loss of the machine gun did little to change the overall situation in favour of the Americans. US casualties continued to mount, and as most of A Company's leaders had been killed or wounded, Moore told the company it had his permission to fall back to the LZ. It had moved only 165 yards (150m).

B Company was also receiving fire, so heavy that it had taken 30 casualties and had to pull back. But the North Vietnamese fire was such that neither company could retreat. A Company's forward observer had been killed and no smoke rounds were available to cover the withdrawal, but Moore recalled how effective white phosphorus rounds had been in the Korean War. Soon the 1st Battalion, 21st Artillery launched a barrage of WP shells, and the star-like bursts of burning phosphorus over the North Vietnamese positions provided the two battered companies with just sufficient time to crawl back with their casualties.

Between 17:00 and 19:00 Moore created as tight a perimeter as he could.

Defensive artillery and mortar patterns were co-ordinated and Moore chose part of the LZ, enough for two helicopters, as his last stand. The 229th Pathfinders (men skilled at guiding in aircraft or paratroops onto improvised landing sites) cleared this final LZ of trees with engineer demolition charges and marked out the lighting panels for nightfall; they were under fire the whole time without suffering any casualties. Around them the exhausted and thirsty cavalrymen dug prone positions and ate the jam from their rations for its moisture. They were heartened when B Company of the 2nd Battalion suddenly swooped in, as promised by Brown, and at 19:15 a re-supply mission skidded in with its crews, pushing out ammunition, water, rations and literally vital medical supplies. Soon after this, the operations officer landed with his two fire controllers, but that was the last movement of the day. The remains of the 1st Battalion, 7th Cavalry lay under a thick pall of smoke and darkness, awaiting the North Vietnamese troops' next move.

The isolated platoon could not move: Savage adjusted artillery to within yards of his position by radio, and soon the 1st Battalion, 21st Artillery knew exactly where Savage's perimeter was. The North Vietnamese attacked three times before 03:45, the sound of their bugle calls coming from the mountain 330 yards (300m) away, indicating the imminence of another attack. As Savage heard the North Vietnamese speaking, he called down a 15-minute barrage with air strikes under illumination. The North Vietnamese retreated slightly, but the light played over the Americans and they had to drive back another major assault in darkness about one hour later.

THE VIETNAM WAR

The main perimeter had also been probed. The 66th North Vietnamese Regiment's 8th Battalion had by now arrived. At first light on 15 November Moore called his commanders together to plan the relief of Savage's platoon. Moore also ordered a thorough check to a distance of 220 yards (200m) made outside the perimeter. Although the Americans did not know it, during the night the North Vietnamese had crawled through the exploding artillery right up to the US perimeter. As the first troopers moved out to sweep around the perimeter, they ran into a withering crossfire. Some men rushed out to help those who had fallen and were themselves hit, and within the space of seconds the commander of C Company and two of his lieutenants had been severely wounded by a machine gun not 45 yards (40m) to their front. Moore now ordered a platoon of A Company to cross the LZ in support of C Company. The commander of A Company took the platoon farthest away from contact, closed the gap with his other men, and despatched the platoon, which lost two men killed and two wounded as it tried to cross the LZ. The other men of the platoon dropped to a prone position on line between the right flank of C Company and the left flank of their own unit. From there they provided defence in depth and protected the command post and aid station in the event that the perimeter was overrun.

The firing on the perimeter defence became dense as D Company, on the left flank of C Company, was attacked. At 07:45 rockets, mortars and automatic weapons fire sealed the LZ. The 7th Cavalry replied to all these new thrusts with all the firepower it had, and large numbers of North Vietnamese were killed. The fighting had grown so desperate by 07:55 that Moore had each platoon mark its position with coloured smoke, for though this advertised the position to the North Vietnamese, it also marked it for the pilots of the attack aircraft to drop bombs and napalm. These were aimed so close that some accidentally dropped inside the perimeter, ignited the reserve ammunition, and burned two men. By this time, the North Vietnamese had pinpointed the position of the consolidated mortars, and now put some of them out of action. Moore had no choice but to ask Brown again for another company. At 09:10 A Company, 2nd Battalion was delivered in heavy fire, and the fresh troopers went into line alongside their own B Company.

Finally, at 10:00, the tons of ordnance from the air attacks and artillery barrages began to achieve results, and the North Vietnamese reduced the pressure of their onslaught to mere harassing fire. This gave the cavalrymen a breathing space to distribute ammunition, move the newly-wounded back to the command post, and then to wait once more. Fortunately, the 2nd Battalion, 5th Cavalry was now completing its approach march from LZ 'Victor' and, after only light resistance, was able to enter LZ X-Ray at about 12:00, bringing the total US strength to about nine companies, four of which had been hard hit.

Moore co-ordinated with the arriving battalion commander, Lieutenant Colonel R.B. Tully. The first task was the recovery of the isolated platoon and, as it knew the way, B Company of the 2nd Battalion, 7th Cavalry was detailed to lead Tully toward Savage at 13:15, while Tully's A and C Companies provided the muscle. In an attempt to divert attention from Tully, Moore mounted another sweep all around the perimeter and scoured the interior, too, in case any North Vietnamese had managed to infiltrate. The troops moved through the blood-stained grass to find North Vietnamese dead stacked up behind anthills. There were craters of churned earth, fragments of North Vietnamese uniforms, and the trails leading toward Chu Pong were soaked in blood and littered with equipment. The unsuccessful sweep of the morning left its evidence of dead American soldiers surrounded by dead North Vietnamese.

Tully advanced without incident up the spur and located the much-relieved lost platoon. In slow order and with only one serious casualty from a sniper, the complete party now retired in good order down to the LZ, carrying the dead and wounded. Once it reached the perimeter, the 2nd Battalion, 5th Cavalry moved to assume an equal share of the defence and everyone dug in.

The cavalrymen had not been forgotten by higher command echelons, and during the afternoon a B-52 raid was made against Chu Pong itself: this was also of significance being the first occasion on which the strategic bombers had been used for the tactical support of ground forces. Throughout the following night, even though artillery ringed the perimeter in depth, the North Vietnamese nonetheless managed to probe the line, finally launching a company-sized attack against B Company of the 2nd Battalion at 05:30 and again an hour later.

THE FATAL COMMITMENT

Cam Canh Bay port, Vietnam.

To avoid falling into the same trap as the day before, Moore instructed the entire perimeter to fire all its weapons into the trees, anthills and elephant grass at first light, in a 'mad minute' of firing. This proved a successful ploy: snipers fell from the trees only a few yards from the cavalry, and a platoon-sized attack was prematurely triggered. After a pause, Moore decided to sweep out to 550 yards (500m), and while doing so B Company of the 2nd Battalion again took the brunt of a determined attack by wounded North Vietnamese, who hurled grenades from where they had fallen. Firing all the way, the company fell back into the perimeter and the forward air controller called in air attacks so close that a 500-lb (227-kg) bomb was delivered on target only 25 yards (23m) in front of the perimeter.

The North Vietnamese were now exhausted, and another US sweep met with little opposition. The LZ was now safe enough for the rest of the 2nd Battalion's companies to land and Moore's weary troopers were carried out. Moore's command had accounted for 634 North Vietnamese known dead and another 581 estimated killed, and six prisoners had been taken. Despite their aversion to abandoning any weapons, the North Vietnamese left more than 100 crew-served and individual weapons, including four Maxim machine guns, rocket launchers and mortars. Moore's losses were 79 killed and 121 wounded.

The battle seemed to be over, and there appeared to be no reason for the US forces to remain in the field. The mission was complete and arguably a success, but Brown was concerned about reports that additional North Vietnamese units were moving into the area over the border. Brown wished to withdraw his command but Westmoreland demanded that the 2nd Battalion, 7th Cavalry and 1st Battalion, 5th Cavalry remain at LZ X-Ray, so that there would be no appearance of retreat.

On the following day the two remaining battalions abandoned LZ X-Ray and began moving to new landing zones: the 2nd/5th under Tully to LZ 'Columbus' about 2.5 miles (4km) to the north-east, and the 2nd/7th under Lieutenant Colonel Robert McDade to LZ 'Albany', about the same distance to the north-north-east, close to the Ia Drang. B-52 bombers had already been despatched from their base on Guam, their target being the slopes of the Chu Pong massif. The US ground forces had to move outside a 2-mile (3.2-km) safety zone by mid-morning to be clear of the scheduled bombardment, and Tully's battalion moved out at 09:00 with McDade's Battalion following 10 minutes later.

The first sign of a Communist presence was detected by the US column's point units, the point squad of the reconnaissance platoon under Staff Sergeant Donald J. Slovak, who saw 'Ho Chi Minh sandal foot markings, bamboo arrows on the ground pointing north, matted grass and grains of rice'. After marching for about 2,200 yards (2000m), A Company leading the 2nd/7th headed north-west, while the 2nd/5th continued toward LZ

124

THE VIETNAM WAR

Columbus. A Company came upon some grass huts which they were ordered to burn. At 11:38 the 2nd/5th reached LZ Columbus.

The Communist troops in the area consisted of the 8th Battalion of the 66th North Vietnamese Regiment, the 1st Battalion of the 33rd North Vietnamese Regiment, and the headquarters of the 3rd Battalion of the 33rd North Vietnamese Regiment. The 33rd North Vietnamese Regiment was

below strength as a result of the casualties it had suffered during the battle at the Plei Me Special Forces camp, while the 8th Battalion was General An's reserve, and as such was fresh and rested.

A Company soon noticed the sudden absence of air cover and its commander, Captain Joel Sugdinis, wondered where the helicopters were. He soon heard the sound of explosions to his rear, and knew that the B-52 bombers were

unloading their bomb loads on the Chu Pong massif.

Leading the reconnaissance platoon, Lieutenant D.P. Payne was moving around some anthills when he came upon a North Vietnamese soldier resting on the ground and took him prisoner, while simultaneously, about 10 yards (9m) away, his platoon sergeant captured a second. Other members of the North Vietnamese reconnaissance team may have escaped and reported to the

THE FATAL COMMITMENT

Candidates practise jumping out of a C-47 mock-up during a training course at the Vietnamese Army Jump School, Airborne Brigade Headquarters, Camp Hoang Hoa Tham, near Tan Son Nhut airbase, Saigon. The school was fashioned after the US Army Jump School at Fort Benning, Georgia, and was commanded by Captain Tran Van Vinh.

they saw around the perimeter. Later, it was discovered that North Vietnamese soldiers had been mopping up, looking for US wounded in the tall grass and killing them.

All the while the noise of battle could be heard in the woods as the other companies fought for their lives. C and A Companies lost 70 men between them in the first minutes, while C Company suffered 45 dead and more than 50 wounded, the heaviest casualties of any unit involved in the LZ Albany engagement. A-1E

Skyraiders of the USAF were soon overhead to provide aerial fire support by dropping napalm. However, because of the smoke, dust and the intermingling of the US and North Vietnamese troops, it is likely that the air and artillery strikes killed Americans as well as North Vietnamese.

The 2nd Battalion, 7th Cavalry had been reduced to a small perimeter at LZ Albany, this containing the survivors of A Company, the reconnaissance platoon, the remnants

of C and D Companies, and the command group. There was also a smaller perimeter at the rear of the column about 500–700 yards (460–640m) due south around Captain George Forrest's A Company of the 1st Battalion, 5th Cavalry. Forrest had run a gauntlet all the way back from the conference called by McDade, when the North Vietnamese mortar fire began to plunge down on the Americans.

At 14.55, B Company of the 1st Battalion, 5th Cavalry under Captain Buse Tully began marching from LZ Columbus toward the rear of the 2nd Battalion, 7th Cavalry's column, about 2 miles (3.2km) distant. By 16:30, they had reached the A Company perimeter, where an LZ large enough for a single helicopter was secured and the wounded were evacuated. Tully's men then began to advance toward the rest of the ambushed column, all the while under North Vietnamese attack. After receiving fire from the tree line, Tully's men assaulted this and pushed back the North Vietnamese. At 18:25 orders were received to secure into a two-company perimeter for the night, with the advance to resume from this coming in the morning.

At 16:00 or thereabouts, Captain Myron Diduryk's B Company of the 2nd Battalion, 7th Cavalry, which had been at LZ X-Ray, was detailed for deployment in the effort to relieve the trapped battalion. At 18:45 the first troop-transport helicopters reached LZ Albany and the troopers were deployed into the tall grass. Lieutenant Rick Rescorla, the sole remaining platoon leader of B Company, led the reinforcements into Albany's perimeter, which was then enlarged to provide better security. LZ Albany's wounded were evacuated at around 22:30 that night, the helicopters involved coming under intense ground fire as they landed and took off. The US troopers holding Albany then settled down for the night.

On the following day, 18 November, the US troopers started to collect their dead, a task which in fact lasted into the next day, the whole of the area being littered with dead Americans and North Vietnamese. On 19 November, the US troopers quit LZ Albany for LZ 'Crooks', 6 miles (9.7km) away.

The engagement at LZ Albany cost the Americans 155 men killed and 124 wounded, bringing the overall toll for X-Ray and Albany fighting to 234 dead and 242 wounded. Within this fighting, the ambush of 17 November had been the costliest for the US forces in the whole of the Vietnam War, with 155 killed and 126 wounded.

The battle can be regarded as a microcosm of the Vietnam War as a whole. The combination of air mobility for the troops with superior air and artillery firepower proved effective in allowing the US forces to accomplish their tactical task. The North Vietnamese and Viet Cong forces learned, however, that they could offset the capabilities of US firepower by closing right up to the American forces. The North Vietnamese later refined this tactic, which they called 'grabbing the enemy by his belt' and with it achieved a kill/loss rate the Americans found politically unsustainable over anything but the very short term. For the time being, however, the North Vietnamese effort to cut South Vietnam in half had been prevented.

While it was a US victory in arithmetical terms, as a result of the 4/1 casualty ratio in favour of the US forces, many considered the battle to have been no more than a draw, since the US Army left the field, allowing the North Vietnamese to reassert control over the area.

The lessons of the Ia Drang operation were clear: moderately inexperienced but well-trained troops could and did acquit themselves well in the face of hardened opponents. They were much aided by supporting fire and reinforcements, but the key factor was the helicopter, which could turn a surrounded force, isolated deep within enemy territory, into an active one with an effective supply line for resupply, reinforcement and evacuation of the wounded. The first engagement between US troops and regular units of the North Vietnamese army, the Ia Drang operation also proved that the helicopter was not a fragile toy but a sturdy weapon.

The North Vietnamese division retreated across the border into Cambodia where, because of restrictions imposed by Washington, US troops were forbidden to follow, and was soon reconstituted as a viable fighting force. The problem of the Communist forces taking refuge in Cambodia and Laos, rebuilding, then returning to fight again, was to trouble Westmoreland for a long time. Although Washington had approved ground patrols to locate the enemy just inside Laos and call in tactical air attacks, Westmoreland had no authority to pursue the Communist forces into Laos or to make any move against Communist sanctuaries in

Cambodia. The Department of State refused every request from the MACV to patrol, bomb or shell North Vietnamese extra-territorial camps. Although it was obvious that the Cambodian head of state, Prince Norodom Sihanouk, had tacitly sanctioned the Viet Cong and North Vietnamese presence in his country, the Department of State thought it better to tolerate that policy rather than risk driving Sihanouk into open collaboration with the Communists.

His hands tied at his waist, a wounded Viet Cong prisoner is forced by his captors, South Vietnamese government forces, to wade through a stream near Bac Lieu in the Mekong delta area as a human detector against mines and booby traps. The guerrilla, recently captured in Operation Eagle Flight by a government ranger battalion, later died from his wounds.

CHAPTER SIX

THE BUILD-UP IN THE NORTH & SOUTH

RIGHT: Marines of G Company, 2nd Battalion, 4th Marines, in action in Operation Rush, near Hills 479 and 500, 2.5miles (4km) south-west of Phu Bai, Vietnam.

BELOW: Marines conduct a search-and-destroy mission along a Vietnamese hillside in 1966.

The command, officers and men of the National Liberation Front learned much from their defeat in the Ia Drang and other combats of the same period, and thereafter opted to avoid fighting the type of confrontational ground war of attrition favoured by the US forces which played to the strengths of their greater weight of fire, tactical air mobility, and air support at all levels by aircraft ranging in size from the Douglas A-1 Skyraider, with its one piston engine, to the Boeing B-52 Stratofortress with its eight jet engines. The forces of the NLF, therefore, switched back to the type of small-unit irregular operations in which they had been so successful up to the middle of 1965.

From a time late in 1964 the North Vietnamese had been despatching units of their regular army into South

Vietnam. At this time some of the politico-military leadership in Hanoi had felt that the time was ripe for an immediate invasion of the south, and this was the reason for the Communist military attempt to split South Vietnam in two with an advance from the Central Highlands east to the sea. This had led to the first major combat operation between North Vietnamese forces in the Ia Drang valley, and to the subsequent revision of the Communist tactics to

reflect the losses suffered by the North Vietnamese. The lesson the US forces drew from the fighting was that the North Vietnamese were not, as they had so wrongly believed, a force of indifferent troops of the light infantry type, little more than irregulars with little discipline and only light weapons, but a force of well-disciplined and highly motivated soldiers with good training and excellent weapons.

On 27 November 1965 the US Department of Defense revealed that it was now thinking that a successful campaign to defeat the North Vietnamese and NLF forces in South Vietnam would require substantially greater strength than had been thought necessary up to this time: major operations were now accepted as necessary, and this would need an increase in the US troop levels in South Vietnam from the current figure of

ABOVE: A Marine from 2nd Platoon 'Vultures' of Bravo Company 'Bushmasters', waves the American flag while others from his unit board a CH-53A Sea Stallion of Marine Heavy Helicopter Squadron 463 in Vietnam in 1967.

LEFT: A sentry on duty with his dog at Da Nang airbase.

THE BUILD-UP IN THE NORTH & SOUTH

120,000 to 400,000. There followed a series of meetings between Johnson and Westmoreland in Honolulu during February 1966, in which Westmoreland argued that, while the presence of powerful US land and air forces had been successful, it was only at the level of preventing the Communist forces from achieving their objective of defeating the South Vietnamese army, overthrowing the South Vietnamese government, and taking control of South Vietnam. To win the war, Westmoreland argued, required the completion of a whole series of major operations to defeat the Communist forces in South Vietnam and to drive

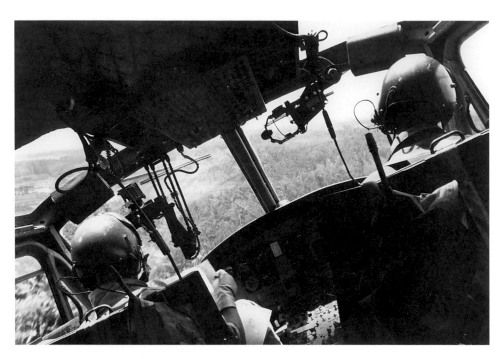

them out of the country. Offensive operations were clearly required, but the problem now to be solved was how the US forces would be employed.

It was the precise nature of the strategic and tactical decisions made by the US military at this time which conditioned the whole nature and prosecution of the war from this time onward to the end of the US commitment in South Vietnam. The basic tenets of US military doctrine, long-established and used with success in the Second World War, indicated that the US forces should attack the main strength of the North Vietnamese army and NLF, or in this instance their source of supply in North Vietnam. Political and diplomatic considerations meant that this was impossible, so the next option was the severing by the US ground and air forces of the Communist forces' lines of reinforcement and supply past the western frontier of South Vietnam in Laos and Cambodia, and by the US naval and air forces along its

THE VIETNAM WAR

eastern frontier on the sea. This would serve to isolate the scattered Communist forces in South Vietnam from all practical means of support, which would leave them in a steadily weakening position for eventual destruction by the South Vietnamese and US ground forces. However, the US leadership was conscious of the effect that standard US military doctrine had created less than 15 years earlier in the Korean War, when the advance of US and allied forces into North Korea had spurred a furious Communist reaction and triggered the Chinese commitment of great ground forces to take over the main weight of the Communist ground operations. Thus the thought was always to the front of the leadership's mind in Washington that direct intervention again North Vietnam carried with it the possibility of a step-by-step escalation that could draw China and then the USSR into the war, with the latter's involvement leading to the possibility of nuclear war.

For this reason, therefore, there could be no real consideration of a direct assault on North Vietnam, the claimed neutrality of Laos and Cambodia would be respected, and the Rolling Thunder air campaign would be held at a level that was sufficiently low that no adversary could claim the US air forces were attempting to destroy North Vietnam in the way they had crippled Germany and Japan during the Second World War.

LEFT: An infantryman of the 2nd Batallion, 5th Marines, on patrol south-east of Da Nang.

BELOW: South of Da Nang, in December 1967, a US Marine fires at a sniper during Operation No Name. The aim of the campaign was to conduct unilateral and combined operations with ARVN forces to locate and destroy the Viet Cong Quang Ngai Provincial Headquarters and the 21st NVA Regiment.

THE BUILD-UP IN THE NORTH & SOUTH

RIGHT: An A-4E Skyhawk of Marine Attack Squadron, VMA-211, on the runway in 1967.

BELOW: A US Navy Iroquois helicopter of Helicopter Attack (Light) Squadron Three (HAL-3), on the flight deck of the tank landing ship, USS Jennings County (LST-846), in the Mekong delta.

This was no knee-jerk reaction to current events, but the result of politico-military leadership thinking from a time before the first men of the US Marine Corps landed on the beach at Da Nang. The Department of Defense appreciated right from the start that this type of restriction would be imposed by the civilian leadership even if the military had had the temerity to ask for the right to wage an all-out conventional military war, and had started to plan a more limited response falling within the restrictions which would be imposed on them, yet still able to complete the task as required. Westmoreland believed he had a strategy that would at best defeat

North Vietnam, or at worst force North Vietnam to undertake serious negotiations about ending the warfare in South Vietnam. As far as Westmoreland was concerned, the key to US success would be attrition of the Communist forces by the greater US military machine, probably to the point at which the North Vietnamese could no longer sustain their effort, or its Communist allies were no longer prepared to support North Vietnam with weapons, fuel, other supplies and diplomatic weight. Westmoreland was firmly convinced that major offensive operations in South Vietnam would wear down the Communist forces to the point at which North Vietnam would call for peace, or that the so-called 'crossover point' would be reached at which Communist losses had become so great that the surviving elements in South Vietnam could be defeated decisively.

Within this overall concept, the US forces were to concentrate their efforts

134

THE VIETNAM WAR

on offensive operations against the North Vietnamese forces, with the aim of driving them back away from urban centres and the heavily populated lowlands along the coast, which produced most of South Vietnam's food, deep into the less densely populated country such as the Central Highlands. This, it was believed, would allow the US forces to make the most effective use of their superiority in firepower and mobility to pin the North Vietnamese forces in set-piece battles and inflict decisive losses on them. As the US forces defeated the North Vietnamese, it was planned, the South Vietnamese army would concentrate on pinning and defeating the more lightly armed and elusive units of the NLF and undertake the pacification of villages which had come under Communist sway.

Westmoreland's basic strategy was now condemned by his US Marine Corps commander, General Lewis W. Walt. Walt had already appreciated that the key element in the whole process of

defeating the Communist forces was the provision of adequate security for rural villages, so ensuring South Vietnamese food supplies and denying both these and recruits to the Communists. Walt had already embarked on such a policy in the area in which his forces were

operating, but Westmoreland did not approve, as he believed this type of action made too little use of the Marines' capabilities. Ultimately the MACV's position prevailed, and the search-and-destroy concept, promoted by Westmoreland as the way to wear away the Communist forces' strength and endurance, became the accepted operational method.

The US forces' search-and-destroy operations were conceived for offensive purposes and as a key element in the second phase of Westmoreland's three-phase plan to defeat the Communist forces and expel their remnants from South Vietnam. The first phase was posited on the checking of the Communist forces, the second on the resumption of fully offensive operations to find, fix and destroy sizeable elements of them, and the third to restore the areas thus freed of Communist control to South Vietnamese government authority. The search-and-destroy

LEFT: The beach at Da Nang, during the landing of the Marines of the 9th Marine Expeditionary Brigade in March 1965.

BELOW: A USAF Douglas C-74 Globemaster at Da Nang in 1966.

ABOVE: A Marine H52 tank in action.

RIGHT: Men of the 2nd Battalion, 4th Marine Regiment in action north-west of Chu Lai, a US Navy base in Dung Quat Bay, whose airfield helped to support the major base at Da Nang.

missions were elements of the second phase in 1966/67, along with a clear-and-secure undertaking to strip the Communist forces of their control of designated areas.

The concept of search-and-destroy missions was to insert ground forces into Communist-held territory on special operations to target and cripple the Communist forces directly before withdrawing immediately afterwards. Westmoreland and his senior US Army advisers believed this to be a strategy ideally suited to counter-insurgency warfare, especially in jungle terrain. The complementary conventional tactics of attacking and taking a Communist position, then fortifying and holding it indefinitely against any and all counter-attacks was known as clear-and-hold or clear-and-secure. The entire concept was based on the advisability and capability of the US forces to achieve their missions and so both secure and enhance the confidence levels of the South Vietnamese.

At the tactical level, the search-and-destroy mission was based on the despatch of a platoon or company or indeed a larger unit as and when the situation dictated, of US ground troops from a fortified position to locate, fix and destroy Viet Cong and North Vietnamese army units in the countryside of South Vietnam. These missions generally involved an approach march ('hiking out into the boonies') and setting an ambush near a trail which, it was thought, was being used by the Communist forces. A typical ambush

was based on the positioning of command-detonated Claymore fixed anti-personnel mines, the establishment of crossing lines of small arms fire, and the organization of mortar support and, possibly, additional artillery support called in via radio from a nearby firebase.

In February 1967, the largest search-and-destroy mission was undertaken in the Iron Triangle region located between Saigon, Route 13 and Route 25. The area was known to accommodate a complex of Viet Cong headquarters and logistics facilities from which operations were planned and despatched into the Saigon area. The offensive began with Operation Junction City, in which the US units destroyed hundreds of tons of rice, killed 720 insurgents, captured 213 prisoners, and destroyed a headquarters, the last disrupting the development of Communist plans for operations in the Saigon area. Both search-and-destroy and clear-and-secure missions extended beyond Westmoreland's second phase into the third phase, which began in 1968. The number of missions mounted, especially after the US forces had been assailed by the Communist forces' Tet Offensive of 1968. As the war grew more aggressive, so did the missions, to the point where the search-and-destroy and clear-and-secure missions blurred one into the other.

Search-and-destroy missions had many faults. First, there was a lack of precision between clearing and search-and-destroy missions. Thus clearing missions, which were specifically designed to be less aggressive, eventually became considerably more so, and in effect blended into the concept of the search-and-destroy mission. Given the

lack of precision between clear-and-secure and search-and-destroy, it was inevitable that the notion of pacification should fall between the cracks in the underpinnings of the US military plan. What seems clear throughout this process was that the US military planners, in South Vietnam as much as in the USA, radically under-estimated the ability of the Communist forces to equal and indeed exceed the US forces in numerical terms. Large numbers of Communists were killed or captured, but these casualties were replaced quickly. Although the US operations did drive Communist forces out of certain areas, the fact that the US forces did not then remain to hold these areas meant that the Communists were able not only to

move back into them, but also to do so in still greater strength. It is arguable, therefore, that search-and-destroy missions were not only unsuccessful in terms of achieving the desired object, but also counterproductive towards the US objective in South Vietnam. They effectively destroyed the country and its all-important rice paddies, thus weakening the economic productivity and creating inflation in South Vietnam. They created millions of refugees, who lost their homes as the result of missions which called for the destruction and firing of the rural population's bamboo houses. Moreover, with many refugees and a damaged economic system, the missions hurt the political and social system in South Vietnam.

An F-4 Phantom on USS Constellation *in the South China Sea.*

THE BUILD-UP IN THE NORTH & SOUTH

Search-and-destroy operations also led to high US and South Vietnamese casualties. In one of the first of these missions, Operation Attleboro, undertaken between 14 September and 24 November 1966 to the north-west of Dau Tieng, 155 US soldiers were killed and 494 wounded, while the North Vietnamese army lost 1,106 men; in Operation Cedar Falls, between 8 January and 26 January 1967 near Cu Chi, 73 US soldiers were killed and 337 wounded and 11 South Vietnamese soldiers were killed and eight wounded, while the Communist forces lost 735 killed and 28 captured; in Operation Junction City, between 22 February and 14 May 1967, 282 US soldiers were killed and 1,023 wounded, while the Viet Cong lost 1,728 men.

The setting for Operation Attleboro was to be found in Westmoreland's decision that, while he could depend on the South Vietnamese army for the close defence of Saigon, he had to position US troops on the approaches to Saigon from the Communist forces' long-established base areas to the north-west of the capital and from Cambodia, a distance of only 30 miles (48km) from Saigon at the closest point. The US 1st Infantry Division, the US 173rd Airborne Brigade and an Australian battalion swept a large rubber plantation, once owned by the Michelin Tyre Company, at a location some 20 to 25 miles (32 to 40km) to the north-west of Saigon, then probed for Communist headquarters and supply bases in two large forested regions, the Boi Loi forest and Ho Bo wood. Two brigades of the US 25th Infantry Division operated in Tay Ninh province to the north-west of Saigon, along the Cambodian border,

while another of the division's brigades swept through the Central Highlands in search of North Vietnamese units. When firm contacts were made in the Central Highlands, Westmoreland moved in a brigade of the US 101st Airborne Division, later reinforced by the whole of the US 1st Cavalry Division, to probe the jungle-covered mountains and prevent the North Vietnamese from massing for attacks on provincial capitals in the region.

When the US 199th Light Infantry Brigade arrived in the late summer of 1966, Westmoreland deployed the unit on the fringes of a major Communist base area in Tay Ninh province, known as War Zone C. When it appeared that the Communists were prepared to fight for this part of the zone, the commander of the II Field Force, Lieutenant General Jonathan Seaman, received reinforcement in the form of the 173rd Airborne Brigade, the 1st Infantry Division, contingents of a South Vietnamese division, and a brigade each of the US 4th and 25th Infantry Divisions. The resulting Operation Attleboro involved about 22,000 US and South Vietnamese troops, and was the largest operation of the war up to that time. After more than six weeks of hit-and-run fighting, the Viet Cong fell back to sanctuary in Cambodia.

Convinced that major North Vietnamese operations were imminent in the northernmost provinces, Westmoreland provided the formations of the US Marine Corps responsible for this area with powerful fire support in the form of two US army battalions of 175-mm (6.89-in) guns, with a range of up to 20 miles (32 km). Westmoreland

also ordered construction of a new airfield far to the north near Quang Tri city, capital of Quang Tri province, instructed that the existing air strip at Khe Sanh be upgraded, and gave Walt, commanding the III Marine Amphibious Force, priority in support by B-52 heavy bombers. As further preparation for battle, he instructed his chief-of-staff, Major General William B. Rosson, to form a headquarters known as Task Force 'Oregon', which would eventually absorb three separate US Army infantry brigades to form the 23rd (American) Infantry Division and assume responsibility for the southern provinces of the I Corps area, thus freeing Walt's Marine forces to concentrate on the area farther to the north.

Quang Tri province was notable in military terms for the sharp contrast in its terrain, which stretched from lofty forested mountains in the west down foothills to a flat and sandy coastal plain. Tortuous valleys emerged from the mountains in the Khe Sanh area down to the plain near Quang Tri city and, farther south in Thua Thien province to the city of Hue. To the south of Hue, the mountains extended right to the South China Sea. Thus, the two northernmost provinces were effectively separated from the rest of South Vietnam, except for the link provided across a high ridge by the Hai Van Pass, through which Route 1 crossed the mountains near the sea. Westmoreland believed that the North Vietnamese army was planning to take the two northernmost provinces before the North Vietnamese authorities would even consider any agreement to negotiate.

THE VIETNAM WAR

Late in March 1967, the North Vietnamese army had apparently completed its build-up, and was preparing to launch its offensive. On 20 March, North Vietnamese artillery fired more than 1,000 rounds against South Vietnamese troops and US Marines manning Con Thien and Gio Linh, two of the forward strongpoints in the area just to the south of the DMZ. A few days later North Vietnamese forces ambushed a US Marine Corps convoy, while US patrols from a number of firebases, including Khe Sanh, elicited sharp reactions from the North Vietnamese forces.

On the morning of 24 April, a platoon of the US Marine Corps patrolling some 5 miles (8km) to the north-west of Khe Sanh became sharply engaged with a substantial North Vietnamese army force. This triggered a series of 'hill fights', centred on three peaks designated as Hill 861, Hill 881 South and Hill 881 North. Elements of a North Vietnamese division had occupied the hills, probably in preparation for an attack on the firebase at Khe Sanh; with the support of tactical fighters and the fire of their 175-mm guns, the Marines gradually fought their way up the hillsides and, in some of the Vietnam War's heaviest fighting, eventually took the three peaks, where they established outposts protecting Khe Sanh, which now enjoyed a period of calm.

The fighting now shifted to other points, most especially the forward base at Con Thien where, for the first time since the Korean War, the US troops were subjected to a deluge of artillery fire comparable with the barrages of the Second World War. The North Vietnamese army was clearly planning an effort to take Con Thien, but the combination of air attacks, artillery fire and sorties from the base by US Marine forces of up to battalion strength adversely affected the North Vietnamese troop concentration. Even so, the US media, or at least that part of it becoming increasingly unsympathetic to the US effort in South Vietnam, began to refer to Con Thien as 'an American Dien Bien Phu', with the clear implication that it was mere military blindness to continue to hold a small piece of tactically insignificant terrain at the probable cost of heavy casualties. But to Westmoreland and Walt, the latter succeeded in command of the III MAF on 1 June by Lieutenant General Robert E. Cushman, Jr., there appeared to be almost no chance that Con Thien would fall, given the weight of fire which the US forces could call down on any North Vietnamese attack. Moreover, the senior command in South Vietnam felt that if the US Marines left Con Thien, and other forward bases of the same type, and fell back to the next line of outposts, they would be ceding much of the two northernmost provinces, which were precisely what the North Vietnamese wanted.

As the fighting around Con Thien continued and intensified, General William M. Momyer, commander of the US 7th Air Force, developed a system to co-ordinate the heavy firepower instrumental in the defence of Con Thien. Creating a forward headquarters, he co-ordinated the full spread of fire support available (tactical aircraft of the US Marine Corps as well as the USAF B-52 heavy bombers and the fire of warships operating close inshore), with locally-based artillery to destroy all North Vietnamese troop and equipment concentrations reported by intelligence sources. This effectively prevented the North Vietnamese from being able to concentrate enough strength for a successful assault on Con Thien. The attacks which were launched were comparatively weak and were fended off with relative ease. By the middle of autumn in 1967, the North Vietnamese 'siege' of Con Thien was over, and the North Vietnamese army pulled back its mauled formations and started to rebuild for other undertakings.

Meanwhile, in other parts of South Vietnam, the arrival of larger US forces opened the way for the launch of the important operations which Westmoreland had been planning for some time. Some of these, including Operation Fairfax, carried out in a defensive grouping of villages and hamlets just outside Saigon and involving an American brigade operating with a group of South Vietnamese rangers, lasted for weeks and even, on occasion, months. For the most part it comprised ambush and intensive patrol work, especially at night, with the object of preventing Viet Cong movements and making it difficult for the Communists to recruit among or terrorize the population of this rural area. Similarly, the US 1st Cavalry Division returned to Binh Dinh province. Here the Viet Cong had been driven out, but then returned with the support of a regiment of the North Vietnamese army. Another long operation took place in the mangrove swamps of the Rung Sat near the mouth of the Saigon river. The region is almost completely covered with salt water at

ABOVE: Troops and equipment of the 1st Cavalry Division (Airmobile) are loaded aboard C-123 and CV-2B Caribou aircraft for flight to the forward area at the start of Operation Masher (Operation White Wing), in January 1966.

RIGHT: A US Marine Corps M50 Ontos self-propelled 106-mm recoilless rifle.

high tide, and the US forces had to be rotated on an almost daily basis to avoid skin diseases and their feet rotting.

Other operations involved larger number of units and formations, and therefore required a higher level of overall planning and co-ordination. One of the first of these major undertaking was Operation Cedar Falls, which took the form of an offensive sweep by two US divisions, one US airborne brigade, one US armoured cavalry regiment and one South Vietnamese army division into the Iron Triangle. This was 60sq miles (155km²) of dense jungle, rice paddies and isolated villages along the Saigon river, some 20 miles (32km) to the north of Saigon in Binh Duong province. The Iron Triangle had for long

been both a Viet Cong stronghold and base area, and also the launching point for terror operations against Saigon.

Cedar Falls began with a surprise landing by a battalion of the 1st Infantry Division, delivered by 60 helicopters right into the middle of the village of Ben Sue, which allied intelligence had decided was the heart of the Communist defences in the region. In order to ensure that the operation began in total secrecy and caught the Viet Cong wholly unawares, the US commanders had not informed their notoriously 'leaky' South Vietnamese counterparts of the landing. While this ensured that tactical surprise was indeed achieved, it meant that the South Vietnamese authorities were suddenly presented with an unexpected refugee problem, and for several days the refugees had to wait in very poor conditions until shelter and food could be provided. US journalists were very critical, further increasing US public disaffection with the war.

The rest of the US forces almost completely surrounded the Iron Triangle, but could create only a loose perimeter through which many Viet Cong slipped. Thus only some 750 Viet Cong were killed. However, the primary objective of Cedar Falls was the elimination of the Iron Triangle as a Communist base area, and to this end the inhabitants of the area had to be relocated outside the area and all building inside the perimeter destroyed. The US force lacked the means to level the forest in this area, so bulldozers were employed to cut wide swaths so that any Viet Cong movement across the lanes so created could be detected. Although the Viet Cong later returned to the Iron Triangle, the relocation of population made the area a 'free fire zone' into which artillery bombardments and air attacks could be directed without concern for civilian casualties. 'Rome plows', developed in World War II to tear through the tall road banks and thick hedgerows of Normandy, were

later brought in to complete the levelling of the whole area, and the Iron Triangle ceased to be a secure sanctuary for the Viet Cong.

In Operation Junction City, 22 US and four South Vietnamese battalions, more than 25,000 troops, 16,000 of them Americans, made another foray into War Zone C, with concentration on the Tay Ninh province close to the border with Cambodia. The operation's objective was again to find and destroy Viet Cong bases and, if at all possible, capture the headquarters of the Central Office for South Vietnam (COSVN), which was the North Vietnamese Communist party's agent for the exercise of military and political control in South Vietnam. For this major undertaking, the US and South Vietnamese troops were deployed around three sides of War Zone C; as these ground forces started to compress the operational area's perimeter and drive forward, one battalion of the US 173rd Airborne Brigade made the only large parachute drop of the war as it jumped into the open end of the horseshoe at Katum to close off the obvious escape route for the Communist forces, who chose not to fight and melted away into a complex system of tunnels in the jungle.

In response, 'tunnel rats' (specially trained tunnel-fighting teams) were used for the first time in an effort to root out the Communists. Almost 3,000 Communist dead were claimed, although the total was in fact only slightly more than half of this, but many Communists, including those at the COSVN headquarters, managed to escape into Cambodia. Of course personnel losses are only one part of the balance sheet for any military undertaking, and Cedar Falls was also reckoned to have severely

disturbed the combat and political control capabilities of the Communists in this area by capturing 100 crew-served weapons, 491 individual weapons, large quantities of small arms ammunition, grenades, mines and rounds for mortars and artillery, more than 5,000 bunkers, tunnels and other military constructions, about 500,000 pages of documents, and about 35.75 tons of sundry foodstuffs and   723 tons of rice, the latter constituting the ration for 2,850 men for one year. The US Army's matériel losses were three tanks, 21 armoured personnel carriers, 12 trucks, five howitzers and two

vehicle-carried quadruple 12.7-mm (0.5-in) machine guns and four helicopters destroyed.

By the time Westmoreland had conceived his three-phase plan to win victory in South Vietnam, and had received approval from Washington for its implementation, the North Vietnamese army had decided it had been wrong to seek to engage and defeat the US forces in conventional large-unit warfare, and therefore reverted to small-unit operations in an effort to avoid direct confrontation with larger US units with superior firepower. As Walt had

Members of Company A, 1st Air Cavalry Division (Airmobile), investigate a hut during Operation Irving, the second phase of Operation Thayer. The division was given the mission of clearing a mountain range, where an estimated two battalions of North Vietnamese regulars were supposed to be massing for an attack on Hammond airstrip.

commanders and men were patently unsuited to the task.

The new pattern of the war was psychologically unsettling for the US ground forces in general, for they were now being committed to a small-unit low-intensity war in an Asian environment when all their doctrine, training and equipment had been geared to the fighting of a large-unit high-intensity war in a European environment. From this time forward most of the fighting involved units smaller than the battalion, and in general of the platoon size. This placed great demands on junior and non-commissioned officers, most of them very young, who were now faced with the task of making independent tactical decisions for a type of war with which they were neither familiar nor trained. The tactical task was no longer the taking and holding of ground but the

pinning and killing of Communist combatants. Thus even after a successful engagement, in which a tactical defeat had been inflicted on a Communist foe who then fell back, the Americans too pulled back to their protected bases and abandoned the ground for which they had shed their blood and lost comrades. This was in itself poor for morale and psychologically unsettling, and was exacerbated into a deep frustration about the US troops' inability to find an effective solution to the Communist forces' use of tactics centred on sniping, creating booby traps, laying mines, and in general using the element of terror against the US soldiers.

Although the task of preventing the infiltration of men, equipment and supplies from North Vietnam into South Vietnam, via the Ho Chi Minh Trail, was extremely difficult, if not impossible, more would have to be done

ABOVE: A member of the 1st Batallion, US 26th Infantry Regiment, in action south-east of Saigon during Operation Workhorse in August 1966.

RIGHT: An Airborne Brigade trooper manning an M60 machine gun in November 1967.

suspected would happen, the war now shifted down in size and focus to the level of the village, where the 'hearts and minds' of the South Vietnamese rural population, whose co-operation was necessary to military success by either side, would be won or lost. According to the Westmoreland plan, however, the pacification of the villages had become the responsibility of the South Vietnamese, whose military

THE VIETNAM WAR

to counter the Communist infiltration of men and supplies along the length of South Vietnam's coast. From the spring of 1965, US ships and South Vietnamese junks and patrol boats patrolled up and down the coast in Operation Market Time. This was primarily the effort of the US Navy, supported by the US Coast Guard, and was one of four US Navy responsibilities launched after the Gulf of Tonkin Incident, the other three being Operation Sea Dragon, Operation Sealords and naval gunfire support for troops operating in the coastal belt.

When a trawler was intercepted landing arms and ammunition at Vung Ro Bay, in the northern part of Khanh Hoa province on 16 February 1965, the first tangible evidence of the North Vietnamese supply operation became known. US Navy destroyers and ocean minesweepers, as well as US Coast Guard cutters, were the workhorses of the operation, with support close up to

the shore provided by the US Navy's Asheville-class patrol gunboats. These last were admirably suited to the task because of their ability to accelerate very rapidly from standard cruising speed on diesel propulsion to a high maximum speed on gas turbine propulsion. These lightweight aluminium and glassfibre vessels were not only fast but also highly manoeuvrable as a result of their variable-pitch propellers.

On 1 August the responsibility for running Market Time passed from the US 7th Fleet to Rear Admiral Norvell G. Ward's Task Force 115, Coastal Surveillance Force. Ward was also the head of the Naval Advisory Group, the overall capability of Market Time being increased by the arrival of the US Coast Guard's Squadron One, with its excellent Swift-class patrol boats. These 50-ft (15.2-m) diesel-engined craft, radar-directed and given fire support by frigates, proved more suited to close inshore patrolling than the US Navy's

164-ft (50-m) Asheville-class patrol gunboats. A brief experiment was also made with the Boeing-built hydrofoil *Tucumcari*, but it was decided not to deploy more such craft to South Vietnam. By December 1965 Operation Market Time included Lockheed P-3A Orion turboprop patrol aircraft,

143

Members of the 4th Battalion, 173rd Airborne Brigade, move up the hill into position as they prepare for the assault on Hill 875, located 15 miles (24 miles) south-west of Dak To in November 1967.

aircraft and the heavily armed riverine assault craft.

In the first phase of the Sealords campaign, the allied forces established patrol 'barriers', often based on the employment of electronic sensors along the waterways paralleling the Cambodian border. Early in November 1968, riverine patrol and assault craft denied use of two canals, between the Gulf of Siam at Rach Gia and the Bassac river at Long Xuyen to Communist use. South Vietnamese paramilitary ground forces helped the naval patrol units to secure the transportation routes in this operational area, soon named 'Search Turn'. Later in the same month, Swift-type riverine patrol craft, riverine assault craft, and South Vietnamese naval vessels penetrated the Giang Thanh/Vinh Te canal system and established patrols along the waterway from Ha Tien on the gulf to Chau Doc on the upper reaches of the Bassac river.

As a symbol of the Vietnamese contribution to the combined effort, the allied command changed the name of this operation from 'Foul Deck' to 'Tran Hung Dao I'. Then in December the US naval forces pushed up the Vam Co Dong and Vam Co Tay rivers west of Saigon, against strong Communist opposition, to sever the infiltration routes from the 'Parrot's Beak' area of eastern Cambodia. The 'Giant Slingshot' operation, so-named for the configuration of the two rivers, severely hindered the ability of the Communists to resupply their forces in the region near the capital and in the Plain of Reeds. Completing the first phase of the Sealords campaign, in January 1969 riverine patrol craft, assault support

activated Task Force 194. Although continuing to function, the 'Game Warden' (patrols of the Mekong river delta and the Rung Sat swamp area between Saigon and the sea by Task Force 116, otherwise the River Patrol Force), Market Time, and Riverine Assault Force operations were scaled down and their personnel and material resources increasingly devoted to Sealords. Task Force 115 patrol craft mounted lightning raids into Communist-held coastal waterways and assumed responsibility for patrolling the delta's larger watercourses. This freed the riverine patrol craft for operations along the previously uncontested smaller rivers and canals. These intrusions into Viet Cong bastions were made possible only by the on-call availability of naval

patrol boats and other river craft established patrol sectors along canals westward from the Vam Co Tay to the Mekong river in Operation Barrier Reef. By a time early in 1969, therefore, a patrolled waterway interdiction barrier extended almost uninterrupted from Tay Ninh, lying to the north-west of Saigon, to the Gulf of Siam.

Meanwhile, as additional US combat units arrived in South Vietnam during the second half of 1965, Westmoreland was able to commit increasing numbers of units to the protection of existing logistical support facilities or the development of new facilities. By the end of 1965, the US strength in South Vietnam had reached 181,000, including the combat forces of three divisions (one infantry, one airmobile and one marine), three army brigades, one marine regiment, and three tactical fighter wings of the USAF. There were, in addition, an Australian battalion and a South Korean division and marine brigade, the latter country's forces totalling some 20,000 men. As well as some 120 New Zealanders, small numbers of troops had already arrived from Thailand, the Philippines and Taiwan. The Thai contingent increased to 11,600 (six battalions) by 1970.

Westmoreland was taking a considerable gamble in deciding to place priority on troops rather than a logistical infrastructure for delivery to South Vietnam from the USA. To a large extent the decision was forced on him by the rapidly crumbling military situation in South Vietnam, which Westmoreland believed had reached a critical state. The decision paid off, for the fresh US troops helped to stabilize the situation and, moreover, were able to

LEFT: A USAF A-1 Skyraider with an HH-53 helicopter behind it in the sky over Vietnam. This combination was a search-and-rescue teaming that did much to keep up the morale of US airmen flying over the battlefields of South Vietnam.

BELOW: Members of Troop B, 1st Squadron, 9th Cavalry, 1st Cavalry Division (Airmobile) await orders while a man ahead is clearing and checking the area before the troops enter it. July 1967.

survive on a minimum logistical infrastructure until more facilities could be built. Here the US Army's Corps of Engineers, the US Navy's 'Seabees' (Construction Battalions), and bought-in US civilian contractor companies, the last a novel feature in modern warfare, undertook a massive, widespread and ultimately successful effort. Within 30 months of the start of the US military build-up in South Vietnam during the middle of 1965, the development of the logistical system in South Vietnam had paved the way for the maintenance of more than 1.3 million men (including almost 500,000 US combat troops), the South Vietnamese armed forces, allied troops, and the personnel of a steadily swelling number of US civilian agencies – also the support of the South Vietnamese civilian economy. Monthly deliveries soon amounted to some 760,000 tons of supplies, including 10 million field rations, 71,000 tons of ammunition, and 80 million US gallons

(303 million litres) of petroleum products. The development of the logistical infrastructure in South Vietnam eventually included new ports or vastly expanded port facilities for six planes (including the modernization and expansion of the facilities in Saigon and a great new port at Cam Ranh Bay, one of the best natural harbours anywhere in South-East Asia). Other elements of the logistical development were enlargement of existing and the creation of new airfields and helicopter operating facilities, vast areas of covered and open storage, a massive volume of refrigerated storage, 1,700 miles (2740km) of road and associated bridges, and 15 large and well-protected base camps.

As the US, South Vietnamese and allied forces continued Westmoreland's campaign to defeat the Communist forces by a process of attritional fighting in the rural areas of South Vietnam, there emerged in the USA a justifiable criticism that in almost all of these US

THE BUILD-UP IN THE NORTH & SOUTH

it possible for Communist forces to move back into the area as soon as the allied forces had departed. This was perhaps an inevitable process, there being never sufficient US troops to occupy even a sizeable portion of South Vietnam in any realistic military sense. But it was nonetheless self-defeating, as Westmoreland and his senior advisers had failed to grasp the fact that attrition was in fact working against the US forces: the Communists were always able to gain new recruits, either voluntary or 'conscripted', whereas the growing strength of the anti-war sentiment in the USA meant that it was politically impossible for the US government to commit the number of men which could have provided a real military victory.

The task of defending the rural population after the end of a US search-

ABOVE: A Cessna A-37A Dragonfly firing 70-mm rockets against Viet Cong positions in South Vietnam in 1966.

RIGHT: A typical US infantryman, equipped with his M16 rifle in South Vietnam.

search-and-destroy undertakings the US forces had merely swept the terrain and deliberately not attempted to hold the ground from which they had eliminated the Communist elements. Thus the rural population of South Vietnam was unwilling to commit itself wholeheartedly and overtly to the South Vietnamese government, because when the US and South Vietnamese forces had completed their defined mission in any one area, they departed to undertake another search-and-destroy operation in a different area, leaving a military, political and administrative vacuum into which the Viet Cong rapidly moved. So while search-and-destroy operations might cause the Communists losses, as Westmoreland hoped, they failed to effect any permanent dislodgement of the Viet Cong's political and administrative power in the rural areas, and also made

THE VIETNAM WAR

and-destroy operation had therefore to be entrusted to the South Vietnamese army, and also to the large number of platoon-sized units which constituted the strength of the so-called Regional and Popular Force. These latter occupied small packed-earth field fortifications on the outskirts of villages and hamlets, but they were woefully under-trained and under-equipped as militia units in that the process of building them into an effective force was inevitably taking time, a commodity which the South Vietnamese did not possess. For lack of anything else, therefore, local defence at the bottom of the organizational ladder had to depend on what were in effect little more than the villagers themselves, with little training and only the lightest of armament.

Behind this altogether illusory screen, the process of 'pacification' continued, largely in urban areas. This was the task of teams organized by the civilian ministries of the South Vietnamese government, with the apparent benefit of advice and aid from US civilians, provided by bodies such as the Central Intelligence Agency, US Information Service, and Agency for International Development. These teams were committed to urban areas with the task of building or revitalizing local government, identifying and removing the personnel of Communist cadres, and the support of local self-help projects with information and money.

Thus the US military element in South Vietnam, and its supporters in the USA, had at least some justification in believing that progress was actually

THE BUILD-UP IN THE NORTH & SOUTH

national support to persevere with his policy of winning a limited war in South Vietnam. Johnson called Westmoreland and Bunker to Washington in November 1967 to make yet another public appearance and confirm that the progress of the war was proceeding according to plan, and that victory was in sight.

Westmoreland and Bunker made several appearances on national TV programmes, and on 21 November Westmoreland made a speech before the National Press Club in Washington. 'We have reached an important point when the end begins to come into view,' Westmoreland said, and proceeded to suggest that the war was on the point of entering a new stage in which the South

Vietnamese forces, and in particular the South Vietnamese army, would be able to assume a steadily increasing part of the burden of fighting the war. This last part of Westmoreland's belief was based on the fact that in June of that year he had received a new deputy in the form of General Creighton W. Abrams, and had assigned this capable officer the responsibility of revitalizing the South Vietnamese forces to a level at which they could play a genuinely useful part in the prosecution of the war against the Communist forces. Assigned the job of upgrading the South Vietnamese forces, Westmoreland added that within a period of two years, that is by November 1969, or perhaps sooner, it should be possible to begin the process of withdrawal of US forces, initially only in token numbers, from South Vietnam. Westmoreland was basing his assertions on what he perceived to be objective military factors, but they were to have enormous political implications out of all proportion to their military background.

While Westmoreland was still in Washington at Johnson's instruction, he learned that there had erupted heavy fighting, involving a division of the North Vietnamese army in the Kontum province of the Central Highlands. Beginning just to the south of the DMZ Con Tien, the epicentre of the fighting had swiftly moved westward to the Laotian border near Dak To, and was characterized by the North Vietnamese army's new willingness to stand its ground and fight. This new readiness of the Communist forces seemed to be just what the US command wanted, for it believed that in such fighting the greater matériel strength of the US Army and US Marine Corps, supported by the

tactical air assets of the US Air Force and the air arms of the US Navy and US Marine Corps, would prevail. Thus the MACV decided to reinforce the northern sector of South Vietnam with US forces from other parts of the country, beginning the phase of the Vietnam War known as the 'border battles', apparently schemed by the Communists as a series of engagements to embarrass the South Vietnamese government on the eve of the inauguration of Nguyen Van Thieu as president and Nguyen Cao Ky as vice president. The fighting was centred on Dak To, one of the border outposts manned by Montagnards, men of the tribes of the Central Highlands, as well

ABOVE: Infantrymen leave their transport and double off across the landing zone.

LEFT: A little rest and home-made entertainment.

as by smaller numbers of US Army Special Forces troopers.

The first such battle was fought at the village of Song Be in Phuoc Long province, where a North Vietnamese regiment attacked the command post of a South Vietnamese battalion and was repulsed with heavy losses. The second was at a small rubber plantation town, Loc Ninh, close to the Cambodian border in the province of Binh Long, where Viet Cong and North Vietnamese regulars attacked an outpost manned by South Vietnamese militia. Reinforcements from a regular division of the South Vietnamese army and from elements of the US 1st Infantry

ABOVE: A USAF B-57 Canberra over South Vietnam.

RIGHT: Wounded personnel await airlift in a USAF medical evacuation aircraft at Cam Ranh Bay airbase, South Vietnam, on 5 May 1970.

THE VIETNAM WAR

Division, delivered by helicopter, helped drive out the Communist forces, but heavy fighting raged from 29 October to 2 November 1967, the Communists on occasion launching 'human wave' attacks and losing some 900 men to the allied total of about 60 dead. The third border battle, the Battle of Dak To, was in fact a series of major engagements fought between 3 and 22 November.

In the summer of 1967 heavy contact with forces of the North Vietnamese army in the area had prompted the launch of Operation Greeley, a combined search-and-destroy effort by elements of the US 4th Infantry Division, the US 173rd Airborne Brigade, and elements of the South Vietnamese army, including the 42nd Infantry Regiment and airborne units. The fighting was intense and lasted into the autumn, when the North Vietnamese forces appeared to pull back. By a time late in October, however, the US intelligence apparatus had received sufficient information to report that Communist forces in the area had been reinforced and combined into the North Vietnamese army's 1st Division, which was tasked with the capture of Dak To and the destruction of a brigade-size US unit. Information provided by a defector from the North Vietnamese army provided the allies with what was believed to be a good picture of the locations and intentions of the North Vietnamese, and this led to the launch of Operation MacArthur as well as to the reinforcement of the allied forces in the area with a number of units which had recently been moved elsewhere, as well as by elements of the South Vietnamese army's airborne division. The battles fought over the hills south and south-

east of Dak To constituted some of the bloodiest and most bitterly contested combats of the Vietnam War.

During the early stages of the US involvement in the Vietnam War, the US Special Forces had created several CIDG (Civilian Irregular Defense Group) camps along the frontiers of South Vietnam, firstly to maintain a watch over and provide intelligence regarding any movements by the North Vietnamese army and National Front for the Liberation of South Vietnam (otherwise the Viet Cong), secondly to guard against infiltration, and thirdly to provide support and training for isolated Montagnard villagers who were bearing the brunt of the fighting in these remote areas. One such camp was constructed near the village and airstrip at Dak To.

After 1965, Dak To was also a forward operating base for the so-called US SOG (Studies and Observations Group), a secret organization which despatched clandestine reconnaissance teams to gather intelligence on activities along the Ho Chi Minh Trail across the border in Laos.

Dak To is located on the floor of a flat valley, surrounded by a series of hills rising to heights at great as 4,000ft (1220m) and extending to the west and south-west in the direction of the region where South Vietnam, Laos and Cambodia meet. This was the western part of Kontum province, and is covered by double- and triple-canopy rain forest in which the only open areas were hemmed in by groves of giant bamboos, the stems often up to 8in (200mm) in

A USAF F-100 Super Sabre, loaded with 500-lb napalm bombs.

THE BUILD-UP IN THE NORTH & SOUTH

RIGHT: A USAF A-7 Corsair, onboard the carrier USS Coral Sea, is readied for take-off.

BELOW: A Douglas A-1 Skyraider of the 1st Air Commando Group dropping napalm.

diameter. LZs large enough to accommodate helicopters were few in number and widely dispersed, and this meant that troop movement usually had to be accomplished on foot. The daytime temperature in this highland region often reached 95° F (35° C), falling at night to 55° F (13° C).

In January 1967 Major General William R. Peers had assumed command of the US 4th Infantry Division responsible for the defence of the western part of Kontum province within the II Corps Tactical Zone in the Central Highlands of South Vietnam. Before the summer monsoon rains started, Peers organized the establishment of blocking positions from the 4th Infantry Division's base camp at Jackson Hole, west of Pleiku,

and on 17 May began Operation Francis Marion. At this time the 4th Infantry Division had its 1st and 2nd Brigades

available, but its 3rd Brigade was operating with the US 25th Infantry Division in the area to the north-west of Saigon.

Throughout the middle period of 1967, however, the western part of Kontum province had become the focus of a series of spoiling attacks by North Vietnamese army forces, and it soon became clear that the North Vietnamese were starting to focus their attention on this area. Immediately after assuming command, Peers laid down procedures designed to ensure that his subordinate units were not isolated and then overrun individually in the region's very rugged terrain, which was also a major factor contributing to the US forces being unable to take maximum advantage of their superiority in matériel. Among the instructions issued by Peers was that battalions should not only operate as single units and not divide into their component companies for search-and-destroy missions, but also that if it became necessary for companies to operate individually, they were not to

Central Highlands, of the altogether different geographical, climatic and operational conditions they would be facing, and also advised them that the regular forces of the North Vietnamese would be altogether tougher nuts to crack than the forces of the NLF, as they were better disciplined, more highly motivated and more comprehensively equipped, especially in the matter of their heavier weapons. Knowing themselves to be members of an elite unit, however, the officers of the 173rd Airborne Brigade paid scant heed to Livsey's warning, paying the penalty for their excess of confidence in the fighting that was soon to embroil them.

On 20 June the men of C Company, 1st Battalion, 503rd Airborne Infantry Regiment, discovered the bodies of

LEFT: A USAF Cessna A-37 Dragonfly.

BELOW: Mini-guns firing from an AC-47 Dragon Ship over South Vietnam.

move farther than 0.6 mile (1km) or a one-hour march from each other, and that if contact with hostile forces was made, the relevant company was to be reinforced immediately. These precautions were eminently sensible, given the terrain over which the 4th Infantry Division was operating, and were instrumental in reducing the formation's casualties.

The number and weight of the summer's contacts with the North Vietnamese forces also persuaded Peers to ask for reinforcements, and on 17 June two battalions of Brigadier General John R. Deane's 173rd Airborne Brigade were moved into the Dak To area to begin Operation Greeley, a major search-and-destroy sweep through the jungle-covered mountains. The 173rd Airborne Brigade had been operating near Bien Hoa air base outside Saigon, and up to this time had seen action only against the more lightly armed forces of the NLF. With this in mind, the 4th Infantry Division's operations officer, Colonel William J.

Livsey, tried to apprise the senior officers of the 173rd Airborne Brigade, before the unit's deployment to the

Field hospital staff wheel a casualty toward a UH-1 Iroquois CASEVAC helicopter.

members of a Special Forces CIDG unit, which had been missing for four days on Hill 1338, the dominant hill mass south of Dak To. Supported by A Company, the men of C Company moved up the hill and prepared for an overnight halt. Just before 07:00 in the morning of the following day, A Company began to move on its own up a ridge finger, and advanced right into an ambush laid by the 6th Battalion of the 24th North Vietnamese Regiment. C Company was immediately ordered to move up in support, but its progress was slowed by the heavy vegetation and difficult terrain. At the same time, artillery support was also rendered generally ineffective, the jungle preventing the spotting of the fall of the projectiles and the issuing of corrective instructions, also by the North Vietnamese's now well-established tactic of 'belt-grabbing', or closing into a very short distance of the Americans, so referred to this action as the 'Battle of the Slopes' and claimed that 475 North Vietnamese had been killed, while the 173rd Airborne Brigade's post-action report claimed 513 North Vietnamese dead, when the men of A Company estimated that during the entire action they had killed only between 50 and 75 North Vietnamese.

Such losses by US forces could not be allowed to pass without the meting out of some form of punishment. Livsey recommended that Deane be relieved of the command of the 173rd Airborne Brigade, but higher up the chain of command it was appreciated that this would merely throw more fuel onto what was already a bonfire of adverse public reaction. Thus it was the commander and junior officers of C Company who

inhibiting them from calling down fire which might affect them as much as the enemy, the same factors making it impossible to call for air support. A Company barely survived a number of attacks throughout the day and the following night, the cost being heavy:

starting with 137 men, the company suffered 76 killed and 23 wounded, while a subsequent search of the battlefield revealed only 15 North Vietnamese soldiers dead.

Press releases from the headquarters of the MACV, issued four days later,

LEFT: US Navy airman Robert Nunes, from Jamestown, Rhode Island, loads the ammunition boxes of the externally-mounted M-60 flex-guns on a US Navy helicopter. There are two ammunition boxes for each set of flex-guns, each holding 600 rounds. In addition there are two boxes of M-79 grenades, which the right door-gunner can fire using a grenade-launcher, and which are used primarily against bunkers and fortifications.

BELOW: A Cobra helicopter gunship pulls out of a rocket and strafing attack on a Viet Cong position near Cao Lanh in the Mekong delta, amid explosions that fill the air in a firework-like display. To all sides lie the large craters left by air and artillery strikes on the area, that is largely uninhabited and scattered with abandoned rice paddies and small coconut groves.

reached the preliminary positions from which they were to assault the North Vietnamese on Hill 875. C and D Companies then moved forward up the hill with two platoons of A Company behind them, while A Company's weapons platoon remained at the foot of the hill to cut out an LZ.

The assault of the three US companies was in effect a frontal assault against a well-prepared enemy, and as events were to prove, it would almost certainly have been better to have used small teams to move into and, with luck, through, past and behind the North Vietnamese positions to pin the opposition, which could then have been destroyed by artillery fire and air attacks. By 10:30 the US soldiers had approached to within about 330 yards (300m) of the top of Hill 885, and here North Vietnamese machine gunners opened fire on them. The advancing paratroopers were taken under fire by rockets and 57-mm recoilless rifles. The Americans tried to put new life into their advance, but the North Vietnamese

ABOVE: A Northrop F-5A Freedom Fighter flying over South Vietnam.

RIGHT: Two mini-guns onboard a USAF Douglas AC-47 Spooky.

(6km) from the border with Cambodia. The task of the 174th North Vietnamese Regiment was to cover the withdrawal of the 66th and 32nd North Vietnamese Regiments, both of which were moving west in the direction of their sanctuary areas across the Cambodian frontier.

On 19 November, Schweiter was informed that a company of the Special Forces Mobile Strike Force had run into a strong North Vietnamese force while undertaking a reconnaissance of the area, and now instructed his 2nd Battalion to take the hill. Just before 09:45 on 19 November, the 330 men of three companies of the 2nd Battalion of the 503rd Parachute Infantry Regiment

were well-concealed in a complex of interconnected bunkers and trenches, and maintained heavy small arms fire together with a constant peppering of grenades. The US advance was checked and the paratroopers went to ground in an effort to find whatever cover they could. Then at 14:30 the situation was rendered still more difficult as more North Vietnamese soldiers, who had remained in concealment at the bottom of the hill up to this time, began a massed assault on A Company. Only now did it become clear to the Americans that they had fallen straight into an ambush prepared in meticulous detail by the 2nd Battalion of the 174th North Vietnamese Regiment.

Fearful they might be cut off and destroyed, the soldiers of A Company retreated, with the North Vietnamese in pursuit, up the hill in the direction of their fellow Americans installed near the summit. All that prevented the North Vietnamese attack, which was being delivered by only one company, from

overrunning the entire US battalion was the determination of the American paratroopers, who stood their ground and died to buy time for their comrades. US air attacks and artillery fire were soon being called in, but these had little effect on the battle because of the hill's dense forest. The US forces were by this time running short of ammunition and water, but resupply was impossible, as indicated by the US Army's loss of six Bell UH-1 Huey helicopters shot down or badly damaged during the afternoon, while attempting to achieve the task.

Just before 19:00 there occurred one of the worst 'friendly fire' incidents of the Vietnam War. A tactical fighter of the US Marine Corps dropped two

ABOVE: A Lockheed AC-130 gunship at Nha Trang airbase, South Vietnam.

LEFT: A 16th Special Operations Squadron airman operating FWR control.

CHAPTER SEVEN
THE SIEGE OF KHE SANH

The Battle of Khe Sanh, the MACV having given the defence of Khe Sanh the designation Operation Scotland, was fought in the north-western portion of Quang Tri province over the period of 77 days between 21 January and 8 April 1968, and involved elements of the US III Marine Amphibious Force and two (later increasing to three) divisional forces of the North Vietnamese army. There had been some warning of the North Vietnamese intentions in this area, for there had been a number of small-scale combat operations around Khe Sanh during the summer of 1967. But the MACV in Saigon felt that these were merely a part of a series of small-scale North Vietnamese offensives in the border regions, and therefore largely

ensure that the US Marines defending the base were supplied in a timely fashion with all that they required. In March 1968 a relief expedition was launched as Operation Pegasus by a combined task force of US Marine, US Army and South Vietnamese army elements, and this finally lifted the siege as it reached Khe Sanh. The battle itself was a tactical victory for the US Marines, but its strategic implications are still disputed.

Though only a village, Khe Sanh was the administrative centre of the Huong Hoa district, an area of Montagnard villages and coffee plantations about 7 miles (11.25km) from the South Vietnamese/Laotian border on Route 9,

LEFT: Khe Sanh airstrip radar, with a control tower in the background. November 1967.

BELOW: A Lockheed C-130 Hercules makes a delivery to Thien Ngon.

irrelevant to the larger-scale conduct of the war. This appreciation was revised when it was discovered that the North Vietnamese army was moving altogether larger forces into the area of the border between South Vietnam, Cambodia and Laos during the autumn and early winter. This led to an increase in the US Marine strength at the Khe Sanh combat base and the hill-top outposts around it.

The Battle of Khe Sanh became one of the decisive elements of the Vietnam War, during which a massive bombing effort, Operation Niagara, was launched by the US Air Force to support the defenders of Khe Sanh. The undertaking was notable for its use of the latest technological advances in order to locate North Vietnamese army forces for targeting. The logistical effort to support the Khe Sanh combat base, once the North Vietnamese army had completed its ground investment of the area, demanded the development and use of other tactical innovations to

THE SIEGE OF KHE SANH

A 105-mm M101 howitzer, deployed during the Siege of Khe Sanh.

impossible. Brigadier General Lowell English, the assistant commander of the 3rd Marine Division, added his own voice to those who felt that Khe Sanh was too remote for effective defence: 'When you're at Khe Sanh, you're not really anywhere. You could lose it and you really haven't lost a damn thing.'

But as far as he was concerned, all that Westmoreland felt he needed to know was that the North Vietnamese had grouped sizeable forces for what could only be an assault on the Khe Sanh Combat Base, and that this offered the opportunity for the type of set-piece battle in which US matériel assets, especially in artillery and air power, could secure a major victory by engaging and destroying an enemy which, up to this

time, had been notable for the elusive nature of its military efforts, but was now apparently considering an offensive on a fixed position. Westmoreland was also encouraged in his decision by the fact that the Khe Sanh Combat Base lay in an unpopulated area, where the full weight of US firepower could be unleashed not only under optimum tactical conditions but also in a location where it need have no concerns about the infliction of losses on innocent civilians.

Marine intelligence confirmed that in slightly more than seven days the North Vietnamese army had brought its 325th Infantry Division into the area around Khe Sanh, and that another two divisions were close enough to provide it with rapid support should this be needed.

These two formations were the 324th Infantry Division in the DMZ, about 10 to 15 miles (16 to 24km) north of Khe Sanh, and the 320th Infantry Division to the north-east of Khe Sanh. All three of the North Vietnamese divisions were within easy reach of the Ho Chi Minh Trail in terms of their logistic support requirements. This intelligence served to emphasize the growing threat to the Khe Sanh combat base; as a result, reinforcement arrived on 13 December in the form of the 1st Battalion of the 9th Marine Regiment.

Over the frontier in Laos, the North Vietnamese army established artillery, mortar and rocket launcher positions to the west of Hill 881South and north of Co Roc Ridge. From these it would be able to bombard the Khe Sanh Combat Base and provide direct support for attacking troops. This part of the North Vietnamese build-up was facilitated by the continuing adverse weather of the winter monsoon, which denied the US forces the opportunity for observation and covert attack.

During the night of 2/3 January 1968, the personnel of a US listening- post spotted six men in black uniforms outside the wire defences of the Khe Sanh Combat Base. The US soldiers challenged these men, received no response and opened fire, killing five of them and wounding the sixth, who nonetheless escaped. This seemed to be incontrovertible proof that the North Vietnamese were on the verge of starting a major undertaking, and Cushman reinforced the forces under Lownds at the Khe Sanh Combat Base with the rest of the 2nd Battalion of the 26th Marine Regiment, all of which was now located at Khe Sanh. F Company of the

THE VIETNAM WAR

C4 and other high explosives, and another wave of explosions rocked the base. Somewhat surprisingly, however, the North Vietnamese forces, under the command of General Tran Quy Lai, did not launch a ground attack on the camp.

As the bombardment of the Khe Sanh Combat Base was proceeding, North Vietnamese forces attacked the Huong Hua district headquarters. Here, parts of the 66th Infantry Regiment of the North Vietnamese 304th Infantry Division were opposed by Montagnard

LEFT: A Sikorsky CH-34 lands at Khe Sanh and loads troops.

BELOW: Pfc Nsyanes of Bravo Company, 1st Battalion, 26th Marine Regiment, with 60-mm mortars ready for a fire mission. February 1968.

2nd Battalion was immediately ordered to occupy Hill 558, which covered a blind spot near the Rao Quan river. On 20 January, Lieutenant La Thanh Tone of the 14th Anti-Aircraft Company of the North Vietnamese 325th Infantry Division entered Khe Sanh as a defector and revealed plans concocted by the North Vietnamese for a series of attacks designed to ensure the capture of Khe Sanh, this series starting with simultaneous assaults on Hill 881 South, Hill 861 and the main base during the coming night. At 00:30 on 21 January, about 300 North Vietnamese soldiers attacked Hill 861, but the US Marine garrison of the hill was fully prepared. Even so, and despite the fall of heavy artillery fire, the North Vietnamese infantrymen managed to penetrate the defence's perimeter, and were repulsed only after vicious close-quarter fighting.

The main base then received an intense barrage of mortar bombs and unguided artillery rockets. Several hundred of these weapons landed inside the perimeter, flattening almost all of the structure above ground level. One of the first North Vietnamese weapons to land also started an explosion in the main ammunition dump, throwing many of the artillery rounds and mortar bombs into the air, which detonated where they landed, most of them inside the base. The misery of the defence was then compounded further by the arrival of a North Vietnamese shell in the separate dump of CS tear gas, which now flowed right over the base. The North Vietnamese bombardment lasted for some time, but the camp's first real bout of danger was by no means over. Hours after the end of the bombardment, at 10:00, the fire ignited a large quantity of

179

THE SIEGE OF KHE SANH

The M107 175-mm self-propelled gun is part of a family of artillery that also includes the M110, being essentially the same but with different barrels. The gun is mounted on an open-tracked body which makes it highly manoeuvrable due to its lighter weight, but extremely vulnerable to attack due to its lack of armour. The M107's combat experience was almost entirely limited to the Vietnam War, where it proved its effectiveness by having one of the longest ranges of any mobile artillery piece.

soldiers of the CIDG, South Vietnamese Regional Force soldiers, led by US Army advisers, and one platoon of the 26th Marine Regiment's O Company, which was an element of the CAP (Combined Action Program). O Company was led by Lieutenant Thomas Stamper, the platoon in Huong Hoa being commanded by Sergeant John Balanco. Another CAP platoon of O Company, in this instance commanded by Sergeant Roy Harper, was stationed at the western end of Khe Sanh village to the north of Route 9, and this was attacked at the same time. This O-2 platoon beat back the North Vietnamese attack and then moved to link with the O-1 platoon in Huong Hoa. Another platoon, O-3, near the combat base, was on alert but was not attacked.

The forces managed to hold out until the morning of 22 January, when helicopters arrived to lift out the Americans of both US Army and US Marine Corps, who were appalled to learn that the helicopter crews had been instructed specifically not to extract any South Vietnamese or Montagnards with weapons. Captain Bruce B.G. Clarke, the senior US Army district advisor for Huong Hoa, and his team's medical orderly, refused to leave under these circumstances and marched their men to FOB 3, the SOG compound adjacent to the Khe Sanh Combat Base, along a hidden pathway. The Special Forces troopers manning FOB 3 also used Montagnards in their CIDG programme, and were happy to take in Clarke's party as well as the US Marines of O Company's CAP element, who aided in the defence of FOB 3, and operated patrols of other military activities throughout the siege.

This first attack revealed that the 304th Infantry Division, just arrived from North Vietnam, was present in full strength with all of its component elements (the 9th, 24th and 66th Infantry Regiments, the 68B Artillery Regiment, and the 14th Anti-Aircraft Battalion) as well as the 24th Artillery Battalion, attached to increase the weight of fire available to the division in its planned attacks. The 304th Infantry Division assumed position to the south-west of the Khe Sanh Combat Base. (It remains uncertain which infantry units of the 325th Infantry Division remained in the Khe Sanh sector. A South Vietnamese study after the battle, and based on captured documents, concluded that only the 95C Infantry Regiment remained at Khe Sanh, with two regiments – the 31st Infantry Regiment of the 341st Infantry Division and possibly one regiment of the 324th

Infantry Division – of other divisions occupying blocking positions on Route 9 to the east of the base. Two battalions of the 3rd Infantry Regiment later moved south to Hue to participate in the battle for that city during the latter stages of the Tet Offensive).

Concerned that there could develop a threat to their right flank, the North Vietnamese decided to call on a Laotian battalion, BV-33, at Ban Houei Sane on Route 9 inside Laos. The Laotian battalion was attacked during the night of 23 January by three North Vietnamese army battalions supported by seven tanks. The Laotian unit was overrun, and many of the survivors made their way to the Special Forces camp at Lang Vei. It should be noted that this action in Laos marked the first occasion on which the North Vietnamese had committed an armoured unit to battle, although it had often been

claimed that the first North Vietnamese use of tanks took place three weeks later during the attack on Lang Vei.

Once it had been established that the North Vietnamese order of battle outside the Khe Sanh Combat Base now included the 304th Infantry Division, Khe Sanh was reinforced still more by the delivery, on 22 January, of the 1st Battalion of the 9th Marine Regiment, and on 27 January by the last reinforcement in the form of the South Vietnamese army's 37th Ranger Battalion. This last was allocated to Khe Sanh for implicitly political rather than overtly military reasons.

The artillery of the North Vietnamese army made its presence felt for the first time on 24 January, when 100- and 152-mm (3.94- and 6-in) guns opened fire on Hill 881 South, then switched to Hill 861 before concentrating their efforts on the main base. The men of the US Marine Corps and South Vietnamese army dug

LEFT: Repairing the runway at Khe Sanh.

BELOW: Refuelling at Khe Sanh.

THE SIEGE OF KHE SANH

themselves deeper into the red earth of the area, drawing hope from the fact that the Tet truce (29–31 January) was approaching and might offer a let-up in the fire During the afternoon of 29 January, however, the US 3rd Marine Division notified the defenders of the Khe Sanh Combat Base that the truce had been cancelled.

During this period the electronic sensors of Operation Muscle Shoals (later redesignated Igloo White), recently installed and currently being evaluated in an area of south-eastern Laos, detected an increase in North Vietnamese army activity along the Ho Chi Minh Trail opposite the north-

western corner of South Vietnam. The inescapable conclusion was that more men, weapons, ammunition and supplies were being moved to the Khe Sanh front, in response to which Westmoreland ordered the launch of Operation Niagara, initially to gather intelligence on North Vietnamese activities in the region of Khe Sanh.

Niagara I was an intelligence-gathering operation by CIA road-watch teams, the reconnaissance teams of the MACV's SOG and photo-reconnaissance aircraft of the US 7th Air Force. As the intelligence data started to arrive, their collation served to confirm that formations and units of the

North Vietnamese army were being grouped, almost certainly for a major offensive. What the data could not provide was any firm indication of the planned offensive's target area. Later in the month US Marine patrols from the Khe Sanh Combat Base triggered a cascade of initial actions which revealed the presence of three North Vietnamese infantry divisions (the 325C, 304th and 320th) as well as one regiment of the 324th Infantry Division, which had either reached or were rapidly approaching the area of Khe Sanh.

It was the combination of the initial actions and intelligence suggestions of the major build-up that led Westmoreland to order the reinforcement of the US Marine Corps' forces holding Khe Sanh, which would be required as the key jumping-off point for any future US or South Vietnamese incursion into Laos. This was a concept with considerable inherent risk, there being every likelihood that the North Vietnamese forces would isolate the Khe Sanh combat base by cutting Route 9, the only road into the area. It was appreciated, therefore, that Khe Sanh would then have to be nourished by air transport, but the continuing north-western winter monsoon would inevitably cover the area in rain, mist and fog, and so make the difficulties considerably greater.

Westmoreland was not overly concerned, however, for he felt that US air power would make impossible any North Vietnamese repeat of the Communist success over the French in the Battle of Dien Bien Phu, which had fallen largely because the French lacked sufficient air power and the Communists had been able to sever the air bridge in

which the French had come to rely after Dien Bien Phu had been isolated on the ground. Not all were so sanguine, however, and comparison of Khe Sanh and Dien Bien Phu soon became commonplace among the military and, most particularly, the media in South Vietnam and the USA.

Westmoreland and his deputy commander for air operations, General William W. Momyer, the commander of the 7th Air Force, had in fact been preparing quietly for the emergence of such an eventuality. The North Vietnamese army would be massing substantial forces in a single geographic area within a remote and unpopulated region, where there would be no restrictions on bombing missions, as noted above. Westmoreland now gave Momyer overall responsibility for the co-ordinated use of all US air assets during the operation to support Khe Sanh. The US Navy was not involved, but the allocation of overall control to the USAF concerned the US Marine Corps, whose own air assets operated under a particular scheme of close air support thinking, optimized for the particular nature of the operations that were the staples of the US Marine Corps' operational diet. The US Marine Corps was therefore unhappy to allow its air assets to be controlled by the USAF.

At this time Westmoreland commanded the US forces only within the geographical extent of South Vietnam, the air element by means of the 7th Air Force. The bombing campaign against North Vietnam was controlled by CINCPAC in Honolulu, and the aerial interdiction campaigns in Laos by the 7th and 7th/13th Air Forces.

This divided command arrangement was not liked by the USAF, whose standard doctrine demanded one command under the 'air manager' concept: in this doctrine, one headquarters allocated and co-ordinated air assets, distributing them as the situation demanded and then transferring them as the situation changed. The US Marines Corps, whose aircraft and doctrine were integral to its amphibious operations concept, was not organized on this basis of centralized command.

On 19 January Westmoreland passed his request for US Air Force control up the chain of command to Admiral U.S. Grant Sharp, Jr., the CINCPAC in Honolulu, from which it proceeded no

further. Meanwhile, there was argument between Westmoreland, the Joint Chiefs-of-Staff, and General Leonard F. Chapman, Jr., the commandant of the US Marine Corps. The US Army chief-of-staff, General Harold K. Johnson, backed the US Marine Corps' opposition to the centralized command position primarily as it would help support his own position against the USAF's ongoing attempt to take control of the US Army's air assets. The argument was therefore not about the best way to proceed in operational terms over Vietnam, but rather a continuation of the inter-service rivalry over missions and assets which had bedevilled the US armed forces since the National Security

A convoy on the move. Such convoys were favoured as targets by the Communist forces, for the destruction of the lead and tail vehicles usually left the convoy immobilized and vulnerable to systematic destruction.

THE SIEGE OF KHE SANH

ABOVE: A Marine takes cover next to a bunker at Khe Sanh during a North Vietnamese army rocket attack in February 1968.

ABOVE RIGHT: A Marine takes the opportunity to eat his C rations, while maintaining a communications watch during a lull in the battle at Khe Sanh. February 1968.

Act of 1947, which created the USAF. Westmoreland threatened to resign if his demand was not met, as a result of which the complete spectrum of air operations was placed, even if on a temporary basis, under single command.

On 21 January the North Vietnamese army opened a continuous artillery barrage directed at Khe Sanh, and on the same day Operation Niagara II was started. The US Marine Corps' DASC (Direct Air Support Center) at the Khe Sanh Combat Base had the primary responsibility for the co-ordination of air attacks with artillery fire. This capability was provided by an airborne battlefield command and control centre, which took the form of a specially adapted C-130 Hercules transport aircraft, and controlled the operations of tactical warplanes against targets designated by the ground troops and marked for attack by FACs (forward air control) aircraft. When weather conditions prevented the use of FACs aircraft, the tactical warplanes operated

on the basis of radar in the form of either the US Marines' TPQ-10 equipment at Khe Sanh, or by the USAF's LORAN (Long-range Air Navigation) system. The latter made it possible for tactical warplanes to attack their targets under all weather conditions by day and night.

Thus there began what may well have been the single most concentrated use of air power in the history of military aviation. Each day's operations in the area of the base included, on average, 350 tactical warplanes, 60 B-52 heavy bombers and 30 observation aircraft. It was Westmoreland who personally ordered the integration of Igloo White, still only in its evaluation stage, into the air operations supporting the defence of Khe Sanh. On 20 January the first Igloo White sensors were dropped, and by the end of January aircraft had delivered 316 acoustic and seismic sensors in 44 strings. The success of the Igloo White effort is attested by the fact that the US Marine Corps

believed that 40 per cent of the intelligence available to its fire support co-ordination centre at Khe Sanh was derived from the Igloo White sensors.

The attacks of the B-52 heavy bombers were at first limited by Lownds, the local commander, to areas not closer than 2 miles (3.2km) from the Khe Sanh perimeter. The North Vietnamese then exploited this fact to close right up to the perimeter and so escape the bombing. The 7th Air Force then demonstrated the fact that closer support could be given by bringing B-52 attacks safely to within 1,300 yards (1190m) of the base's perimeter, and Lownd's restriction was removed. Evidence of the devastation caused by the B-52 attacks was provided by a North Vietnamese prisoner, who reported that 755 of his regiment had been killed in just one B-52 attack.

Despite the fact that he was already deploying huge quantities of fire power against the North Vietnamese forces around Khe Sanh, Westmoreland was

concerned that this would be insufficient, and for the first time actively considered the employment of a tactical nuclear weapon, but was immediately instructed by Washington to terminate the small study group he had established. Had the fact that the Americans were investigating the use of an atomic weapon leaked out, the diplomatic and political ramifications would have been huge, and all to the detriment of the USA.

During the Niagara II effort, the warplanes of the USAF flew 9,691 sorties and delivered 14,223 tons of ordnance. The US Marine Corps' aviation wing flew 7,098 sorties and delivered 17,015 tons of ordnance. Naval Aviation, whose main undertaking at this time was the continuing Rolling Thunder campaign against North Vietnam, contributed 5,337 sorties and delivered 7,941 tons of ordnance. By the end of March the North Vietnamese had begun to withdraw from the area. Westmoreland accepted the USAF's estimate that its warplanes had been responsible for the killing or wounding of somewhere between 9,800 and 13,000 North Vietnamese troops, and gave

Though rendered technically obsolete by the development of the turbine-powered Bell UH-1 series, the helicopters of the piston-engined Sikorsky H-34 series nonetheless saw extensive service in the Vietnam War.

THE SIEGE OF KHE SANH

Dropping supplies at the Khe Sanh Combat Base.

Back in South Vietnam, meanwhile, the Tet Offensive was launched, prematurely in some areas, on 30 January, and on the following night combined North Vietnamese army and NLF attacks were reported from locations throughout South Vietnam. One of the few exceptions was Khe Sanh, but the beginning of this huge widespread offensive, representing the largest Communist military effort to date, over most of South Vietnam, did not distract Westmoreland from the situation at Khe Sanh. This is indicated by the fact that on 1 February Westmoreland prepared but did not in fact release a press report which included the following: 'The enemy is attempting to confuse the issue...I suspect he is also trying to draw everyone's attention away from the greatest area of threat, the northern part of I Corps. Let me caution everyone not to be confused.'

While larger-scale activities were continuing around the Khe Sanh combat base, slightly farther way at Lang Vei there had been little more than patrol activity of the standard type by the garrison, comprising the Green Beret troopers of Detachment A-101 and their four CIDG companies of Montagnards. Then early in the morning of 7 February the situation changed completely. The US force had been told by Laotian soldiers, fleeing camp BV-33, that the North Vietnamese were using armour, but while it was known that the North Vietnamese army did have two armoured regiments, it had not yet deployed any such unit in South Vietnam. The Americans also believed that no armour could have reached the area of Khe Sanh

much of the credit for the 'victory' at the Khe Sanh Combat Base to the timely and effective employment of US air power.

Although it is jumping forward somewhat, it is worth noting that the description of the Battle of Khe Sanh as a victory has been disputed. The US forces certainly achieved a notable tactical success, and certainly many thousands of North Vietnamese troops were killed, but claims that this was a major victory depend on the question of North Vietnam's strategic motive. Known by historians as the 'riddle of Khe Sanh', this remains an imponderable. Did the North Vietnamese intend to take the base by direct assault but call off their effort when the task became too difficult? Did the collapse of the Tet Offensive in South Vietnam's urban areas prompt the withdrawal? Or was the Battle of Khe Sanh connected with the border battles of the previous year as just one element of the North Vietnamese effort to divert the attention of the MACV to the remote north and so persuade it to withdraw forces from the south and coastal lowlands to reinforce those in the north?

A rifleman of the US Marine Corps expresses the sentiments of the period.

without being detected by American reconnaissance aircraft.

For this reason the Special Forces troopers at Lang Vei were taken completely by surprise when their base came under attack by 12 tanks. These were Soviet-built PT-76 amphibious light tanks of the North Vietnamese army's 202nd Armoured Regiment, and though only lightly protected and armed with only a 76-mm (3-in) main gun, the Americans lacked the weapons to defeat

them and the tanks therefore rolled though or over the defences of Lang Vei. In the wake of the tanks followed the men of the 7th Battalion of the 66th Infantry Regiment and the 4th Battalion of the 24th Infantry Regiment, both part of the 304th Infantry Division, with equipment including satchel charges, tear gas and flame throwers. The Lang Vei camp's outer defences were overrun in just 13 minutes, but the fighting inside the perimeter lasted for several hours, during

which the Special Forces troopers and Montagnards knocked out at least five of the tanks.

The US Marines at Khe Sanh drafted a contingency plan for such an eventuality, but Colonel Lownds was concerned about the possibility of a North Vietnamese ambush of any ground relief force and refused to order the implementation of the plan. Lownds also refused to approve a helicopter extraction of the survivors. At a MACV meeting,

THE SIEGE OF KHE SANH

held at Da Nang at 07:00 the following morning, Westmoreland and Cushman accepted Lownds' decision, but a more junior US Army officer, Lieutenant Colonel Jonathan Ladd, commanding the 5th Special Forces Group and freshly arrived by air from Khe Sanh, said he was amazed 'that the Marines, who prided themselves on leaving no man behind, were willing to write off all of the Green Berets and simply ignore the fall of Lang Vei'.

Ladd and the commander of the SOG compound, now part of the Khe Sanh Combat Base, suggested the US Marines provide helicopters for the SOG soldiers to undertake the rescue of any survivors. Even so, the Marines were still opposed to the effort, and Westmoreland finally had to order Cushman to sanction the rescue effort. It was not until 15:00 that the relief effort was launched, yet it nonetheless proved successful. Even so, 200 of the 500 CIDG troops were dead or were missing and another 75 wounded; of the 24 US personnel, 10 hhad been killed and 11 wounded.

The Special Forces personnel were already furious at the mishandling of the relief effort for Lang Vei, and Lownds now worsened the situation even further when the indigenous survivors from Lang Vei, their families, civilian refugees from the area, and Laotian survivors from the camp at Ban Houei Sane, reached the entrance to the Khe Sanh Combat Base. Fearing that North Vietnamese infiltrators might have mingled with the survivors, now totalling more than 6,000 with civilian adherents, Lownds ordered that the Montagnard soldiers be disarmed and compelled to sit, under armed guard, in bomb craters. Lacking water and food, many of the Laotians decided to walk back along Route 9 to Laos. The Montagnards were specifically denied the chance of evacuation from the highlands by order of the South Vietnamese army's local

commander, who ordained that no Montagnards were to be allowed to move into the lowlands.

In mid-January Lownds estimated that the logistical needs of the Khe Sanh Combat Base were 60 tons per day, this figure rising to 185 tons once all five battalions of the defence force had arrived. At this stage the greatest problems in the logistical procedure of getting supplies through to Khe Sanh were the North Vietnamese closure of Route 9 and the weather typical of the winter monsoon. Right from the start of the Battle of Khe Sanh to a time early in March, low cloud and fog of varying densities shrouded the area from early morning until about midday. Even during the afternoon the clouds seldom rose above 2,000ft (610m), effectively denying use of the airstrip to all but the most courageous pilots. To make matters worse, any aircraft whose pilots

When the Khe Sanh Combat Base was reinforced, the delivery of infantry was paralleled by that of artillery. By a time early in January 1968 the defence could call on the fire support of 46 artillery pieces in various calibres, five tanks armed with 90-mm (3.54-in) guns, and 92 106-mm (4.17-in) recoilless rifles, some of the last mounted sextuply on M50 Ontos light armoured vehicles created initially for the anti-tank role. The base could also call on the fire support of the US Army's 175-mm

LEFT: Cpl G.E. North, 1st Battalion, 26th Regiment H & S repairing a communications wire on the perimeter. February 1968.

BELOW: The pointman studies the terrain as members of H Company, 2nd Battalion, 26th Marines, move out during operations against the enemy outside Camp Carroll in 1968.

were prepared to chance the weather and attempt a landing at Khe Sanh were targeted by North Vietnamese anti-aircraft fire as they came in to land, and once they did touch down, they immediately received the attentions of large numbers of North Vietnamese artillery and mortars. The whole process was reversed on flights out of the base, and presented aircrews and aircraft with a very high degree of risk. As a result, the majority of the supplies, amounting to some 65 per cent of the total, was delivered by paradrops from C-130 transports. The USAF claimed that during the siege it delivered 14,356 tons of supplies (8,120 of them by paradrop), while the 1st Marine Aircraft Wing delivered 4,661 more tons of cargo into the Khe Sanh Combat Base.

The resupply of the numerous but isolated outposts on the hills outside the main perimeter was perhaps even more difficult and dangerous, and could be undertaken only by helicopter or paradrop. The North Vietnamese anti-aircraft gunners exacted a steady toll of the aircraft, and especially of the helicopters involved in this effort. The US Marines Corps found a solution to the problem in the 'super gaggle' tactics, in which 12 Douglas A-4 Skyhawk light attack and tactical warplanes flew in the flak-suppression role allowing a force of some 12 to 16 helicopters to delivery supplies to all of the hill-top bases simultaneously. This was introduced late in February, and marked the turning point in the logistic effort. In February the pilots of the US Marine Corps delivered an average of some 16 tons of supplies per day, but in the following month the combination of the super gaggle and improving weather allowed a rise in the average to 40 tons per day.

THE SIEGE OF KHE SANH

ABOVE: Colonel David E. Lownds, USMC (right), commanding the Khe Sanh Base, is introduced to Colonel Hubert S. Campbell, Commander 3rd Brigade, and Ltc Roscoe Robinson, 2nd Battalion Commander, by Brigadier Oscar E. Davis, ADC, 1st Cavalry Division (Airmobile), on their arrival at Khe Sanh. April 1968.

RIGHT: Sgt H.C. Behrens, a photographer with the 3rd Division, checking M-14 rifles belonging to Charlie Battery, which were destroyed along with the whole supply tent during the rocket attack on Khe Sanh in January 1968.

artillery projectiles, mortar bombs and unguided artillery rockets into the base.

During the night in which Lang Vei was overrun, three companies of the North Vietnamese army's 101D Infantry Regiment moved into jump-off positions to attack the Alpha-1 outpost just outside the Khe Sanh combat base. This was occupied by 66 men of the 1st Battalion of the 9th Marine Regiment. Under cover of a mortar barrage, the North Vietnamese penetrated the perimeter and pushed the remaining 30 defenders into the south-western part of the defended area. For reasons which remain unknown, the North Vietnamese soldiers did not attempt to complete their seizure of Alpha-1. A relieving force had meanwhile emerged from the main base and attacked through the North Vietnamese force, driving the men into supporting tank and artillery fire.

(6.89-in) guns at Camp Carroll, to the east of Khe Sanh. In the course of the Battle of Khe Sanh, the artillerymen of the US Marine Corps fired 158,891 rounds, and it is believed that the North Vietnamese artillery fired 10,908

On 23 February the Khe Sanh combat base was at the receiving end of the heaviest North Vietnamese artillery barrage of the whole battle. During one eight-hour period the combat base took 1,307 North Vietnamese rounds mostly from 152-mm (6-in) and 130-mm (5.12-in) pieces, the latter being used for the first time in this battle. These heavier and longer-ranged pieces of artillery were located in Laos and were therefore effectively immune to US counter-fire and air attack. The US losses, as a result of this bombardment, were 10 killed and 51 wounded. Two days later, the Americans spotted the first North Vietnamese trenches, extending due north to points within 27.5 yards (25m) of the perimeter of the Khe Sanh Combat Base. On the same day a patrol of B Company of the 1st Battalion of the 26th Marine Regiment was ambushed by a North Vietnamese force estimated as being of about battalion-size. The US Marines suffered nine men killed, 25 wounded, and 19 missing and presumed dead.

At the end of February, US intelligence suggested that the 66th Infantry Regiment of the 304th Infantry Division was preparing to attack on the positions of the South Vietnamese 37th Ranger Battalion on the eastern perimeter of the base. On the night of 28–29 February, an artillery bombardment and air attacks targeted the possible staging areas and routes for any North Vietnamese advance in this part of the perimeter. The North Vietnamese attack was launched at 21:30, but was driven back with comparative ease by the small arms force of the South Vietnamese, which was supported by thousands of artillery

had began on 1 November 1967 were 205 killed in action, 1,668 wounded, and 25 missing and presumed dead, but these figures do not include the casualties among Special Forces troops at Lang Vei, aircrews killed or missing in the area, or US Marine replacements killed or wounded while entering or exiting the base aboard aircraft. It is believed,

rounds and air attacks. Two further attacks later in the morning were halted before the North Vietnamese finally withdrew. The North Vietnamese clearly perceived the sector of the perimeter held by the South Vietnamese as being the most vulnerable at Khe Sanh, and five more attacks against this sector were launched during March, but with no greater success than the first.

By mid-March, US intelligence discerned that the North Vietnamese forces around the Khe Sanh combat base were noticeably fewer, and in fact the North Vietnamese were starting to leave the area. First to depart was the headquarters of the 325C Infantry Division, followed by the 95C and 101D Infantry Regiments, all of which moved off to the west, while at the same time the 304th Infantry Division withdrew to the south-west. This did not mean that the Battle of Khe Sanh was over, however, for on 22 March more than

1,000 rounds fell on the base, and once again the base's ammunition dump was hit and exploded. On 30 March B Company of the 1st Battalion of the 26th Marine Regiment launched an attack on the place in which the 25 February ambush had killed so many of its brother Marines. After a rolling barrage fired by nine batteries of artillery, the US Marines' attack advanced through two lines of North Vietnamese trenches, but no remains of the men lost in the ambush were discovered. Even so, the US Marines' attack had killed 115 North Vietnamese soldiers, while the US losses were only 10 dead, 100 wounded, and two missing.

At 08:00 on the following day, Operation Scotland was officially terminated, and responsibility for the Khe Sanh area was transferred to the US Army's 1st Air Cavalry Division for the duration of Operation Pegasus. The overall butcher's bill for Scotland, which

THE SIEGE OF KHE SANH

Marine UH-1E Huey helicopters touch down with their loads at Fire Support Base Cunningham, dominating the A Shau valley, where artillerymen of the 12th Marines are supporting elements of the 9th Marines conducting search-and-clear operations.

therefore, that the overall allied losses were 730 killed, 2,642 wounded and seven missing out of a total strength in the order of 6,000 men. As far as North Vietnamese casualties were concerned, it is believed that up to 30,000 men were deployed at Khe Sanh, and out of this strength the allies counted 1,602 bodies, and also took seven prisoners as well as receiving two defectors. US intelligence estimated that between 10,000 and 15,000 North Vietnamese soldiers were killed during the operation, many of

them in air attacks. There must be caution about the US estimates, however, which must be seen in the light of the methods by which they were obtained, mostly indirectly by sensor readings, sightings of secondary explosions, reports of defectors or POWs, and a highly inaccurate process of inference and extrapolation.

The development of a plan for the overland relief of Khe Sanh had been started as early as 25 January 1968, when Westmoreland instructed Major

General John J. Tolson, commanding the 1st Air Cavalry Division, to prepare a contingency plan. The only realistic overland route from the east, Route 9, was impassable for the twin reasons of its poor state of physical repair and the presence, along much of its western extent, of North Vietnamese troops. Tolson was reluctant to assume the task allocated to him, feeling that in the current military situation, the best use of his formation would be in an offensive into the A Shau valley. Westmoreland was thinking farther ahead, however, for he had already set in motion the development of a plan to use the relief of the Khe Sanh Combat Base as a precursor for a pursuit of the North Vietnamese forces into Laos.

Tolson briefed the MACV's senior officers on 2 March, and in this laid out the basic elements of Operation Pegasus, the largest operation launched by III MAF in the Vietnam War to date. The core of the plan was very simple: the 2nd Battalion of the 1st Marine Regiment and the 2nd Battalion of the 3rd Marine Regiment would be delivered by air to LZ 'Stud' at Ca Lu, some 10 miles (16km) to the east of Khe Sanh, and move along Route 9 while elements of the 1st Air Cavalry Division used helicopters to 'leapfrog' along the length of the road and take the major terrain features from which it could cover the advance of the two US Marine battalions. The advance would be supported by the fire capability of 102 pieces of artillery.

The advance of the two US Marine infantry battalions would be accompanied by the US Marines' 11th Engineer Battalion to repair the road as the US advance pushed to the west. The

THE VIETNAM WAR

forces used in the first stage of Pegasus would later be supplemented by the 1st Battalion of the 1st Marine Regiment and 3rd Airborne Task Force (3rd, 6th, and 8th Airborne Battalions) of the South Vietnamese army.

The plan angered the US Marine Corps, which had not felt it important to hold Khe Sanh in the first place and which had since taken much criticism about the way its men had defended Khe Sanh, seen by many as indifferent at best. The US Marine Corps believed that the Battle of Khe Sanh was not, in the technical sense, a siege, as the combat base had never been wholly isolated from resupply or reinforcement; General Cushman, no doubt, echoed the sentiments of all US Marines when he said that he was truly dismayed by the 'implication of a rescue or breaking of the siege by outside forces', that is, that the US Marines had to be rescued.

Whatever the feelings and arguments of the US Marine Corps, Pegasus was launched on 1 April. Only light North Vietnamese opposition was encountered, and the only real difficulty which affected the advance was the morning cloud cover, which was sufficiently heavy and sustained to slow the rate at which the helicopter operation could be undertaken. As the relief force made progress, the US Marines at Khe Sanh emerged from their positions to begin a programme of patrols at a greater range from the combat base. The 1st Air Cavalry Division's 3rd Brigade encountered stronger opposition on 6 April, when it was checked by a North Vietnamese blocking force and was forced to fight a one-day engagement to open its path for a resumed advance.

On the following day the 1st Air Cavalry Division's 2nd Brigade captured the old French fort near Khe Sanh village after a three-day battle. The relief force and the US Marines at Khe Sanh finally met at 08:00 on 8 April, when the 2nd Battalion of the 7th Cavalry Regiment entered the camp. Route 9 was declared open to traffic on 11 April, and on the same day Tolson ordered his formation to make immediate preparation for operations in the A Shau valley. At 08:00 on 15 April Pegasus was officially ended. The US losses had been 92 killed in action, 667 wounded and five missing, while the South Vietnamese army had lost 33 men killed and 187 wounded. Estimates of North Vietnamese casualties were 1,100 killed, with 13 North Vietnamese soldiers having been captured.

Lownds and the 26th Marine Regiment were now pulled out of the Khe Sanh Combat Base, the defence now resting in the hands of the 1st Marine Regiment. Westmoreland demanded the continued retention of this combat base until his departure from South Vietnam on 11 June as he was succeeded as head of the MACV by his erstwhile deputy, General Creighton W. Abrams. Abrams waited for seven days and then ordered the implementation of Operation Charlie, in which the Khe Sanh Combat Base was evacuated and then destroyed. Charlie was completed on 6 July.

When the news of Khe Sanh's end as a combat base broke, the US media immediately questioned the thinking behind its termination, on the grounds that if the combat base had been of significant strategic importance in

January, why was it not still important in July? The explanations of the MACV were that 'the enemy had changed his tactics and reduced his forces; that PAVN [North Vietnamese army] had carved out new infiltration routes; that the Marines now had enough troops and helicopters to carry out mobile operations; that a fixed base was no longer necessary'.

What must be said is that by this phase of the Vietnam War the long-term demands of the US Marine Corps for an enhanced degree of mobility were no longer valid. The gradual withdrawal of the US forces, which started in the following year, and the adoption of the policy of Vietnamization meant that, by 1969, 'although limited tactical offensives abounded, US military participation in the war would soon be relegated to a defensive stance'.

CHAPTER EIGHT

THE TET OFFENSIVE

A sniper team comprising two men, one with binoculars serving as the spotter for the man with the rifle, whose telescopic sight offers only a very small field of vision.

During the first days of 1968 the signs that the Communist forces were on the verge of launching a major undertaking continued to increase, while it was more obvious that the North Vietnamese army was concentrating two, if not three, divisions around the Khe Sanh Combat Base in the far north-west of South Vietnam; these divisions, as a defecting lieutenant had revealed, were to launch their attempt to seize Khe Sanh in the course of the upcoming Tet (lunar New Year) holiday. A captured document revealed that the Communists now felt that the time was right for a 'general offensive and general uprising' of the South Vietnamese population 'to take over towns and cities' and 'liberate' Saigon, while another such documents dealt with the Communist plans for a major offensive in Pleiku province to begin 'before the Tet holidays'.

The commander of the II Field Force, Lieutenant General Fred C. Weyand, drew the conclusion from all the evidence available to him that the Communist forces in the III Corps operational zone around Saigon were moving up from their sanctuary areas along the South Vietnamese/Cambodian frontier in the direction of Saigon. Other signs of an impending offensive included the capture, in the central coastal city of Qui Nhon, of 11 NLF soldiers in a house raided by South Vietnamese troops. These soldiers, who had with them a tape recorder and two pre-recorded tapes, revealed under interrogation that there were to be Communist attacks on Qui Nhon and other cities during the Tet period, and that the tapes were propaganda messages to be broadcast over the air as soon as the government radio station had been taken.

The MACV's most senior intelligence officer, Major General Phillip B. Davidson, another of the senior US officers who appreciated that the Communist forces might be preparing to unleash a 'make or break' offensive, cancelled the period of leave he had planned to take, and warned Westmoreland in explicit terms that the intelligence branch of the MACV expected major attacks all over South Vietnam. What Davidson could not provide, however, was a precise date on which the Communists were going to target urban areas.

On 20 January 1968, 10 days before the start of the traditional Tet truce period, Westmoreland reported to the

THE VIETNAM WAR

Joint Chiefs-of-Staff in Washington that the 'enemy is presently developing a threatening posture in several areas in order to seek victories essential to achieving prestige and bargaining power. He may exercise his initiative prior to, during, or after Tet'.

By this time the situation had become so critical, and so threatening to the allied cause in South Vietnam, that Westmoreland persuaded President Thieu to cancel the ceasefire which had been planned for the Tet period in the northern provinces, and to trim the ceasefire to a mere 24 hours everywhere else. Because neither he nor his senior subordinates could state with any accuracy the places and timing of the Communist effort, Westmoreland did not consider it worthwhile to alert the US media and thus the American public; the closest he came to this was in a TV interview in which he said that the Communists were planning 'a major effort to win a spectacular battlefield

success along the eve of Tet'. Weyand also issued a similar warning, informing one journalist that the Communists seemed to be on the verge of undertaking 'critical – perhaps spectacular – moves'.

In Washington, the chairman of the Joint Chiefs-of-Staff, General Wheeler, stated publicly that 'there may be a Communist thrust similar to the desperate effort of the Germans in the Battle of the Bulge in World War II'. Strangely enough, none of these individually limited but collectively significant intimations of major events about to unfold received major coverage in the US media. Another oddity of the period was that when he was on a state visit to Australia, President Johnson

ABOVE: Allied armour on the move.

LEFT: A sniper's extemporised firing loophole.

THE TET OFFENSIVE

warned the Australian government of 'dark days ahead', but did not think it appropriate to give the people of the USA any similar warning.

What cannot be disputed, however, is that any such warning might well have been ignored by the people of the USA, or in any case have been lost on an American public which by now was highly suspicious of all apparent information put out by the US forces, the Department of Defense, and the Johnson administration with regard to the Vietnam War: so many claims had been made, either as a fudging of the truth if not outright lies, about matters such as body counts, that ever larger numbers of Americans were coming to doubt all that was promulgated by the US authorities. Meanwhile, the more trusting chose to take at face value the statement made by Westmoreland at his recent appearance at the National Press Club, that the war had now 'reached an important point when the end begins to come into view'. Prepared to accept what they deemed to be an assurance that matters were well in hand, such Americans had little reason to suspect that a crisis was looming over the course of the Vietnam War.

At this time the Tet Offensive, known to the Communists as the Tong Cong Kich/Tong Khoi Nghia (General Offensive/General Uprising), was in the final throes of preparation as a three-phase campaign to be waged between 30 January and 23 September 1968 by the combined forces of the NLF (National Front for the Liberation of South Vietnam, universally known to the US forces as the Viet Cong, and the People's Army of Vietnam (North Vietnamese army). The entire undertaking, which

was of unprecedented size and ferocity, was designed to hit and destroy military and civilian command and control centres and capabilities right through South Vietnam, and thus trigger a general uprising among the population to overthrow the South Vietnamese government and so bring the war to a successful end with the Communists in control of a reunified Vietnam.

The operation is generally known in the West as the 'Tet' Offensive, as its scheduled start was the early morning of 31 January, the beginning of the Tet Nguyen Dan, or lunar New Year holiday. The offensive, in fact, got off to a premature start during the morning of 30 January in the I and II Corps Tactical Zones, but the reasons for this remain completely unexplained. Also unexplained are the reasons why the reports of these attacks, which were launched on a large scale and over a substantial geographical area, did not set off alarms in Saigon and thus the implementation of major defensive measures. When the main weight of the operation by the North Vietnamese army and NLF started during the morning of the following day, therefore, the allies had made few preparations, let alone implemented them, to handle the major offensive that was now erupting all over South Vietnam on a well co-ordinated basis. More than 80,000 Communist troops were in action in more than 100 cities and towns, including 36 of the 44 provincial capitals, five of the six autonomous cities, 72 of the 245 district towns, and even Saigon itself. The Tet Offensive was the largest military operation yet attempted by either side in the Vietnam War up to this time.

It would be an understatement to say that the initial attacks took the allied forces by surprise and totally stunned them, but after the allies had recovered from the shock of the offensive they quickly contained most of the attacks and beat them back, in the process inflicting huge losses on the North Vietnamese army and NLF. The two major exceptions to this general rule were the bitter and devastating combat which tore apart Hue, the old imperial capital of Vietnam, where the fighting lasted for a month, and the action around the US combat base at Khe Sanh, which had started just before the launch of the Tet Offensive and would continue for two more months.

In overall terms, therefore, the Tet Offensive was a military disaster at the operational and tactical levels for the Communist forces in terms of their extremely adverse loss/kill ratio from the allied forces and their failure to take and hold major physical objectives or to spark a general uprising among the civil population of South Vietnam. At the strategic and psychological levels, however, it was a major success for the Communists, for the very fact that they could plan and launch such an endeavour throughout South Vietnam had a devastating impact on the US administration and genuinely shocked the American public.

Whatever the scepticism with which the members of the US population accepted the pronouncements of their government regarding the situation in the Vietnam War, most had been prepared to accept that while the allies were not actually winning the war they were at least holding their own. The obvious conclusion from this acceptance was that the Communists were therefore incapable of planning, launching and sustaining a major military effort, and yet now they were doing just that. Thus, while the losses of men and matériel by the allies may have been significant, they paled into insignificance in the face of the shock to the American people, among whom those opposed to the war now grew rapidly in number, determination and willingness to demand that their voices be not only heard but also heeded.

Although most Western historians feel that the Tet Offensive ended in June, a supposition which allows it to be slotted neatly into the framework of US political and military decisions that then completely altered the US commitment to the Vietnam War, the offensive in fact lasted, entirely in accordance with its original plan, through another two and fully distinct phases. The second phase began on 5 May and continued until the end of the month, while the third started on 17 August to end finally on 23 September.

During the autumn of 1967 there had been two major questions in the minds of the US people and President Johnson's administration. The first of these was whether or not the USA's strategy of attrition, based on the search-and-destroy operational and tactical method, was working in South Vietnam, the second being which side was in fact winning the war. According to General William C. Westmoreland, commander of the MACV (Military Assistance Command, Vietnam), the answer could be found by a mathematical process: take the total number of North Vietnamese army and

NLF soldiers estimated to be in South Vietnam and subtract the number killed (or rather claimed to have been killed) or captured during military operations, and this would establish the so-called 'crossover point' at which the number of those killed or captured was greater than the number of those raised by the North Vietnamese or NLF to replace those lost. The major problem with this simplistic approach to establishing the balance of the war was that there was a significant difference between the MACV's and the CIA's order of battle estimates for the strength of the Communist insurgent forces operating within South Vietnam. In September 1967 members of the MACV's intelligence branch and of the CIA had met to prepare a 'Special National Intelligence Estimate', which would then be used by the Johnson administration to assess whether of not the USA was actually winning the Vietnam War.

On the basis of documents captured in the course of Operations Cedar Falls and Junction City, in which vast numbers of papers were seized, the CIA came to the assessment that the number of NLF guerrillas, irregulars and cadremen operating within the south could be as high as 430,000. On the other hand, the MACV's Combined Intelligence Center was sure that the number could be no more than 300,000. Westmoreland was distinctly concerned how the US public might interpret any revelation of such an increased estimate, Communist troop strengths having been a routine feature of press briefings and hand-outs. According to the MACV's current head of intelligence, Major General Joseph A.

McChristian, the new and very much increased figures 'would create a political bombshell', proving that the North Vietnamese army and NLF now 'had the capability and the will to continue a protracted war of attrition'.

During May, the MACV attempted to obtain a compromise from the CIA by maintaining that the various NLF militia forces did not constitute a fighting force as such, but were rather low-level 'fifth columnists' used for the collection of information. The CIA's response was that any such notion was specious, in that they were directly responsible for half of the casualties suffered by the US forces. With the two parties effectively deadlocked, George Carver, the CIA's deputy director for Vietnamese affairs, was invited to mediate, and emerged during September with a compromise solution whereby the CIA would drop its insistence on including the irregulars in the final tally of forces, and add a section to the estimate explaining the agency's position. This did not sit well with most of the CIA's leadership, and George Allen, Carver's deputy, went as far as to say that the agency had capitulated, and that the responsibility for this lay with Richard Helms, the CIA's director. Allen believed that 'it was a political problem...[Helms] didn't want the agency...contravening the policy interest of the administration'.

During the second half of 1967 the Johnson administration had become positively alarmed by criticism, both inside and outside government circles, of the manner in which the war was being prosecuted, and also by increasing numbers of reports concerning the rapid decline of public

THE TET OFFENSIVE

US soldiers had neither training nor experience in urban fighting, but learned the art of this difficult military tactic very rapidly in the hard school of experience.

support for the administration's policies with regard to the Vietnam War. Public opinion polls now suggested that the percentage of Americans believing that the USA had been wrong to send troops to South Vietnam had almost doubled, from 25 per cent in 1965 to 45 per cent by December 1967. Analysis of this trend suggested that the shift in public opinion resulted not from any belief that the struggle was in itself not worthy of US commitment, but from concerns about the steadily rising casualty rate, the increased level of taxation required to pay for the war effort, and a feeling of despondency that there appeared to be no end to the war in sight. A poll of

November 1967 indicated a 55 per cent majority in favour of a tougher and more telling US commitment, suggesting that while most Americans felt it might have been wrong to have become involved in the first place, the way forward rested with a greater determination to win, now that US forces were committed, expressing itself in more intensive operations, or alternatively in a complete withdrawal. What the US people wanted, therefore, was a speedy resolution of the Vietnam War in victory or withdrawal.

It was principally this last which prompted the administration to commit itself to a 'success offensive', which was

an attempt to shift public perception from the idea that the war had reached a stalemate position to that of the success of the Johnson administration's policies. As part of this effort, Walt W. Rostow, the National Security Advisor, co-ordinated a programme to saturate the media with indications of optimism, based largely on interpretation of statistics such as kill/loss ratios, body counts and village pacifications, with all such 'data' being spoon-fed to the media and also to the Congress. The senior figures of the administration were also wheeled out for public consumption: in mid-November 1967, for example, Vice President Hubert H. Humphrey, during a TV interview said: 'We are beginning to win this struggle…We are on the offensive. Territory is being gained. We are making steady progress.'

The 'success' offensive peaked at the end of the same month as Johnson called Westmoreland and Ellsworth Bunker, the new US ambassador to South Vietnam, to Washington for what was apparently a 'policy review', but which was more realistically another opportunity to strengthen the administration's case with public utterances, further bolstered by pronouncements from Saigon by men such as Robert Komer, the head of the pacification programme, that his task in the rural areas of South Vietnam was paying handsome dividends and clearly succeeding, with 68 per cent of the South Vietnamese population now under the control of the South Vietnamese government and only 17 per cent under that of the NLF; no comment was passed concerning the other 15 per cent. General Bruce Palmer, one of the three field force commanders

popularity of the Johnson administration which, by the end of the year, had increased by 8 per cent. But public opinion is always fickle and by a time early in January 1968, a poll suggested that 47 per cent of Americans still disapproved of the administration's handling of the war, and many could not help but remember, during and after the Tet Offensive, Westmoreland's statement to a journalist: 'I hope they try something, because we are looking for a fight.'

On the other side of the non-existent 'front line', the Communists had begun work on the planning of a 1968 winter/spring offensive early in 1967, the politico-military leadership in Hanoi persevering in this effort until a time

LEFT: Casualties arrive by CASEVAC (casualty evacuation) helicopter.

BELOW: US soldiers with a recoilless rifle, a lightweight form of weapon that allows the firing of heavier projectiles than would be practical with a recoiling weapon.

in South Vietnam, claimed that 'the Viet Cong has been defeated' and that 'He can't get food and he can't recruit. He has been forced to change his strategy from trying to control the people on the coast to trying to survive in the mountains'.

It was Westmoreland, perhaps, who was strongest and most public in his support of the US policy on South Vietnam, and who therefore was responsible in large measure for the US people's later despondency and anger when the Tet Offensive broke in South Vietnam. Addressing the National Press Club on 21 November, Westmoreland said that the Communist forces were now 'unable to mount a major offensive...I am absolutely certain that whereas in 1965 the enemy was winning, today he is certainly losing...We have reached an important point when the end begins to come into view.'

The success offensive certainly paid dividends in terms of boosting the

THE TET OFFENSIVE

An airfield after an NLF visit, with a destroyed Douglas C-47 transport immediately behind the M60-armed Jeep and other matériel burning in the background.

early in 1968. It is difficult to assess why and how the Tet Mau Than (Tet Offensive) was conceived, for even 30 years after the end of the Vietnam War there is still a great reluctance to reveal anything. In North Vietnamese official literature the decision to launch the offensive is still generally presented as

the direct response to the North Vietnamese perception that the USA had failed to win the war quickly, that the Rolling Thunder bombing campaign was not achieving its objectives, and that there was a growing anti-war movement in the USA. In overall terms, however, the decision to launch the Tong Cong

Kich/Tong Khoi Nghia (General Offensive/General Uprising) was considerably more complex. When finally reached, the decision marked the conclusion of a hard-fought and decade-long debate within the Communist party leadership, initially involving two and finally three factions.

THE VIETNAM WAR

The moderate faction within the leadership believed that North Vietnam's economic viability should be the driving force behind the development of the nation, and thus should receive greater attention than the support of a large-scale conventional war in what the Communist party believed to be the occupied southern part of the country. This faction also believed in the Soviet philosophy of peaceful co-existence and the reunification of Vietnam through political means, and was led by Truong Chinh and General Vo Nguyen Giap, the party theoretician and the minister of defence.

The militant faction adhered to the foreign policy concept practised by Communist China, which was based on the advisability of reunifying the country by military means without any thought of negotiation with the USA. This faction was led by the party's first secretary, Le Duan, and Le Duc Tho. General Nguyen Chi Thanh, who was head of COSVN (the headquarters controlling the Communist war effort in South Vietnam), was the political commissar and commander-in-chief of the Communist forces in South Vietnam, and was another prominent member of the militant faction which, up to the

mid-1960s, had been in the ascendancy and therefore controlled the manner in which the war was fought and, somewhat oddly given its adherence to the Communist Chinese concept of how such a war should be fought (i.e. emphasis in the early stages on irregular warfare), based its strategy on the adoption of large-scale conventional military operations using main-force formations, and not on the type of protracted irregular warfare suggested by the writing and practices of Mao Zedong. Under Thanh's command, therefore, the North Vietnamese army strove to match the US military escalation in South Vietnam on a steady stage-by-stage basis.

By 1966/67 the North Vietnamese army and National Liberation Front forces fighting in South Vietnam had suffered very heavy losses, there was in effect a battlefield stalemate, and the economy of North Vietnam was being steadily destroyed, albeit on a piecemeal basis, by the US forces' Rolling Thunder air bombardment campaign, in which it

ABOVE: Marines of Company C, 1st Battalion, 5th Regiment, are engaged in a fire fight in the streets of Hue City.

LEFT: Pfc Roger D. Coon, a rifleman of Company A, 2nd Battalion, 12th Cavalry Regiment, 1st Cavalry Division (Airmobile), drinks some water after accomplishing his first patrol at Camp Evans, 14 miles (22km) north of Hue. January 1968.

THE TET OFFENSIVE

was appreciated that, should these conditions continue, North Vietnam would sooner rather than later lack the financial, military, political and social strengths to gain the advantage in the war in South Vietnam. This led to the renaissance of the moderate faction, which called for the start of negotiations and a revision of North Vietnam's basic strategy. The militant faction was sure that a return to irregular warfare was the most useful course for the Communist forces to pursue, it being clearly impossible to defeat the USA in any conventional military conflict. The moderate faction was also confident that the policy of rejecting negotiations was wrong as the USA could have its determination to support South Vietnam worn down only by means of a 'war of wills' over an extended period of what the members of the moderate faction called 'fighting while talking'.

During 1967 matters were going so badly for the Communist forces, in overt battlefield terms, that Le Duan instructed Thanh to incorporate into his overall strategy of the war several aspects of protracted irregular warfare. It was during this period that there emerged the new centrist faction, led by the party chairman, Ho Chi Minh, Le Duc Tho, and the foreign minister, Nguyen Duy Trinh, which called for the leadership to commit the nation to negotiations. From October 1966 to April 1967 there was an open debate over military strategy in the North Vietnamese media between Thanh and his rival Giap, the latter having long suggested that North Vietnam and the Communist elements in South Vietnam would benefit from the use of a defensive and essentially irregular warfare strategy against the forces of the USA and South Vietnam. Thanh countered with the claim that Giap and his supporters were focused too much in their thinking on their experiences during the 1st Indo-China War with the French, and therefore that they were too 'conservative and captive to old methods and past experience...mechanically repeating the past'.

Much of the argument would be conducted at the level of what was politically and militarily the optimum course for North Vietnam to pursue, but there was also a foreign policy aspect to the argument. This resulted from the fact that North Vietnam lacked the resources to fight a war against the USA over any extended period, and was therefore almost entirely dependent on military and economic aid from one or more third parties. These were, of course, Communist China and the USSR. Communist China naturally advised the North Vietnamese to switch entirely to the Maoist concept of irregular warfare, its primary concern being to support a fellow Communist state but without the possibility of being drawn into a conventional war as it had been by its support for the Communists of North Korea during the Korean War. The Communist Chinese were also against any move toward negotiation with the Americans. The USSR, on the other hand, indicated its approval for the notion of negotiation, but was prepared at the same time to provide the weapons which allowed the North Vietnamese forces to embroil themselves in a conventional war along Soviet tactical precepts.

North Vietnamese politics thus took the form of a balancing act between the demands of a war policy, internal and external policies, domestic antipathies, and foreign allies known to possess 'self-serving agendas' not necessarily coincident with the best interests of the Vietnamese Communist party. Then, on 27 July 1967, and in an attempt to break the will of their domestic opponents and reaffirm their autonomy vis-à-vis their foreign allies, several hundreds of pro-Soviet party moderates, military officers and members of the intelligentsia were arrested in the 'Revisionist Anti-Party Affair', the factor determining whether any individual was arrested being that person's position on the political leadership's choice of tactics and strategy for the proposed general offensive. This made the militant faction pre-eminent, an immediate result being the end of all talk of negotiation, the termination of the concept of fighting a lengthy war, and a strengthened adherence to the concept of the Tong Cong Kich/Tong Khoi Nghia to take place in the cities and towns of South Vietnam. The position of the militant faction was further consolidated by more waves of arrests during November and December 1967.

The plan for the Tong Cong Kich/Tong Khoi Nghia was initially conceived as the 'COSVN proposal' at Thanh's headquarters in South Vietnam during April 1967, and had been forwarded to Hanoi in the following month. Thanh was then summoned to Hanoi to lay out his thinking before the Military Central Commission. But in July, after receiving authorization to start preparing the offensive, Thanh suffered a heart attack and died.

After consolidating its pre-eminent position in the crackdown, the militant

THE VIETNAM WAR

faction speeded the planning process for a major conventional offensive as the most effective means available to break the military stalemate in South Vietnam, drawing strongly on its belief that there was so great a disaffection in South Vietnam's population with the US forces and the South Vietnamese administration that the population would rise in support of any major military success by the Communist forces, and so pave the way to a swift and comprehensive victory for the Communists. The militant faction had reached this conclusion about South Vietnam's overall condition on the basis of its belief that the South Vietnamese armed forces had been rendered effectively impotent by losses and a wholly ineffectual administration, that the wholesale disaffection of the population with the civil government had been reflected in the popular vote of a mere 24 per cent for Nguyen Van Thieu's and Nguyen Cao Ky's party in the presidential election of the autumn of 1967, that the Buddhist uprisings of 1963 and 1966 reflected religious antipathy to the current administration, that there was a growing and very vociferous anti-war movement in the south, as reflected by demonstrations in Saigon, and that there was continuous criticism of Thieu's administration in the South Vietnamese media. The militant faction was therefore highly confident of success, and also felt that the commitment of the offensive would quell the last vestiges of what it termed 'dovish calls for talks, criticism of military strategy, Chinese diatribes of Soviet perfidy, and Soviet pressure to negotiate – all of which needed to be silenced'.

In October the politico-military leadership of North Vietnam decided that the Tong Cong Kich/Tong Khoi Nghia should be launched on the first day of the Tet holiday in January 1968, a decision that had been reaffirmed in December and formalized as party policy at the 14th Plenary Session of the Party Central Committee in January 1968. This formalization was ratified in Resolution 14, which was a major blow to all left in the Vietnamese Communist party, and in foreign Communist parties which wanted to see a concentration on longer-term irregular warfare. Despite its strength, the militant faction nonetheless had to yield some concessions to the centrist faction by stating that negotiation was possible.

Although he is credited in most of Western literature as the planner of the Tong Cong Kich/Tong Khoi Nghia, General Giap did not plan the offensive. Thanh's basic concept was developed by a party committee headed by Thanh's deputy, Pham Hung, and then modified by Giap, whose earlier opposition may well have been tempered by the arrest and incarceration of most of the members of his staff during the Revisionist Anti-Party Affair. Giap's task was therefore to ensure that an existing plan had the maximum chance of success, and to this end introduced guerrilla operations into what was basically a conventional military offensive, shifting the task of triggering the anticipated popular rising from the North Vietnamese army to the forces of the NLF. As far as Giap was concerned, any success gained by the plan would reflect well on all concerned, while any failure would reflect primarily on the militant faction which had demanded

this major undertaking. The moderate and centrist factions took at least a measure of comfort from the fact that there was still the possibility of negotiations, predicated on an end to the US aerial bombardment of North Vietnam.

The planning of the Tong Cong Kich/Tong Khoi Nghia was based on three main phases of offensive operations, preceded by a preliminary phase in which the Communist forces would launch attacks in South Vietnam's border areas to divert US attention and forces from the cities and towns of South Vietnam. The campaign proper would then get under way with simultaneous offensive actions in most of the urban areas of South Vietnam and attacks on major allied bases, these being Saigon and Hue. Over this same period, as noted above, the Communist forces would maintain their pressure on the Khe Sanh Combat Base.

Giap admitted that this would deny the services of three of the North Vietnamese army's divisions to the offensives into South Vietnam's cities and towns, but he felt that the pressure should nonetheless be maintained on Khe Sanh to protect the North Vietnamese lines of communication and keep the attention of the US forces focussed in the north. Giap was also convinced that the main focus of the offensive should not be the US forces but those of the South Vietnamese and their political masters, whose destruction or major weakening would, it was felt, trigger the popular uprising on which the success of the undertaking was predicated. The offensive was accordingly aimed most deliberately at the task of convincing the population

THE TET OFFENSIVE

The airs and graces assumed by a victorious soldier.

of South Vietnamese, rather than that of the USA.

According to General Tran Van Tra, Thanh's successor as head of the COSVN, the offensive was to have three distinct phases: Phase 1 was scheduled to begin on 31 January, taking the form of a country-wide assault on the cities and towns of South Vietnam primarily by the forces of the NLF, while at the same time a propaganda offensive would be started in an effort to persuade South Vietnamese troops to desert and the South Vietnamese population to rise up against the government. Even if outright victory did not result from this, it was believed that there might emerge a coalition government paving the way for a US withdrawal. But if Phase 1 failed to achieve these objectives, other operations would be launched to wear down the physical strength and moral

resolve of the South Vietnamese and Americans, and so pave the way toward a negotiated settlement: these operations were to be Phases 2 and 3, scheduled to begin on 5 May and 17 August respectively.

The Communist forces' preparations were already well under way. The logistical build-up to ensure that the forces committed to the offensive had sufficient weapons, ammunition and other essential supplies had begun in the middle of 1967, and by January 1968 81,000 tons of supplies and 200,000 troops, including seven infantry regiments and 20 independent battalions, had passed along the Ho Chi Minh Trail from North Vietnam to South Vietnam. This logistical effort was designed to support not only the North Vietnamese army but also the units of the NLF; the latter were thus largely

equipped with new Soviet-supplied weapons, including the AK-47 assault rifle and B-40 rocket-propelled grenade-launcher, which gave the NLF firepower superior to that of the less well-armed formations and units of the South Vietnamese army.

The North Vietnamese build-up was not limited to the military and logistical fields, but in an effort to confuse the South Vietnamese and Americans included a diplomatic initiative. The North Vietnamese foreign minister had announced on 30 December 1967 that North Vietnam would (as opposed to its earlier assertions that it might) start to negotiate with the USA if the latter unconditionally terminated its Rolling Thunder aerial bombardment of North Vietnam. This announcement led to a spate of diplomatic activity during the last part of 1967, but amounted to nothing.

At this juncture of the Vietnam War, the South Vietnamese and US military intelligence departments estimated that the number of Communist troops deployed in South Vietnam during January 1968 amounted to 323,000 men in the form of 130,000 North Vietnamese regular troops, 160,000 NLF insurgents and members of the NLF infrastructure, and 33,000 service and support troops. The assessment suggested that these men were organized as nine divisions totalling 35 infantry and 20 artillery or anti-aircraft artillery regiments with 230 infantry and six engineer battalions.

The Communist forces had no chance of achieving their build-up without the allied forces gaining some impression of what was afoot and, as

LEFT: The Communist forces fought tenaciously during the Tet Offensive, and suffered very heavy losses.

BELOW: This Viet Cong officer, captured during the Tet Offensive, was executed moments later by the South Vietnamese.

noted above, the South Vietnamese and US intelligence departments in Saigon soon began to suspect that a major undertaking was being prepared, although its nature could not be deduced, and that large and well-equipped forces were being moved into South Vietnam. In the period of the late summer and autumn of 1967 both South Vietnamese and US intelligence agencie collected clues that indicated a significant alteration in the strategic planning of the North Vietnamese army and NLF, and by the middle of December many in Saigon and Washington were confident that they were right to suspect the imminence of a major offensive. Conventional military intelligence systems, and both aerial and electronic reconnaissance, made it clear that a major logistical effort was being undertaken during the last three months of 1967. During October, for example, the number of trucks observed moving to the south through Laos on the Ho Chi Minh Trail rose from a monthly average of 480 to 1,116, with 3,823 in November and 6,315 the following month. This persuaded Westmoreland on 20 December to signal the Department of Defense that he believed with a high level of certainty that the Communist forces would 'undertake an intensified countrywide effort, perhaps a maximum effort, over a relatively short period of time'.

Despite the intelligence warnings and other indications received over a

205

THE TET OFFENSIVE

ABOVE: An aerial view of Hue City, taken in June 1968.

ABOVE RIGHT: Marines of Company A, 1st Battalion, 1st Marine Regiment, fire from the window of a house in a search-and-clear mission during the Battle of Hue.

considerable period, the allied forces were nonetheless taken completely by surprise when they began to appreciate the great size of the Tong Cong Kich/Tong Khoi Nghia undertaking in the days after it began. It has been suggested, with considerable likelihood, that the reason for this was a basic flaw in the way the allied intelligence staffs analyzed the data received: it tended in general to look at the Communists' probable plans on the basis of capabilities rather than intentions. Thus the allies estimated that the Communist forces had little in the way of capability,

certainly by American standards, and could therefore not be planning to launch an offensive of strategic implications. It must be admitted, however, that another way in which error may have entered the calculation was the general lack of co-ordination and co-operation between the allied intelligence outfits with each other and also with those of the other nation.

Further difficulty was added to the process of assessing the Communist forces' intentions by the so-called 'border battles' just to the south of the DMZ. On 24 April 1967 a US Marine Corps patrol had prematurely triggered a North Vietnamese offensive aimed at taking the airstrip and combat base at Khe Sanh, the western anchor of the US Marine Corps' defensive positions in Quang Tri province. The fighting lasted until May, resulting in 940 North Vietnamese and 155 US Marine Corps dead.

Over a 49-day period from early in September and into October, the North Vietnamese shelled the US Marine Corps' outpost of Con Thien at the rate of some 100 to 150 rounds per day, persuading Westmoreland to launch Operation Neutralize as an intense aerial bombardment campaign of 4,000 sorties into and just north of the DMZ. On 27 October a South Vietnamese army battalion at Song Be, the capital of Phuoc Long province, was attacked by the whole of a North Vietnamese regiment, and two days later another attacked the US Special Forces border outpost at Loc Ninh in Binh Long province, triggering a 10-day battle which drew in elements of the US 1st Infantry Division and the South Vietnamese 18th Infantry Division before the fighting ended with 800 North Vietnamese dead.

The most severe of these border battles started in October and continued

achieving, was the preliminary phase of the Tong Cong Kich/Tong Khoi Nghia plan, which was to focus the attention of the US forces on an area well away from the regions where the main operations were to take place, and to keep the Americans off balance.

Further grist was added to this mill by the unfolding of events around the US Marine Corps' combat base at Khe Sanh where, on 21 January 1968, a force of between 20,000 and 40,000 North Vietnamese troops laid partial siege to the garrison. The MACV was sure they intended to make a major effort and overrun the base, which would have secured the Communist forces a major psychological and propaganda victory as well as pave the way for an maximum-

LEFT: Flares, dropped from aircraft, illuminate the night sky over the city of Saigon.

BELOW: A soldier of the 9th Infantry Division in Saigon.

into November around Dak To, another border outpost in Kontum province. The 22 days of fighting involved four regiments of the North Vietnamese 1st Infantry Division against the US 4th Infantry Division, US 173rd Airborne Brigade, and a number of South Vietnamese infantry and airborne units: by the end of the fighting between 1,200 and 1,600 North Vietnamese and 262 US soldiers had been killed.

The military intelligence department of the MACV was unable to establish what motives the North Vietnamese may have had in triggering such large-scale actions in remote regions, where the decisive factor would certainly have been US aerial and ground firepower. At the tactical and operational levels, as far as the Americans were concerned, these North Vietnamese undertakings lacked any real purpose. But it seems likely that what the Communists had attempted to do, and to a large extent succeeded in

THE TET OFFENSIVE

ABOVE: *An infantryman stands guard, armed with an M60 machine gun.*

RIGHT: *A captured Viet Cong nurse in Cholon, the Chinese area of Saigon.*

outskirts of Saigon. Thus, when the Tong Cong Kich/Tong Khoi Nghia undertaking started, 27 allied manoeuvre battalions were in position to defend the South Vietnamese capital and the area surrounding it. It is probable that this redeployment was one of the most critical tactical decisions of the Vietnam War.

By the first day of 1968, the US had deployed to South Vietnam 331,098 personnel of the US Army and 78,013 from the US Marine Corps, in nine divisions, one armoured cavalry regiment, and two independent brigades. This US commitment in South Vietnam was complemented by the 1st Australian Task Force, one regiment of the Thai army, two South Korean infantry divisions, and a South Korean marine brigade. The South Vietnamese strength was 350,000 regular personnel in the

effort offensive to take the two most northern provinces of South Vietnam. To deter any such possibility, Westmoreland deployed 250,000 men, including half of the MACV's US manoeuvre battalions, into the I Corps Tactical Zone.

This disturbed Lieutenant General Frederick C. Weyand, commanding the US forces in the II Corps Tactical Zone, which included the Capital Military District centred on Saigon. A former intelligence officer, Weyand, already concerned about the emerging pattern of North Vietnamese and NLF activities in his area of responsibility, had made his worries known to Westmoreland on 10 January. Westmoreland agreed with Weyand's thinking and ordered 15 US battalions to drop back from positions near the Cambodian border to the

208

army, air force, navy and marine corps, supported by the 151,000 personnel of the Regional Forces and 149,000 personnel of the Popular Forces, which were the equivalent of regional and local militias.

In the days just before the Communist forces launched their Tet Offensive, the allied forces were at a comparatively low level of preparedness; North Vietnam had announced that its forces would be observing a seven-day truce from 27 January to 3 February for the Tet holiday, with the South Vietnamese military planning to release about half of its strength on leave. Westmoreland had already cancelled the truce in the I Corps Tactical Zone, and now requested the South Vietnamese to cancel their leave programme. President Thieu had already reduced the ceasefire period to 36 hours but refused to shorten the leave period further, on the grounds that any such change would adversely affect the morale of the armed forces, and in fact benefit only the Communist propaganda machine.

As noted above, on 28 January 11 NLF cadremen were captured in Qui Nhon city with a pre-recorded tape containing a message to the people of 'already occupied Saigon, Hue and Da Nang'. During the afternoon of the following day, General Cao Van Vien, chief of the South Vietnamese army general staff, ordered his four corps commanders to place their troops on alert, but even at this very late stage in the approach to the Tet Offensive, and with several warning indications already received, the allies seemed beset by a certain lethargy in increasing their level of preparedness, and even if he was aware of the potential disaster facing his

own forces, as well as the forces and population of his allies, he did not make this plain to other senior officers for transmission down the chain of command. Thus during the evening of 30 January, and of the outbreak of the Tet Offensive, 200 American colonels, all of them officers of the MACV intelligence staff, were at a pool party at the officers' quarters in Saigon. According to one man present: 'I had no conception Tet was coming, absolutely zero...Of the 200-odd colonels present, not one I talked to knew Tet was coming, without exception.'

Westmoreland was also deficient in conveying to the Department of Defense, and then to the administration, the extent of his concern. Although he had warned the President between 25 and 30 January that large-scale Communist attacks were imminent, his reports were all so oblique or couched in terms designed to persuade the recipients of his sense of optimism, that there was not the slightest inkling in Washington of the storm that was about to break.

Probably as a result of some error, the first wave of Communist attacks began shortly after midnight on 30 January rather than on the following day, as all five provincial capitals in the II Corps Tactical Zone, as well as Da Nang in the I Corps Tactical Zone, came under attack. Nha Trang, where the headquarters of the US I Field Force was located, was the first to be attacked, followed in short order by Ban Me Thuot, Kontum, Hoi An, Tuy Hoa, Da Nang, Qui Nhon and Pleiku. In all of these places, the Communist attacks were based on essentially the same tactical method: an initial barrage of

mortar and/or rocket attacks was followed by ground assaults undertaken by battalion-strength elements of the NLF, which were in some places supported by North Vietnamese soldiers. These assault forces linked up as swiftly as possible with local NLF cadremen, who served as guides to lead the regulars to the most important South Vietnamese headquarters and the radio station. What was evident almost from the first moments of the offensive was that the operations were not well-co-ordinated at the local level, and by the break of day almost all of the Communist assault forces had been driven back from their objectives.

Major General Phillip B. Davidson, the new head of the MACV's intelligence branch, now informed Westmoreland that the same was going to happen in the rest of the country that night and the following morning. All American forces were immediately placed on maximum alert and similar orders were issued to all South Vietnamese army units, although the South Vietnamese still showed no real sense of the need for speed and decision in raising the level of their preparedness, and orders cancelling leave arrived too late or were simply ignored.

At 03:00 on 31 January, NLF and North Vietnamese army forces launched the larger main wave of attacks against Saigon, Cholon and Gia Dinh in the Capital Military District within the south-central III Corps Tactical Zone; then Quang Tri again, Hue, Quang Tin, Tam Ky and Quang Ngai, as well as the US bases at Phu Bai and Chu Lai in the northern I Corps Tactical Zone; Phan Thiet and Tuy Hoa, as well as the US installations at Bong Son and An Khe in

THE TET OFFENSIVE

The US ambassador in Saigon, Ellsworth Bunker, views the casualties and damage (above and right) within the US Embassy compound in the aftermath of a Viet Cong attack during the Tet Offensive.

In most cases the defence was primarily the task of the South Vietnamese forces. Local militia and elements of the South Vietnamese army, with the support of the national police force, generally managed to drive back the attackers within two or three days, and on some occasions in a matter of just hours. But heavy fighting continued for several days longer in Kontum, Ban Me Thuot, Phan Thiet, Can Tho and Ben Tre. The outcome in each instance was usually based on the military capability of the local commander: some proved themselves to be very capable but there were also some who revealed themselves as cowards or incompetents or, worst of all, as both. During this crucial phase of the crisis, however, no South Vietnamese unit had broken or defected to the Communists as the latter had so confidently expected.

By his own account, Westmoreland rose to the occasion with optimism, both in media briefings and in his reports to Washington. But many surrounding the commander of the MACV said that Westmoreland had been 'stunned that the Communists had been able to co-ordinate so many attacks in such secrecy' and had been rendered 'dispirited and deeply shaken'. Although his assessment of the situation in purely military terms was essentially correct, Westmoreland seemed to have lost sight of the larger picture when he claimed steadily that it was the Khe Sanh Combat Base which was the real objective of the Communist effort, and that the 155 attacks by 84,000 Communist troops over the whole of South Vietnam was merely a diversion: Westmoreland maintained this position right up to 12 February or perhaps later.

Although the city was at the heart of their effort, the Communist forces did not attempt to take the whole of Saigon. Instead they targeted five main points in the downtown area of the South

the north-central II Corps Tactical Zone; and Can Tho and Vinh Long in the southern IV Corps Tactical Zone. On the next day, Bien Hoa, Long Thanh, Binh Duong in III Corps and Kien Hoa, Dinh Tuong, Go Cong, Kien Giang, Vinh Binh, Ben Tre and Kien Tuong in the IV Corps Tactical zone were assaulted. The last attack of the Communist offensive's Phase 1 initial operation was launched against Bac Lieu in the IV Corps Tactical Zone on 10 February. It is believed that some 84,000 Communist troops were involved, with thousands more ready to move in as reinforcements or as blocking forces. The Communist forces also launched mortar or rocket attacks on every major allied airfield, attacking 64 district capitals and many more smaller towns.

THE VIETNAM WAR

Vietnamese capital: the headquarters of the South Vietnamese army general staff, the Independence Palace, the US Embassy, the Long Binh naval headquarters, and the national radio station. These were all attacked by small elements of the local C10 Engineer Battalion. Elsewhere in the city or its outskirts, ten NLF Local Force battalions attacked the central police station and the headquarters of the South Vietnamese Artillery Command and Armoured Command headquarters, both located at Go Vap. The Communist plan for operations in and around Saigon called for these initial forces to take and hold their objectives for 48 hours, by which time reinforcements were to have arrived to relieve them.

The defence of the Capital Military Zone was primarily a South Vietnamese

responsibility, and was initially based on a strength of eight South Vietnamese army infantry battalions and the local police force. By 3 February they had been reinforced by five South Vietnamese ranger battalions, five marine battalions and five airborne battalions, making for an overall strength of 23 battalions. US Army units involved in the defence included the 716th Military Police Battalion, seven infantry battalions (one of them mechanized), and six artillery battalions.

Erroneous intelligence and poor co-ordination at the local level adversely affected the Communist attacks right from the start. At the headquarters of the South Armoured Command and South Vietnamese Artillery Command headquarters on the northern edge of Saigon, as just one example, the

Communist plan was based on the capture of armoured fighting vehicles (in particular tanks) and artillery to support their offensive, but only after

ABOVE: Removing a casualty from the US Embassy in Saigon.

BELOW LEFT: During the attack on the US Embassy, American military police kneel behind a wall at the entrance to the US Consulate, next door to the US Embassy, as they and soldiers of the 101st Airborne Division fight a Viet Cong suicide squad for control of the embassy compound. In the foreground are two dead American soldiers killed in earlier fighting.

THE TET OFFENSIVE

A bullet fired by Brigadier General Nguyen Ngoc Loan strikes the head of a Viet Cong officer, killing him instantly. The officer was captured near a Quang Buddhist pagoda in Saigon on 1 February 1968, during a day-long battle. General Loan, the chief of South Vietnam's national police, said after the execution: 'They killed many Americans and many of my peoples.'

the attacks had been launched did the Communists discover that the tanks had been moved to another base two months earlier and that all the artillery had been rendered useless by the removal of their breech blocks.

One of the most important NLF targets was the national radio station, so that the insurgents could broadcast their message calling for a national uprising. The NLF forces involved had with them a tape recording of Ho Chi Minh announcing the liberation of Saigon and calling for a general uprising against the Thieu administration. The NLF forces took and held the building for six hours, but could not make their broadcast as the lines between the main studio and the transmitter tower, which was situated in a different place, were severed as soon as the station had been seized.

The US Embassy in Saigon, a very substantial six-floor building located inside a 4-acre (1.6-hectare) compound,

had been completed as recently as September of the preceding year. At 02:45 the embassy came under attack by a 19-man sapper team, which blew a hole in the 8-ft (2.4-m) surrounding wall, rushing through it into the compound. With their officer killed in the initial attack and their attempt to gain access to the building defeated, the NLF sappers then simply milled around in the chancery grounds until they were all killed after US reinforcements had arrived. By 09:20 the embassy and its grounds were secure once more.

Elsewhere in Saigon small parties of NLF troops raced to attack a number of the billets used by enlisted men as well as officers, the homes of South Vietnamese army officers, and district police stations. The teams had lists of military officers and civil servants, and used these as they seized and killed any they could find. However, it should be emphasized that the brutality was not a one-way matter: on 1 February General Nguyen Ngoc Loan, chief of the national police force, in the presence of a photographer and a film crew executed Captain Nguyen Van Lem, an NLF officer captured in civilian clothing. The resulting photographs and footage were widely distributed, but what was not made clear in any accompanying documentation or sound track was the fact that the executed man had just been involved in the murder of one of Loan's most trusted officers and his entire family.

Outside the city, two NLF battalions attacked the US headquarters and logistical base at Long Binh, one battalion attacking the Bien Hoa airbase and another the nearby headquarters of the South Vietnamese army's III Corps.

Three battalions attacked the Tan Son Nhut airbase in the north-western part of the city, but here the allies were fortunate inasmuch as one combat-ready battalion of South Vietnamese airborne troops, awaiting air transport to Da Nang, was able to go straight into action, halting the attack.

In all, some 35 Communist battalions, many of whose personnel were undercover cadremen who had lived and worked within the capital or its general area for some years, had been committed to the attacks in and around Saigon. By dawn, most of the attacks in the city centre had been checked, but severe fighting erupted in the Chinese suburb of Cholon around the Phu Tho racetrack, which the NLF was using as a staging area and also as a command and control centre. The fighting was characterized by house-to-house fighting, and on 4 February the residents were ordered to leave their homes so that the area could be declared a free fire zone. Fighting in the city came to a close only after a fierce battle between NLF and South Vietnamese rangers on 7 March.

Except at Hue and in the course of clearance operations in and around Saigon, the first surge of the Tet Offensive had been terminated by the second week of February. The MACV estimated that during the first phase of the fighting, between 30 January and 8 April, some 45,000 NLF and North Vietnamese soldiers had been killed, with many more wounded. For some years this figure was thought by many to have been considerably exaggerated, but was confirmed in Hanoi during 1981. Westmoreland claimed that during the same period 32,000 Communist troops

THE VIETNAM WAR

southern portions as a vital transport artery connecting the coastal city of Da Nang, where the US had built a major port facility and associated logistic dumps, to the DMZ. Hue was also a base for the US Navy, so in the light of its strategic and operational value, as well as its distance of only 50 miles (80km) from the DMZ, Hue should have been well-fortified, garrisoned and prepared for any Communist attempt to take it. The city was, in fact, only poorly defended, and was unprepared because the allied forces had expected the Tet truce to be respected, but Hue was actually one of the most important targets for the Communist offensive.

Early in the morning of 31 January, a division-sized force of North Vietnamese army and NLF troops launched a co-ordinated attack on the

LEFT: Members of Company C, 206th Infantry, 101st Airborne Division, with the support of members of the 3rd Platoon, 2nd Squadron, 11th Armored Cavalry Regiment, conduct house-to-house searches for Viet Cong snipers during the lunar New Year celebrations in Bien Hoa.

BELOW: The men of Company A, 30th Ranger Battalion, are on the alert, looking for Viet Cong terrorists near Saigon during the lunar New Year offensive.

had been killed and 5,800 captured. The South Vietnamese losses were 2,788 killed, 8,299 wounded and 587 missing in action, while the US and other allied forces suffered 1,536 killed, 7,764 wounded and 11 missing.

The battle for Hue was one of the bloodiest and longest of the entire Vietnam War, during which forces of the South Vietnamese army and three under-strength battalions of the US Marine Corps, totalling fewer than 2,500 men, checked, counter-attacked and finally defeated more than 10,000 men of the North Vietnamese army and NLF.

By the time the Tet Offensive had begun on 30 January, the US forces had been involved in a combat role within South Vietnam for almost three years. Route 1 passed through Hue and over the Perfume river, which ran through the city dividing it into northern and

city. Their targets were the Tay Loc airfield, the headquarters of the South Vietnamese 1st Infantry Division in the Citadel, and the MACV compound in the New City, on the southern side of the Perfume river, the Communist strategic objective being the 'liberation' of the entire city within the context of triggering a general uprising of the South Vietnamese population to oust the current South Vietnamese administration, eject the Americans from the country, and sweep the Communist party into power over a reunified Vietnam.

At 02:33 a flare signalled the start of the attack, and two battalions of the North Vietnamese 6th Infantry Regiment began their offensive on the western side of the Citadel in the northern part of the city, their objectives being the Mang Ca compound, Tac Loc airfield and the imperial palace. A simultaneous attack by the North Vietnamese 4th Infantry Regiment was directed at the headquarters of the MACV compound in the southern part of the city. At the Western Gate of the Citadel, a four-man North Vietnamese sapper team, dressed in South Vietnamese army uniforms, killed the guards and opened the gate, flashing a pre-arranged signal that opened the way for the leading elements of the North Vietnamese 6th Infantry Regiment to enter the Old City.

North Vietnamese soldiers now streamed into the old imperial capital, their 800th and 802nd Battalions driving through the Western Gate before advancing to the north. On Tay Loc airfield, the South Vietnamese 'Black Panther' Company, reinforced by an ordnance company, stopped the 800th

Battalion. Although the Communist battle report states that the South Vietnamese 'offered no strong resistance', the North Vietnamese army report acknowledged that 'heavy enemy [South Vietnamese] fire enveloped the entire airfield. By dawn, our troops were still unable to advance'.

As the fighting for the airfield remained in the balance, the 802nd Battalion fell on the headquarters of the 1st Infantry Division at Along Ca. Although the Communist battalion penetrated the division's compound, a hastily concentrated force of 200 men, mostly staff officers and clerks, were able to check the attack. Lieutenant General Ngo Quang Truong, commander of the 1st Infantry Division, called back most of his Black Panther Company from the airfield to strengthen the defences of the divisional headquarters, and the Communists failed in their objective. At 08:00 North Vietnamese troops raised their flag over the Citadel.

At this time three battalions of the US Marine Corps, the officer commanding them in Hue being Major General Foster C. LaHue, were protecting the air base at Phu Bai, about 10 miles (16km) to the south-east of Hue, Route 1 and all the western approaches to Hue, when there should have been two complete regiments. Across the Perfume river in southern Hue, much the same situation existed. US advisers to the 1st Infantry Division in the MACV compound, which was a complex of two- and three-storey buildings, including a former hotel, awoke in the early hours as mortar bombs and artillery rockets began to rain down. The US personnel manned

the defences and drove back the first Communist assault. The North Vietnamese troops then surrounded the compound but tried no further direct assault. The MACV's Advisory Team 3 was in the region to provide fire and logistic support for the South Vietnamese 1st Infantry Division and the Thua Thien provincial forces. The provincial headquarters was located just to the north of the MACV compound, and the adviser team was accommodated in an area of about one city block on the south side of the Perfume river in the New City of Hue. The North Vietnamese 4th Infantry Regiment, together with the North Vietnamese 804th Battalion, supported by local force companies and elements of the Hue City Engineer Battalion, launched its offensive against the modern city. Divided into several attack groups, the Communists sought out key civil and military facilities.

The Communist preparations and assaults in the New City were lacking the precision and timing of those in the Citadel, a fact even recorded in the North Vietnamese official account. Indeed, one unit became lost in the dark and did not reach the city until 06:00. Despite confusion and some reverses, the North Vietnamese army nonetheless gained control of most of the southern part of Hue during the morning, apart from the prison, the MACV compound, and the LCU (landing craft utility) ramp on the waterfront to the compound's north-east.

Embattled in the Citadel, Truong called in reinforcements during 1 February, ordering his 3rd Regiment, 3rd Troop of the South Vietnamese 7th Cavalry Regiment and 1st Airborne

Task Force to relieve the pressure on his Mang Ca headquarters. Responding to the call at PK 17, the South Vietnamese base on Route 1, 10.5 miles (17km) north of Hue, the 3rd Troop and the 7th Battalion left as an armoured convoy, moving south in the direction of Hue. A North Vietnamese blocking force stopped this relief force about 440 yards (400m) short of the Citadel wall. Unable to force their way through, the paratroopers requested assistance. The South Vietnamese 2nd Airborne Battalion reinforced the convoy and the South Vietnamese were finally able to drive though the North Vietnamese line to enter the Citadel in the early hours of the next day. The cost was heavy: the South Vietnamese had lost 131 casualties, including 40 dead, and had lost four of the 12 armoured personnel carriers which had left PK 17. According to the South Vietnamese, the Communists had also been hard hit, losing 250 men killed, five taken prisoner, and 25 crew-served as well as 71 individual weapons.

The South Vietnamese 3rd Regiment had a still more difficult time. On 31 January its 2nd and 3rd Battalions advanced east from an area to the south-west of the city along the northern bank of the Perfume river, but the heavy weight of North Vietnamese defensive fire drove them back. Unable to enter the Citadel, the two battalions established their night positions outside the south-eastern wall of the Old City. Communist forces, meanwhile, surrounded the 1st and 4th Battalions of the same regiment, operating to the south-east as they attempted to reinforce the units in Hue. Captain Phan Ngoc Luong, commanding the 1st Battalion,

ordered his unit to fall back to the coastal outpost at Ba Long, reaching it with most of his surviving men who were down to their last few clips of ammunition. At Ba Long the battalion embarked in motorized junks and finally managed to reach the Citadel during the following day. The 4th Battalion was not able to break out of its encirclement for several days.

To the south of the city, on 31 January, Lieutenant Colonel Phan Huu Chi, commanding the South Vietnamese 7th Armoured Cavalry Squadron, attempted to break the Communist stranglehold. He led an armoured column toward Hue but found it impossible to break through. With the promise of US Marine Corps reinforcements, Chi's column made another attempt with three tanks in the lead. This time the South Vietnamese force crossed the An Cuu bridge into the New City and, reaching the central police headquarters in southern Hue, tried to relieve the police defenders. But a rocket struck Chi's tank, killing the colonel, and the South Vietnamese armour pulled back. After this the US Marines at Phu Bai were asked to intervene in support of the South Vietnamese, and were soon on the move. This US Marine element was part of the 1st Battalion of the 1st Marine Regiment, part of Task Force X-Ray.

On the night of 30/31 January, even as they were attacking Hue, the Communist forces launched a barrage of mortar bombs and artillery rockets at the US Marine forces holding the Phu Bai airstrip, and Communist infantry units moved forward against the US Marine Corps and South Vietnamese militia forces in the region, including

those in the Truoi river and Phu Loc sectors. At the key Truoi river bridge, at about 04:00, a North Vietnamese company attacked the South Vietnamese bridge security detail and the nearby H-8 platoon of the US Marine Corps. Lieutenant Colonel Cheatham instructed Captain G. Ronald Christmas, the commander of H Company, to relieve the embattled platoon unit. The US Marines caught the Communist force as it was starting to pull back and took it under fire. Seeing an opportunity to trap the North Vietnamese, Cheatham reinforced H Company with his command group and F Company. With his other companies in blocking positions, Cheatham hoped to catch the Communists against the Truoi river. Cheatham was able to inflict significant casualties on the Communist forces, but his plans were overtaken by events in Hue. At 10:30 on 31 January, G Company departed for Phu Bai as the task force reserve and later, in the afternoon of the same day, Cheatham was also deprived of operational control of F Company, which departed at about 16:30; the North Vietnamese successfully disengaged and E and H Companies assumed night defence positions.

As the fighting continued in the Truoi river and the Phu Loc sectors, the 1st Battalion of the 1st Marine Regiment began to advance into Hue. In the early hours of 31 January, following the rocket bombardment of the airfield and the initial attack on the Truoi river bridge, Task Force X-Ray received reports of Communist attacks right along the length of Route 1, between the Hai Van Pass and Hue. In overall terms, the Communists attacked 18 targets, including bridges, tactical units and

A grenadier of Company B, 1st Battalion, 505th Infantry Regiment, 3rd Brigade, 82nd Airborne, stands security while a house is being searched.

company defensive positions. With A Company of the 1st Battalion of the 1st Marine Regiment as the Phu Bai reserve, Colonel Hughes directed Lieutenant Colonel Gravel to organize the company to meet any contingency. At 06:30, Hughes ordered the company to reinforce the Truoi river bridge.

Up to this point the fighting inside Hue had been entirely a South Vietnamese matter, and LaHue, commanding Task Force X-Ray, had very little reliable intelligence on which to base his preparations for a US

intervention. All LaHue knew was that Truong's headquarters had been attacked, as too had the MACV compound. Because of the Communist mortaring of the LCU ramp in the southern part of Hue, the allies had stopped all river traffic into the city. As the US Marines approached the southern suburbs, they began to come under heavy sniper fire. In one village, the troops dismounted and cleared the houses on either side of the main street before proceeding, and the convoy stopped several times to eliminate

resistance in heavy house-to-house and street fighting before moving forward once again. At about 15:15, and after bloody fighting, the US Marines managed to push forward in the direction of the MACV compound, from whose immediate vicinity the Communists had pulled back their forces by this time. Colonel Gravel eventually met a US army officer, Colonel George O. Adkisson, the senior adviser to the 1st Infantry Division. Leaving its A Company to secure the MACV compound, the US Marine battalion commander took G Company, reinforced by the three tanks of the 3rd Tank Battalion and a few South Vietnamese tanks of the 7th Armoured Squadron, and attempted to cross the main bridge over the Perfume river. Gravel left the armour behind on the southern bank to provide direct fire support. As the US Marines started to cross the bridge, a Communist machine gun at the other end of the bridge fired, killing several of the Americans before one of the men ran forward and hurled a grenade, which silenced the machine gun. Two platoons then made their way over to the other end of the bridge, where they wheeled left and immediately came under automatic weapon and recoilless rifle fire from the wall of the Citadel. The US Marines then decided to withdraw.

This was no easy task, for the Communists were positioned and firing from virtually every building in the part of Hue north of the river. The number of wounded was rising and the US Marines commandeered abandoned South Vietnamese civilian vehicles for temporary service as ambulances to carry them out. By 20:00 the 1st

THE VIETNAM WAR

Battalion of the 1st Marine Regiment had established defensive positions near the MACV compound and a helicopter LZ in a field just west of the LCU ramp. On that first day, the two companies of US Marines in Hue had lost 10 men killed and 56 wounded. During the night, the battalion called a helicopter into the LZ to evacuate the worst of the wounded.

The US commanders still had little real information concerning the situation in Hue, and at 07:00 on the following morning Gravel committed a two-company assault, supported by tanks, in the direction of the jail and provincial building. The US Marines managed to advance only one block before once again coming under sniper fire. One of the tanks was knocked out by the projectile of a recoilless rifle, after which the attack was stopped and the battalion returned to the MACV compound.

The South Vietnamese 1st Infantry Division was able to obtain limited success to the north of the Perfume river on 1 February. Although the 2nd and 3rd Battalions of the 3rd Regiment remained outside the walls of the

Citadel, unable to penetrate the North Vietnamese defences, the 2nd and 7th Airborne Battalions, supported by armoured personnel carriers and the Black Panther Company, recaptured Tay Loc airfield. At about 15:00 the 1st Battalion of the South Vietnamese 3rd Regiment reached the command post of the South Vietnamese 1st Infantry Division at the Mang Ca compound, and later in the day US Marine helicopters delivered about half of the 4th Battalion of the South Vietnamese 2nd Regiment from Dong Ha into the Citadel; however, deteriorating weather then forced the cancellation of a second airlift to deliver the rest of the battalion.

Shortly after 15:00, F Company of the 2nd Battalion of the 5th Marine Regiment made a helicopter landing in the southern part of Hue with the object of effecting the relief of a MACV communications facility surrounded by an NLF unit. The company tried to achieve its task through most of the

ABOVE: An area off Plantation Road outside the south-western perimeter of Tan Son Nhut airbase. Attacking NVA forces were able to capture the US Forces' headquarters, located at the base, which assisted them in the capture of Saigon.

LEFT: Members of the 4th Battalion, 173rd Airborne Brigade, pinned down by mortar fire during an assault.

THE TET OFFENSIVE

RIGHT: A US Navy armed gunship helicopter fires a rocket in support of two river patrol boats, firing on enemy positions in the Mekong delta of South Vietnam. They were working together in the US Navy's Operation Game Warden to deny use of the delta's waterways to the Viet Cong.

BELOW: Wherever space could be created for it to land, the Boeing CH-47 Chinook twin-rotor helicopter was able to deliver men and supplies and evacuate the wounded.

afternoon, but could not break through. On this same day, General Cushman alerted the commander of the US 1st Air Cavalry Division, Major General John J. Tolson, to prepare his formation's 3rd Brigade for deployment into a sector west of Hue. By 22:15 Tolson's command had requested the III MAF to co-ordinate with the I Corps and Task Force X-Ray in its designated area of operations within the Hue sector. Tolson's plan called for the delivery of two battalions of the 3rd Brigade to the north-west of Hue: the 2nd Battalion of the 12th Cavalry Regiment would arrive first, and be followed by the 1st Battalion of the 7th Cavalry Regiment as well as elements of the 3rd Brigade. Once on the ground, the force would attack to the south-east and attempt to cut the Communist lines of communication into Hue.

In the middle of the afternoon of 2 February, the 2nd Battalion of the 12th Cavalry Regiment descended on its LZ to the north-west of Hue, then pushed forward in the direction of the city. In the southern part of Hue, on the same day, the US Marines made slight progress and brought in further reinforcement, the 1st Battalion finally relieving the MACV radio facility during the morning before fighting a three-hour battle to reach the university. Although the North Vietnamese had destroyed the railroad bridge across the Perfume river, to the west of the city, during the night, they had left the bridge across the Phu Cam

Canal. At about 11:00, H Company of the 2nd Battalion of the 5th Marine Regiment, under the command of Captain G. Ronald Christmas, crossed the An Cuu bridge over the canal. As the US Marine convoy, accompanied by US Army trucks equipped with quadruple 12.7-mm (0.5-in) machine guns and two Ontos vehicles, each armed with six 106-mm (4.17-in) recoilless rifles, entered the city, Communist snipers opened up on the US Marine reinforcements. Near the MACV compound, the US Marines came under heavy machine gun and rocket fire, to which the quadruple machine guns and sextuple recoilless rifles responded. In the resulting confusion, the convoy managed to

exchange fire for a short time with a US Marine unit already in the city.

By about 12:00 the North Vietnamese troops were continuing to block all advance to the south, and a 75-mm (2.95-in) recoilless rifle knocked out one of the supporting tanks. By the end of the day, the US Marines had suffered two killed and 34 wounded, but claimed to have killed nearly 140 Communist soldiers. The battalion consolidated its night defensive positions and waited to renew its attack on the following day.

LEFT & ABOVE: B-52 Stratofortress long-range, subsonic, jet-powered strategic bombers, carrying out raids on North Vietnamese targets.

THE TET OFFENSIVE

A USMC McDonnell Douglas F-4 Phantom bombing targets in North Vietnam.

Heavy street fighting followed as the US Marines battled their way through the city for more than three weeks. Men of the 1st and 5th Marine Regiments, fighting alongside the South Vietnamese 1st Infantry Division and supported by the US Army's 7th and 12th Cavalry Regiments, drove the North Vietnamese and NLF forces out of Hue only in incremental bites as they retook the city little by little. Most of the US Marines had little or no experience of street fighting, and none in the US unit was trained for urban close-quarter combat, so the battle was notably hard. Because of Hue's religious and cultural position as the capital of imperial Vietnam, the allied forces were ordered not to bomb or shell the city lest they destroy the historic buildings. Moreover, as the

fighting was taking place during the winter monsoon, it was virtually impossible for the US forces to call in any form of air support as there was almost always rain, low cloud or fog. As the intensity of the battle increased, however, the policy had to be changed; the Communist forces were using snipers, hidden inside buildings or in small holes, firing intensively from improved machine gun bunkers, making local counter-attacks in an effort to keep the allied forces off balance and, during the nights, creeping out to set explosive booby traps.

The Communist forces were finally compressed into the Citadel with the imperial palace at its centre. With casualties already high and the prospect of still greater losses looming over the

allied forces, it was decided to make use of tactical air power in an effort to bring about a speedy final resolution, to which end Douglas A-4 Skyhawk light attack warplanes dropped bombs and napalm on the Citadel. The allied forces moved forward once again and the imperial palace was secured on 24 February. A few days later the North Vietnamese and NLF pulled their last men out of Hue.

The Communist forces suffered notably heavy casualties in the battle for Hue. The South Vietnamese claimed to have killed nearly 3,000, though this may be too high a figure, while the Americans claimed 1,500; it is estimated that about another 3,000 were killed outside of the city.

There had also been large massacres by North Vietnamese forces of the civilian population during their month-long control of the city. In the battle's aftermath, South Vietnamese and American soldiers unearthed numerous shallow mass graves inside and on the outskirts of the city containing the bodies of about 2,800 people killed by the North Vietnamese and NLF within the context of their programme of systematic 'elimination' of those considered to be a threat, or even a potential one, to the eventual Communist victory. There have also been claims that some of the bodies discovered may have been people killed by a South Vietnamese intelligence unit on the grounds that they were Communist 'fifth columnists' or had otherwise aided the Communist forces.

In purely military terms, Hue was considered a victory for the allies as the forces of the North Vietnamese army and NLF (thought to have numbered more than 10,000 men, equivalent to more than one division) had been thwarted in their objectives. At the strategic level, however, Hue was an allied defeat, in that it finally swayed the American people into thinking that the Vietnam War could no longer be won.

Thus Hue was the beginning of the end for the US commitment to the Vietnam War. It marked the point when the American people became increasingly loath to commit their sons, the vast majority of whom were teenage conscripts lacking the education and families affluent enough to pay for the college education which would have earned them a draft deferment from what was increasingly seen as the meatgrinder of the war in South Vietnam. Another bone of contention, where the American public was

concerned, was that the drafted men were often sent into the war with only the barest of training and under the command of non-commissioned officers with little more age and experience than themselves. This was because the Johnson administration felt that a strong posture had to be maintained in other areas, most notably in Europe, and it was these formations, facing the possibility of a tank-spearheaded grand offensive of the Warsaw Pact under Soviet command which kept the best

men and much of the best equipment. Thus in the following five years, as noted below, the anti-war sentiment and public opinion would force the US administration to decrease its commitment on a slow but steady basis to Vietnamize the war effort, until the last US combat troops left South Vietnam in 1973.

During the first two weeks of the Tet Offensive, the Communist forces lost about 32,000 men killed and 5,800 captured, the combined figure of 37,800

November 1971. An F-4 refuels from a KC-135 Stratotanker, while two others fly overhead, armed with 500-lb laser-guided bombs.

THE TET OFFENSIVE

A US Navy A-4E Skyhawk. Skyhawks were the navy's primary light bomber over both North and South Vietnam during the early years of the Vietnam War.

being little short of half the total Communist strength committed to the offensive. Among the allied forces, about 2,800 South Vietnamese and 1,000 US troops were killed. Only at Hue did the attackers take and hold any objective for a significant period, and this may be the reason why the North Vietnamese did not commit any of the troops held in reserve to exploit success. Although they were at many locations below strength, as a result of the absence of many men on Tet leave, the South Vietnamese regular and militia force, which in fact bore the brunt of the fighting, performed for the most part with courage and capability. And still more dishearteningly for the North Vietnamese, nowhere had there been the slightest suggestion of a popular uprising of the type on which the

whole concept of the Tet Offensive had been based.

As noted above, therefore, the defeat of Phase 1 of the Tet Offensive was regarded as a major military success for the allies, and rightly so. But the media were giving an altogether different impression of events, and it was this which the American people readily believed. The reasons for what had in effect become a tide of misinformation were firstly the tight deadlines to which the journalists were working, which constantly led to error; and secondly the wilful disregard of logical analysis and anything that might interfere with the filing of a 'good' story – one that echoed Westmoreland's wild and almost culpable over-optimism in suggesting that victory was foreseeable. Of course, few among the US media personnel

involved in the reporting of the Vietnam War, either from inside the theatre or outside of it in the USA, had combat experience themselves, and fewer still had any understanding of military history. To media personnel, therefore, the Tet Offensive was rightly a great shock, as it was to most of the US military, but also (and more short-sightedly in an effort to secure a by-line and column inches) an unmitigated disaster, as it was clearly a US and South Vietnamese defeat.

None of the media personnel thought to draw a parallel, even if they knew of such a one, with other wars in which a side on the verge of losing the battle launched a grand offensive in the hope of wresting victory out of defeat: classic examples were and remain Germany's last offensives in 1918, toward the end of the First World War, and in 1944 toward the end of the Second World War. Like the Tet Offensive, they caught their opponents off-balance, at the cost of many lives, but ultimately speeded the defeat of Germany in the two world wars. The media personnel believed with a most steadfast and unprofessional certainty that the Johnson administration had been lying to the American people for years, and now saw their opportunity to expose the chicanery and trickery that 'must' lie behind the administration's claims that real progress was being made in the prosecution of the war.

Though light by the standards of many recent wars, especially the Second World War and the Korean War, the damage suffered by South Vietnam's cities and towns during the Tet Offensive seemed enormous to the militarily inexperienced media personnel, whose

THE VIETNAM WAR

training to extract the maximum 'shock' value from still and moving imagery meant that tight focusing could create the impression that a badly damaged urban area was representative of a whole city or town. Perhaps the most unfortunate quotation secured by media in the entire course of the Vietnam War was that of a US officer in the town of Ben Tre, some 25 per cent of which had been badly damaged, who said that 'it became necessary to destroy the town to save it'. This became the implicit mantra of the media: damage and destruction were everywhere, and those responsible for it were not the Communist forces, which had now translated a rural conflict into an urban war, but the US and South Vietnamese armies with their artillery, tanks and warplanes. A related concept was the US media concentration on the approximately 7,000 civilian casualties and almost 700,000 refugees that resulted from the fighting, rather than the 5,000 or more South Vietnamese civilians who had been seized, tortured and then executed by the Communists in Hue and other cities and towns.

Exaggeration is, of course, always a good avenue towards a headline, so reporters said that the imperial palace in Hue had been wholly destroyed, although the damage was in reality comparatively light. Saigon, in which had been inflicted, was portrayed on American TV as a great city destroyed, with smoke rising from the ruins. This was all part of the same media syndrome which portrayed the ongoing Battle of Khe Sanh as the Dien Bien Phu of the US military adventure in South Vietnam, and therefore prophesied great US and South Vietnamese casualties when the North Vietnamese overran this combat

base. Wholly ignored was the inconvenient fact that 6,000 allied troops at Khe Sanh, only slightly more than 1.5 per cent of the manpower available to Westmoreland, were holding up to 20,000 North Vietnamese troops, who could have been far better used in the Tet Offensive. The constant media message was that the North Vietnamese had tied down large number of allied troops for inevitable defeat.

Whenever there was an official statement claiming an allied victory (generally in terms to deliberately put

the best possible appearance on the matter, it must be admitted), the media responded only grudgingly with a report that accepted it only with reluctance and reservations, and at the same time that it must somehow or other have been a psychological victory for the Communists.

Remarkably enough, however, opinion polls later showed that while such reporting 'played well' with those already against the US commitment to the war, it did not turn the majority of the population against the

The North American OV-10 Bronco was conceived for the battlefield observation and light attack roles, offering its two crew members exceptional fields of vision.

THE TET OFFENSIVE

Johnson administration or the war until after Johnson had failed to take strong retaliatory action against the Communists.

Thus the anti-war bias of the media appealed most strongly to the membership of the US Congress and middle-level civilian bureaucrats and presidential advisers in Washington. The congressional 'doves' gained ground on the 'hawks', while many civilian officials found it increasingly hard to separate fact from fiction when they were faced with official reports on the one hand and reporting which presented an altogether different view on the other.

General Wheeler, the chairman of the Joint Chiefs-of-Staff, visited Saigon and came away highly concerned with the progress of the war, all the more so as Westmoreland, though optimistic about an allied victory against the Tet Offensive, revealed that the Communists might be able to launch other offensives. As far as the Department of Defense was concerned, the Vietnam War was merely the largest of several difficulties it was facing at this time: the North Koreans had recently seized the US communications ship, *Pueblo*, and there was always the possibility that Berlin or the Middle East might flare up into major hotspots. Concerned with the difficulties he faced in building up the US strategic reserves, already eroded by the demands of the Vietnam War, and in preparing for the possibility of other major Communist undertakings in South Vietnam, Wheeler urged Westmoreland to ask for major reinforcement. Westmoreland saw this as an opportunity to gain sufficient strength for incursions into Laos and Cambodia, should he receive

authorization, to sever the Ho Chi Minh Trail and destroy Communist base areas, or for an amphibious assault on the coast of North Vietnam to trap sizeable North Vietnamese formations in the DMZ. Westmoreland also felt that the calling-up of US reserve forces, hitherto denied for political reasons, would impress on the North Vietnamese that the USA was determined to win the war.

Faced with a request for an additional 206,000 men, to be divided equally between Vietnam and the strategic reserve, Johnson could not make up his mind and demanded a pair of studies on what such reinforcements might achieve: one of these was allocated to a committee chaired by the new defence secretary, Clark M. Clifford, and the other to a group of senior ex-officers. Both groups recommended against any major reinforcement. Johnson accepted this, but before any public announcement had been made a US newspaper published the fact that the administration was considering 206,000 more troops for Vietnam. The media then reacted in their typically antagonistic manner, and this is often credited with causing Johnson's poor result in the Democratic presidential primary in New Hampshire. Though construed by the media as a vote against Johnson's 'pro-war' stance, it was in fact more of a protest about the president's refusal to react more positively to the Tet Offensive.

Events in South Vietnam over the next few months proved that Westmoreland had been entirely correct in his assertion that the Communists had been hard-hit by their failure in the Tet Offensive.

As had already been planned, the Communists attempted their Phase 2 and Phase 3 offensives in May and August, but these were little more than short-lived attacks, mainly by artillery rocket and mortar rather than infantry. The pacification programme, which had been declared dead by the media, now began to gain greater success. The control of the South Vietnamese government was swiftly restored to those rural areas lost in the Tet Offensive, and was in fact considerably expanded. Again, quite contrary to the picture offered by the media, the South Vietnamese forces emerged with a higher level of morale and improved overall capabilities. South Vietnamese recruitment programmes fared well, and the USA increased and speeded its programme to provide new and improved weaponry and equipment for the militia as well as the regular forces. The South Vietnamese people also revealed, for the first time, wholehearted support for the Saigon government, and this allowed the creation of a national self-defence force with many thousands of personnel and modern arms.

By this time, however, Johnson had come to the conclusion that Westmoreland, after presiding over the US effort in South Vietnam for four and a half years, should be elevated to US Army chief-of-staff, his place in South Vietnam going to his deputy, General Creighton W. Abrams. The president made this decision in mid-January 1968, before the Tet Offensive broke over South Vietnam, but the delay in announcing it made it possible for Westmoreland's opponents to portray the situation as Johnson's adverse reaction to Westmoreland, as a result of the Tet Offensive, to get him out of South Vietnam.

It was primarily the opposition of the media and civilian officials in his administration to the US handling of the Tet Offensive which led Johnson to make concessions to anti-war critics and to order a halt in the US bombing of North Vietnam. Johnson also invited the North Vietnamese, yet again, to negotiate a peace agreement. Johnson also announced that he would not stand for re-election as president in the election of autumn 1968. Johnson had told Westmoreland of his decision, which resulted mainly from his poor health and the desires of his family, at a time late in 1967, but the ever-more vociferous anti-war lobby quickly claimed to have hounded Johnson out of office; there may have been an element of truth in the assertion, inasmuch as Johnson had been very seriously disturbed by the tenor of the anti-war lobby's protests against him.

Much to Johnson's surprise, the North Vietnamese agreed to negotiate, but it was the usual delaying tactic, and during the next four years the North Vietnamese steadfastly refused to agree to anything but the shape of the conference table in Paris. But in acceding to Johnson's offer, the North Vietnamese were effectively chaining the United States to the negotiating table until they could effect a more conventional land invasion of South Vietnam, and until the US population was so heartily tired of the war that a new president, Richard M. Nixon, would make concessions that extricated the USA from the Vietnam War, but at the same time ensured that North Vietnam succeed. So while the North

Vietnamese were defeated in the Tet Offensive, victory would eventually be theirs.

Wishing to exert increased pressure on the Americans in the Paris negotiations, scheduled to start on 13 May, the North Vietnamese launched Phase 2 of the Tet Offensive at a time late in April. US intelligence sources estimated that between February and May about 50,000 men had been moved south along the Ho Chi Minh Trail to replace the losses which the North Vietnamese divisions and NLF forces had sustained in Phase 1. Some of the most protracted and bitter combat in the whole of the Vietnam War began on 29 April, lasting until 30 May as the 8,000 men of the North Vietnamese 320th Infantry Division, backed by artillery firing across the DMZ from sites in North Vietnam, threatened the US logistical base at Dong Ha in the north-western part of Quang Tri province. In what became known as the Battle of Dai Do, the North Vietnamese clashed savagely with men of the US Marine, US Army and South Vietnamese army before being forced to pull back after suffering the loss of about 2,100 men to the allies' casualties of 290 killed and 946 wounded.

In the early morning of 4 May, Communist units launched Phase 2 of the offensive (known by the South Vietnamese and Americans as 'Mini-Tet') with attacks on 119 targets throughout South Vietnam, including Saigon. On this occasion, however, the allied intelligence machine was better informed of the Communists' plans and strengths, so there was no element of tactical surprise to aid them in the first wave of attacks. As a result, most of the

Communist forces were intercepted by allied forces before reaching their targets, but 13 NLF battalions managed to evade interception even so, driving once again into Saigon where chaos ensured. Two days' of severe fighting occurred at Phu Lam before the NLF's 267th Local Force Battalion was defeated around the Y-Bridge, and at Tan Son Nhut. By 12 May the Communists' second foray into Saigon was over and the surviving Communist forces pulled back, leaving behind them more than 3,000 dead.

The fighting had no sooner died down around Saigon than the US forces in Quang Tin province were attacked and suffered the most serious defeat of the Vietnam War. The Battle of Kham Duc was fought for a US Army Special Forces camp located at Kham Duc, and lasted from 10 to 12 May 1968. The Kham Duc camp was occupied by the 1st Special Forces detachment, consisting of US and South Vietnamese special forces as well as Montagnard irregulars of the CIDG. From September 1963 the camp had been used as an intelligence-gathering post, and patrols in strength from the camp often checked or slowed the Communist efforts to infiltrate their forces into the Central Highlands.

During May 1968, therefore, the North Vietnamese decided to take the camp in an undertaking parallel to Phase 2 of the Tet Offensive. With the fighting for the Khe Sanh Combat Base and other places over, the North Vietnamese could focus more tightly on Kham Duc, consequently from a time early in May the Communists began to move the North Vietnamese 2nd Infantry Division and the NLF 271st

THE TET OFFENSIVE

An OV-10 Bronco manoeuvres into position to call in more heavily armed warplanes and so support troops hard-pressed on the ground.

Regiment into the area; this was detected by the allied forces who, alarmed at what this movement might portend, had A Company of the 1st Battalion of the 46th Infantry Regiment flown in, followed a day later by the 2nd Battalion of the 1st Infantry Regiment of the US 196th Light Infantry Brigade from Chu Lai.

On 10 May the outpost of Ngok Tavak was attacked by the North Vietnamese regulars and the soldiers of the NLF. Although it was not the main target, Ngok Tavak obstructed the approach of the Communist forces to Kham Duc, and even as they attacked the Ngok Tavak outpost, Communist

forces began artillery bombardment of the Kham Duc camp. An Australian officer, Captain John White, led a small company of Chinese Nung soldiers and US Marines to engage the Communist attackers. The fighting at Ngok Tavak confirmed White's suspicion that a CIDG platoon had been infiltrated by the Communists. At 03:00 a group of soldiers approaching the Ngok Tavak position claimed to be 'friendlies', but were challenged by machine gunners, and shortly after this two North Vietnamese companies surged forward to attack the machine gun positions, and at the same time set the allied mortar positions on fire with flamethrowers.

The fighting lasted for ten hours until White's force had used up all its ammunition. With no sign of reinforcement evident, White's force abandoned the position and escaped in the direction of Kham Duc. They had covered about half the distance to Kham Duc before helicopters arrived to lift them the rest of the way.

When the survivors from Ngok Tavak reached Kham Duc the fighting there was still in its early stages, but the North Vietnamese mortars were proving especially effective, and several of the allied outposts received direct hits. Appreciating that the camp could not be reinforced any further, Westmoreland decided that the best course was to order the evacuation of the camp, and so avoid the adverse publicity which would result from the killing or capture of a sizeable force of allied troops.

On the morning of 11 May a Lockheed C-130 tactical transport aircraft of the 21st Tactical Airlift Squadron landed on Kham Duc's airstrip. South Vietnamese civilians immediately rushed onto the aircraft, overwhelming the loadmaster as the C-130 came under enemy fire, and minor damage was suffered as a result. Despite the fact that their aircraft had a flat tyre on one of its wheels, the crew of the C-130 tried to take off, but failed. So while work to repair the damaged C-130 was begun, a Fairchild C-123 twin-engined tactical transport arrived to fly the civilians out. During the afternoon US tactical warplanes were instrumental in driving back a massed assault on the main compound; napalm and cluster bombs were used to good effect as had been the case in many other episodes of this nature.

THE VIETNAM WAR

On 12 May the North Vietnamese 2nd Infantry Division and NLF 271st Regiment tightened their noose around Kham Duc, attacking and overrunning three outposts by 9:30. The USAF was tasked with completing the evacuation of Kham Duc, and while the evacuation was being undertaken, B-52 heavy bombers were summoned to pound the North Vietnamese positions around the camp with large loads of conventional ordnance. Under heavy mortar bombardment, the officers of the American Infantry Division requested immediate extraction. Men of A Company of the 1st Battalion of the 198th Light Infantry Brigade's 46th Infantry Regiment were being ferried out by a Boeing CH-47 Chinook twin-rotor helicopter when this machine was hit by anti-aircraft fire, forcing it to land under intense fire. One soldier was killed by ground fire and was left on the crashed Chinook. The evacuation of Kham Duc was complicated when Montagnard fighters and their families boarded helicopters which had been designated for the extraction of US soldiers. Men of 'A Company of the 1st Battalion of the 46th Infantry Regiment were sent in to remove the Montagnards so that they could board the helicopters instead, the decision having been taken that all the Montagnards would be evacuated by C-130 transports. One C-130 carrying Montagnards and some South Vietnamese was shot down, and all aboard were killed.

During the afternoon, as a succession of aircraft lifted off from Kham Duc airfield, helicopters of the US Army and US Marine Corps landed to evacuate what was left of these services' personnel. Though most of the camp's personnel were lifted out by air, there was not room for all and those left behind had to try to escape through the Communist lines. When the last special forces team was flown out, another C-130 landed on the airstrip carrying Major John Gallagher, Sergeant Mort Freedman and Sergeant James Lundie, who ran into the camp. Lieutenant Colonel Jay Van Clee, the pilot of the C-130, took off after it was reported that the evacuation had been completed, but on receiving reports that the three men had been left behind, Lieutenant Colonel Alfred Jeanotte landed his C-123, but no one appeared. Another C-123, piloted by Lieutenant Colonel Joe M. Jackson, landed on the airfield under North Vietnamese fire and was able to extract the men, who had been hiding in a ditch.

At 16:33 on 12 May the Kham Duc camp was abandoned and was immediately overrun by the North Vietnamese and NLF forces. Kham Duc was the second CIDG camp to be taken by Communist forces in 1968, the first having been Lang Vei, and was the last special forces camp in the north-western part of South Vietnam to be destroyed. The evacuation of Kham Duc had been undertaken amid a level of disorder verging on panic, but despite coming under heavy fire the pilots of the USAF managed to extricate most of the special forces personnel and civilians. The forces

US troops deploy during a jungle patrol.

ABOVE & RIGHT: Armourers prepare their charges before the start of a sortie.

pagodas in the mistaken belief that they would not be targeted for artillery and air attack. The fiercest fighting once again took place in Cholon. One notable event occurred on 18 June when 152 members of the NLF's Quyet Thang Regiment surrendered to South Vietnamese army forces, the largest Communist surrender of the war. The Communist action also brought more suffering to the city's civilian population: another 87,000 were rendered homeless, more than 500 were killed and 4,500 were wounded. During Phase 2 of the Tet Offensive, between 5 and 30 May 1968, US casualties amounted to 1,161 killed and 3,954 wounded, with those of the South Vietnamese being 143 killed and 643 wounded.

Phase 3 of the Communist offensive began on 17 August, and this time comprised attacks on targets in the I, II and III Corps Tactical Zones. Significantly, during this phase of the operation, only North Vietnamese forces were involved. The main offensive was preceded by attacks on border towns, these being Tay Ninh, An Loc and Loc Ninh, in an effort to lead the allies to move troops as reinforcements to these areas and so at last partially to denude the defences of the larger cities and towns which were the North Vietnamese forces' primary objectives. A North Vietnamese attack on Da Nang was pre-empted by an operation by the US Marine Corps on 16 August, but as part of their continuing effort to clear the borders of South Vietnam of allied forces, and so facilitate the infiltration of Communist forces and supplies, three regiments of the North Vietnamese army moved up against the US Special Forces camp at Bu Prang in Quang Duc province, only 3.1 miles (5km) from the Cambodian border. There were two days of combat before the North Vietnamese broke off the contact after suffering 776 killed to

involved had been in the order of some 5,000 to 10,000 Communists soldiers against slightly more than 1,760 allied personnel, and while the Communist losses remain unknown and not even estimated, the allies lost more than 270 persons killed or missing together with nine aircraft.

The Communists returned to Saigon on 25 May, launching a second wave of attacks on the city. The fighting during this phase differed from that of the Tet Mau Than and 'Mini-Tet' inasmuch as no US installations were attacked on this occasion. During this series of actions, NLF forces occupied six

THE VIETNAM WAR

the allies' figure of 116 killed (114 South Vietnamese and two US).

Saigon was once again attacked during this phase of the ongoing offensive, but on this occasion the attacks were less sustained and, once again, were defeated and driven off without difficulty. As far as the MACV was concerned, the North Vietnamese effort during August had been a complete failure, for in five weeks of combat and with the loss of some 20,000 men, they had reached, taken and held absolutely none of the objectives set for them. In this same period 700 US soldiers had been killed.

The great casualties sustained by the forces of the North Vietnamese army and NLF in the course of these extended operations was finally beginning to exert a pronounced influence on the nature of the politico-military leadership's thinking in Hanoi, and the loss of so many men and equipment for the achievement of no practical gain whatsoever merely made the situation worse. Almost certainly as an indirect if not actually direct result of their losses, and the overall pain of the 1968 campaigns, over the course of the first six months of 1969 more than 20,000 Communist troops defected to the allies, this being three times the number who had changed sides in 1968. Another indicator of the pain which the Communist forces had suffered was the directive issued on 5 April 1969 by the COSVN, which included the words 'Never again and under no circumstances are we going to risk our entire military force for just such an offensive. On the contrary, we should endeavour to preserve our military potential for future campaigns.'

The politico-military leadership in Hanoi was decidedly unhappy about the failure of the Tong Cong Kich/Tong Khoi Nghia (General Offensive, General Uprising), which had signally failed in all its objectives. Its first and most ambitious goal, to produce a general uprising, had ended in dismal failure, moreover the Border Battles of 1967 and the nine-month winter/spring campaign had resulted in between 75,000 and 85,000 North Vietnamese army and NLF troops being killed in action. While the North Vietnamese losses might be made good, given time and opportunity, the comparatively greater losses suffered by the NLF could not so easily be made good, and also struck deeply into the essentially irreplaceable infrastructure that had been built up in South Vietnam over a period of ten or more years. This is reflected in the fact that from this time onward, about one-third of the NLF's strength had to be provided by North Vietnamese troops. This had little practical effect on the conduct of the war, however, as North Vietnam had little difficulty in replenishing the depleted ranks.

In the aftermath of the Phase 1 fighting, the Communist politico-military leadership began to see that while the offensive may have failed in its primary objectives, some benefit had accrued to the Communist cause. As General Tran Do, the North Vietnamese commander in the Battle of Hue, put it: 'In all honesty, we did not achieve our main objective, which was to spur uprisings throughout the South. Still, we inflicted heavy casualties on the Americans and their puppets, and this was a big gain for us. As for making an impact in the USA, it had not been our intention – but it turned out to be a fortunate result.' Thus it was the gradually developing failure of

will among the American leadership and people in the aftermath of the Tet Offensive that was now perceived as the victory which the Communists had achieved, and this was altogether more important than any purely military success would have been.

The North Vietnamese had not anticipated the political and

A Bell UH-1 Huey helicopter of the US Army.

THE TET OFFENSIVE

A piece of US self-propelled artillery, in this instance an M110 203-mm (8-in) howitzer, in action. The rear-mounted spades stabilized the equipment in the firing position and so boosted accuracy, allowing the 200-lb (91-kg) projectile to prove devastating in plunging fire.

psychological effect the offensive would have on the US leadership and people, but now started to build a propaganda offensive on the idea of a Communist 'victory', and the start of negotiations and the diplomatic effort that went with this, which had been something to be feared in Hanoi, swiftly came to occupy a position equal to that of the military struggle.

On the other side of the DMZ, the human and material impact of the Tet Offensive on South Vietnam had been enormous. The number of civilian dead was estimated by the government at

14,300, with another 24,000 wounded, while the number of refugees within the country had increased by 630,000 over the total of almost 800,000 already rendered homeless by the war: by the end of 1968 8.33 per cent of the South Vietnamese population was living in a refugee camp. More than 70,000 homes had been destroyed in the combat, with another 30,000 more badly damaged, while South Vietnam's infrastructure had been virtually destroyed. The South Vietnamese forces had performed altogether more creditably than the MACV had thought likely, but had

suffered psychological as well as physical blows as reflected in an increase in the desertion rate from 10.5 per 1,000 men before the start of the Tet Offensive to 16.5 per 1,000 during July.

The Tet Offensive, however, also seemed to galvanize the Thieu administration into the display of greater energy. On 1 February the president declared a state of martial law, the National Assembly approving Thieu's request for general mobilization of the population on 15 June and the drafting of another 200,900 men into the armed forces by the end of the year, even though the same proposal had been rejected a mere five months earlier. This increase would bring South Vietnam's military strength to more than 900,000 men. Not ignored in this process of increasing the capability of South Vietnam's armed forces was the need to improve their administration, and this was reflected in the start of an anti-corruption campaign and administrative reform. Thieu also created a National Recovery Committee to oversee food distribution, resettlement, and the building of new housing.

Thieu also saw the opportunity to consolidate his personal power. His only real political rival was Vice President Ky, formerly the commander of the South Vietnamese air force, who had been outmanoeuvred by Thieu in the presidential election of 1967. In the aftermath of the Tet Offensive, supporters of Ky among the military and the administration were quickly removed, arrested or exiled, and there was also a crackdown on the South Vietnamese press and the restoration of some members of ex-President Ngo Dinh Diem's Can Lao party to high positions in the government and military. By the summer of 1968, Thieu had increasingly come to be known as the 'little dictator'.

Unlike most South Vietnamese, Thieu was unwilling to accept that the Americans had been taken by surprise in the Tet Offensive, and saw President Johnson's decision of 31 March to trim the bombing of North Vietnam as the first step in a secret US policy of disengagement from the Vietnam War. After a meeting with Johnson in Honolulu on 18 July, however, Thieu was somewhat bolstered by Johnson's statement that Saigon would be a full partner in all negotiations, and that the US would not support the forcible imposition of any form of government on South Vietnam.

In the USA there was an ever-widening 'credibility gap' between what the Johnson administration and the Department of Defense claimed to be the case, and what the American people perceived to be the situation. This paved the way toward an eventual feeling of national shock, other milestones in this process being the 18 February revelation by the MACV of the highest US casualty figures for a single week during the entire war, with 543 killed and 2,547 wounded; the 23 February announcement by the US Selective Service System of a new draft call for 48,000 men, the second highest of the war; and the resignation on 28 February of Robert S. McNamara as Secretary of Defense, who had overseen the escalation of the war in 1964/65 but had later turned against it.

In May 1968, as noted above, peace negotiations began between the USA and North Vietnam. The talks achieved nothing for five months until Johnson gave orders to halt the bombing of North Vietnam. The Democratic presidential candidate, Vice President Hubert Humphrey, was running against the Republican former Vice President Richard Nixon who, via an intermediary, advised Thieu to refuse to participate in the talks until after the US presidential election, claiming that he would give the South Vietnamese a better deal once he had been elected. Thieu obliged, which meant that almost no progress had been made by the time Johnson left office.

During the election Nixon promised 'peace with honor', his overarching plan being to build up the South Vietnamese forces in every respect so that they would be able to assume the primary burden in the defence of South Vietnam, and so pave the way for the gradual withdrawal of US forces. This became known as the policy of 'Vietnamization', which had the unfortunate corollary of implying that up to this time only the US forces had been protecting South Vietnam. However, it is worth noting that this was in some respects a   harking back to the thinking of the Kennedy administration, the major difference being that while Kennedy demanded the South Vietnamese fight the war themselves and seek to find ways to limit the scope of the war, Nixon was prepared to look at other options, including a major widening of the conflict.

Nixon also pursued the avenue towards possible US withdrawal by negotiation, and within South Vietnam Abrams was ordered to shift the emphasis to smaller-scale operations aimed at NLF logistics, with better use made of firepower and more co-operation with the South Vietnamese forces. Other changes which came in with the Nixon administration were a more open relationship between the administration and the media, the pursuit of a policy of détente with the USSR, and an attempt to reach a rapprochement with Communist China. This combination of policies helped to decrease global tensions, and détente led to nuclear arms reduction by both superpowers. But the Nixon administration was much disappointed that the USSR and Communist China each continued to supply North Vietnam with aid.

In September 1969 Ho Chi Minh died at the age of 79.

CHAPTER NINE
EXCURSIONS & THE FALL OF SOUTH VIETNAM

A C-130 Hercules transport lands on an extemporised airstrip with reinforcements or supplies to keep up the momentum of the misconceived offensive into eastern Cambodia.

America had by now lost the Vietnam War, but failed to understand the fact, pressing ahead with its efforts to stem the Communist tide and preserve South Vietnam as a 'democratic' state, whose defeat of Communism would prevent the start of the much-feared domino-effect loss of other non-Communist states in the region, starting with Cambodia and

Laos, then proceeding to Thailand and finally to Malaysia and possibly Burma.

In 1955 Prince Norodom Sihanouk had proclaimed Cambodia to be neutral, but the North Vietnamese and National Front for the Liberation of South Vietnam used Cambodian soil for the establishment of major bases, in the belief that in this neutral state they would be free from attack. The southern

portion of the Ho Chi Minh Trail also extended through the eastern part of Cambodia. Sihanouk was prepared to put up with the presence of the Communist forces as the price he had to pay to avoid being dragged more fully into the Vietnam War. Under pressure from the USA, however, Sihanouk revised this policy during 1969, making it clear that the North Vietnamese and NLF were no longer welcome. The newly inaugurated President Richard M. Nixon took the opportunity to launch a huge bombing campaign, Operation Menu, against the Communist sanctuary areas on the Cambodian side of the border with South Vietnam, which violated a long succession of pronouncements from Washington supporting Cambodian neutrality.

Nixon communicated with Sihanouk in April 1969, assuring the Cambodian leader that the USA fully respected 'the sovereignty, neutrality and territorial integrity of the Kingdom of Cambodia'. But over a time lasting some 14 months, US warplanes began to drop something in the order of 2.75 million tons of ordnance on eastern Cambodia, although this massive exercise in the use of major air power was carefully concealed from the US people. In 1970 Sihanouk was deposed by a pro-US army officer, General Lon Nol. The country's borders were closed, and US and South Vietnamese forces launched incursions into Cambodia to attack

THE VIETNAM WAR

been raped and/or sexually molested, beaten, tortured or maimed, and some of the bodies were also mutilated. The reaction to the incident by the Nixon administration was seen as both callous and indifferent, generating more support for the anti-war movement.

The South Vietnamese launched Operation Lam Son 719, which was intended to cut the Ho Chi Minh Trail inside Laos, the offensive being a clear violation of the neutrality of Laos, which neither side respected. Encountering resistance stronger than they had anticipated, the South Vietnamese forces retreated in a confused rout, fleeing back toward South Vietnam along roads littered with

LEFT: A cache of ammunition. US warplanes were committed to destroy abandoned equipment, including tanks, to prevent them from falling into Communist hands.

BELOW: Abandoned trucks found by men of Company C, 1st Battalion 5th Cavalry, 1st Cavalry Division, in a large NVA military complex known as 'The City', located in the Fishhook area of the Vietnam border with Cambodia.

North Vietnamese and NLF bases and buy time for South Vietnam to rebuild its capabilities to survive against the Communist forces as the US military commitment was cut back. The combination of the US bombing, followed by the coup d'état, destabilized Cambodia, thereby increasing the level of popular support for the Khmer Rouge, the indigenous Cambodian analogue to the NLF.

The invasion of Cambodia triggered a great surge of protest in the USA. Four students were killed by National Guardsmen at Kent State University during a protest in Ohio, and this provoked public outrage, as too had the revelation of the My Lai massacre, this being the mass murder of from 347 to 504 unarmed South Vietnamese citizens, most of them civilians and the majority of them women and children, by an element of the US Army on 16 March 1968, in the hamlets of My Lai and My Khe during the Vietnam War. Before being killed, some of the victims had

the operation were killed or captured, and the operation was a complete failure. It also emphasized the complete failure, up to this time, of the concept of Vietnamization.

During 1971 Australia and New Zealand withdrew their troops. The number of US forces was further reduced to 196,700, with a deadline to remove another 45,000 by February 1972. As peace protests spread across the USA, there was a comparable and parallel development of total disillusionment within the ranks of the draftee troops in South Vietnam. During this period drug use, already a major problem, increased rapidly, race relations grew tense, especially as it became clear

ABOVE: Men of the 409th Radio Research Detachment aboard an M113 armoured personnel carrier during the 1970 Cambodian Incursion.

RIGHT: A member of Company C, 75th Ranger Battalion, in the vicinity of Da Lat airfield, Vietnam, aboard a Bell HU-1D Iroquois helicopter in March 1970.

their own dead. When they ran out of fuel, South Vietnamese soldiers abandoned their vehicles and attempted to force their way onto US helicopters sent to evacuate the wounded. Many South Vietnamese soldiers even hung onto the skids of the helicopters in their desperation to escape. US warplanes were committed over the rout to destroy abandoned equipment, including tanks, and so prevent them from falling into Communist hands. Some 50 per cent of South Vietnamese troops committed to

THE VIETNAM WAR

regardless, but US air power came to the rescue with the launch of Operation Linebacker, and the offensive was halted. It became clear, however, that without US air power South Vietnam could not survive. The last remaining US ground troops were withdrawn in August, although there were still civilian and military advisers in South Vietnam.

Linebacker was the designation of the air interdiction campaign

LEFT: The 79th Engineers check hundreds of NVA supply crates, left behind by a fleeing enemy in The City.

BELOW: US Army HU-1H helicopters, with an AH-1G Cobra trailing behind, return from patrol in the jungles of Vietnam and Cambodia. After refuelling at Bu Dop Special Forces Camp, 80 miles (129km) north of Saigon, they resumed their guard of resupply operations. 15 May 1970.

that the proportion of the draftees were from the poorer, and most especially black, sectors of the US population, and the number of soldiers disobeying their officers rose alarmingly: this latter also involved an increase in the incidence of 'fragging', or the murder of unpopular officers with fragmentation grenades.

The concept of Vietnamization was again tested by the Communist forces' 'Nguyen Hue' Offensive (known in the West as the Easter Offensive) in the spring 1972. This was a huge conventional invasion of South Vietnam by the Communist forces, which swiftly and easily overran the northern provinces of South Vietnam and, in co-ordination with other forces, attacked the western part of South Vietnam from their base areas in Cambodia, threatening to cut the country in half. US troop withdrawals continued

EXCURSIONS & THE FALL OF SOUTH VIETNAM

undertaken by the warplanes of the US 7th Air Force and the US Navy's Task Force 77 against North Vietnam between 9 May and 23 October 1972. Its purpose was to halt or slow the transportation of supplies and materials for the Nguyen Hue Offensive. Thus Linebacker became the first continuous bombing effort against North Vietnam since the halt of Rolling Thunder, ordered by President Lyndon B. Johnson in November 1968.

At 12:00 on 30 March 1972, 30,000 North Vietnamese troops, supported by regiments of tanks and artillery, moved south across the DMZ separating the two Vietnams. Comprising three divisions, the invasion force caught the forces of the South Vietnamese army and the limited number of US troops still in the theatre completely by surprise and wholly unprepared. The North Vietnamese force struck the defensive positions of the South Vietnamese 3rd Infantry Division and threw the

formation into disarray. South Vietnamese forces then fell back, and there developed a race between the antagonists to the bridges at Dong Ha and Cam Low. By 4 April, the South Vietnamese had managed to cobble together a new defensive line which checked the North Vietnamese, albeit only temporarily. Although the conventional attack by the North Vietnamese, which included the

extensive use of armour and considerable quantities of medium and heavy artillery, riveted the attention of the allies on the northern provinces, it was only the first of three such operations launched during the spring of 1972. On 5 April, a North Vietnamese force of 20,000 crossed the border from their sanctuaries in Cambodia in another three-division force to attack Binh Long province to the north of

Saigon. They quickly seized the town of Loc Ninh before surrounding the town of An Loc, cutting the road to the capital. On 12 April the North Vietnamese struck again, this time moving in from the eastern part of Laos and seizing a series of border outposts around Dak To in Kontum province in the Central Highlands. The North Vietnamese then pushed to the east in the direction of the provincial seat of Kontum. Hanoi had initiated the offensive to coincide with the winter monsoon, when continuous rain and low cloud cover would render air support most difficult.

The USA's first response to the offensive was tardy, indifferent and confused. The Department of Defense was not unduly alarmed, and the US ambassador and the commander of the US forces in South Vietnam, General Creighton W. Abrams, were both out of the country. President Nixon's initial response was to consider a three-day attack by Boeing B-52 Stratofortress heavy bombers on Hanoi and the port city of Haiphong, but he was persuaded by the national security adviser, Dr. Henry Kissinger, to reconsider on the basis that a heavy-handed US response might jeopardize the first Strategic Arms Limitation Treaty with the USSR, due to be formalized in May. Another stumbling block was Abrams' desire to make use of all the available bombers, with their all-weather navigation and attack capabilities, to support the South Vietnamese defence.

Nixon and Kissinger each thought the plan proposed by the Joint Chiefs-of-Staff to be unimaginative and

ABOVE: Men of the 2nd Battalion, 12th Cavalry, Companies D and E, uncover tons of ammunition and equipment in lightly camouflaged bunkers, 80 per cent of which are above ground. Seven men were lost and 27 wounded in the operation.

LEFT: 23 May 1970. The site of an enemy grenade factory, destroyed by air strikes 6 miles (10km) north-east of Krek, Cambodia.

EXCURSIONS & THE FALL OF SOUTH VIETNAM

insufficiently aggressive. On 4 April, Nixon authorized that the bombing of North Vietnam, which up to now had been limited to retaliatory raids just above the DMZ, as far north as the 18th parallel. To prevent a total rout of the South Vietnamese forces and bolster US prestige during a forthcoming summit meeting with Leonid Brezhnev, the Soviet premier, Nixon decided to risk a massive escalation of force.

At the start of the Communist forces' offensive there had been fewer than 10,000 US troops still left in South Vietnam, and most of this now very

limited military force was scheduled to leave within the next six months. The number of US warplanes stationed in South-East Asia was less than half that of its peak strength in 1968/69, the strength of the USAF in South Vietnam being three squadrons of McDonnell Douglas F-4 Phantom II multi-role warplanes and one squadron of Cessna A-37 Dragonfly light attack aircraft, totalling 76 machines. There were another 114 tactical warplanes at bases in Thailand, and also 83 B-52 bombers at U-Tapao airbase in Thailand and at Andersen Air Force Base on Guam

Island in the Marianas. The US Navy's Task Force 77, operating in the Gulf of Tonkin, had four aircraft carriers assigned to it, but only two were available at any one time to conduct operations. Its air wings totalled about 140 aircraft.

US and South Vietnamese warplanes had been supporting the defence as and when the weather permitted since the start of the Communist offensive. These attacks were flown in support of the South Vietnamese forces, and included the missions flown by the air wings of the carriers *Coral Sea* and *Hancock*. But the steady prevalence of adverse weather had severely trimmed the ability of the US warplanes to aid the South Vietnamese in halting the North Vietnamese onslaught. By 6 April the US air forces had been put on a higher state of alert at naval and air bases around the world, and as US forces were put on alert, ships and aircraft began to redeploy to South-East Asia.

The USAF deployed 176 F-4 Phantom and 12 Republic F-105 Thunderchief strike fighters from bases in South Korea and the USA to Thailand between 1 April and 11 May in Operation Constant Guard, and between 4 April and 23 May Operation Bullet Shot saw the despatch, by the Strategic Air Command, of 124 B-52 bombers from the USA to Guam, bringing the total B-52 strength available for operations to 209. The US Navy cut short the in-port periods for the carriers *Kitty Hawk* and *Constellation*, and ordered the *Midway* and *Saratoga* to augment the US 7th Fleet so that four or more carrier air wings were available for the conduct of simultaneous missions. The 7th Fleet in the waters off

THE VIETNAM WAR

South-East Asia thus rose from 84 to 138 ships.

USAF tactical attacks against North Vietnam north of the 20th parallel were authorized on 5 April as 'Freedom Train'. The first major attack by B-52s on targets in North Vietnam was flown on 10 April, when 12 of these heavy bombers, supported by 53 tactical warplanes, attacked petroleum storage facilities around Vinh. By 12 April, Nixon had informed Kissinger that he had decided on a more far-ranging and aggressive bombing campaign which would include attacks on Hanoi and Haiphong. On the following day, 18 B-52 bombers struck Thanh Hoa's Bai Thuong airfield. Three more days then followed before another attack was delivered, in this instance flown by 18 bombers in a pre-dawn attack against an oil tank farm outside Haiphong.

They were followed by the daylight attacks of more than 100 tactical warplanes on targets around Hanoi and Haiphong. In the period 6–15 April US warplanes also struck and destroyed the Paul Doumer and Thanh Hoa bridges and the Yen Vien railway marshalling yard. This marked the introduction of laser-guided bombs against strategic targets in North Vietnam, both bridges having previously been attacked unsuccessfully with conventional bombs and even missiles. The B-52 bombers were then withdrawn from operations in the north, their missions to be limited to the southern panhandle when they returned in June.

By the middle of the month almost the whole of North Vietnam had been cleared for bombing raids for the first time in over three years. USAF and US Navy commanders and pilots were

Lt Col Stratton, commander 23rd Tactical Air Support Squadron, scans the ground for hostile forces during a Forward Air Control mission in September 1972.

EXCURSIONS & THE FALL OF SOUTH VIETNAM

US troops in a helicopter flying over South Vietnam.

relieved that Nixon had not followed Johnson's lead and interfered with the planning and execution of the attacks, whose planning was thus left to local commanders, whose remit was also somewhat less constrained than it had been in Rolling Thunder. Between 1 May and 30 June B-52 bombers, tactical warplanes and gunships flew 18,000 sorties against formidable anti-aircraft artillery defences with the loss of 29 aircraft.

The USA now also began to interdict the flow of supplies into North Vietnam. On 20 April Kissinger and Brezhnev met secretly in Moscow and, not wanting the USSR's increasingly

normalizing relations with the West to be jeopardized, and also wary of the USA's improving relationship with China, Brezhnev agreed to exert pressure on North Vietnam to end the offensive and embark on a programme of realistic negotiation in Paris.

Brezhnev then arranged for another secret meeting, this time between Kissinger and the senior North Vietnamese negotiator, Le Duc Tho, on 2 May in Paris. On the assigned day, the two men met for a session that Kissinger later described as 'brutal and insulting'; sensing that North Vietnam was on the verge of victory, Le Duc Tho was not prepared to make concessions.

As a result of this meeting and the fall of Quang Tri City, Nixon was now prepared to raise the stakes, stating that 'the bastards have never been bombed like they're going to be bombed this time'.

On 27 April, the South Vietnamese defences in Quang Tri province began to fail, and as a result of conflicting orders, a swelling number of South Vietnamese units joined the southward flow of refugees, in the process abandoning Quang Tri City. The North Vietnamese entered the city on the same day as the meeting between Kissinger and Le Duc Tho took place. The North Vietnamese offensive had by this time become a general offensive, being undertaken simultaneously on three fronts by the equivalent of 15 divisions and 600 tanks. As the North Vietnamese continued to gain ground in three of South Vietnam's four military regions, the US Joint Chiefs-of-Staff updated their contingency plans for the resumption of bombing in the north and recommended it to the president, who approved it on 8 May.

Shortly after his inauguration, Nixon had ordered the preparation of a contingency plan known as Operation Duck Hook, designed to guarantee the defeat and include an invasion of North Vietnam as well as the mining of that country's major ports. The plan had been shelved at the time as too extreme, but had not been forgotten. The US Navy had also been updating its own contingency plans for just such a mining operation since 1965. On 5 May, the president ordered the Joint Chiefs-of-Staff to prepare the launch of the aerial mining portion of Duck Hook within three

THE VIETNAM WAR

days, under the designation of Operation Pocket Money.

At precisely 09:00 on 8 May, six Vought A-7 Corsair IIs and three Grumman A-6 Intruder attack warplanes of the US Navy flew over Haiphong harbour and dropped 36 1,000-lb (454-kg) Mk 52 and Mk 55 mines into the water. The aircraft were themselves protected from attack by North Vietnamese fighters by the long-ranger guided missiles of the cruisers *Chicago* and *Long Beach*, and by flights of F-4 Phantom warplanes. The precise timing of the strike became apparent when Nixon simultaneously delivered a televised speech, explaining the

escalation to the US people. The mines were activated five days after their delivery in order to allow any vessels then in port to escape without damage. Over the next three days other carrier aircraft laid 11,000 more mines into North Vietnamese secondary harbours, effectively blockading all maritime commerce.

Both before and during Pocket Money, Nixon and Kissinger had been concerned about the possible Soviet and Communist Chinese reactions to this escalation of the war. Hours before the president's speech announcing the mining, Kissinger had delivered to the Soviet ambassador, Anatoly Dobrynin, a

letter setting out the US plan, but also making clear Nixon's willingness to proceed with the summit. Although both the USSR and China publicly denounced the US operation, they were not willing to jeopardize their thawing relationship with the USA, so the requests of the North Vietnamese for support and aid received only a cool reception in Moscow and Beijing. Thus US diplomacy had proved successful and the USA was free to react as it pleased.

Operation Linebacker, as the new interdiction campaign was designated, had a quartet of objectives: the isolation of North Vietnam from outside sources

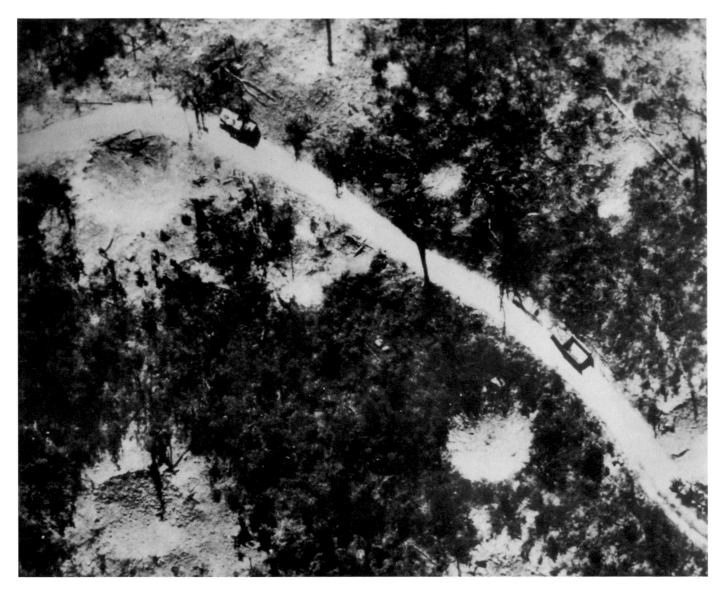

Laos: an aerial view of the Ho Chi Minh Trail, showing a North Vietnamese truck convoy destroyed by the US Air Force circa 1970.

yards at Yen Vien and the Paul Doumer Bridge on the northern outskirts of Hanoi. Some 414 sorties were flown on this first day of the operation, and the aircraft were met by the most concentrated period of air-to-air combat during the Vietnam War, resulting in the loss of 11 North Vietnamese Mikoyan-Guryevich fighters (four MiG-21 and seven MiG-17 machines) and two USAF F-4s. Heavy anti-aircraft artillery fire and more than 100 surface-to-air missiles also brought down two US Navy aircraft.

By the end of the month the US attacks had destroyed 13 bridges along the rail lines running from Hanoi to the Chinese border, and another four between Hanoi and Haiphong, the latter including the notorious 'Dragon's Jaw' across the Song Ma river near Thanh Hoa, while several more bridges were brought down along the rail line leading to the south toward the DMZ. The US targeting then shifted to the petroleum and oil storage and transportation networks, and also to North Vietnam's airfields, making an immediate impact on the battlefield in South Vietnam. North Vietnamese artillery fire was reduced by 50 per cent between 9 May and 1 June, this reflecting not so much an immediate shortage of artillery rounds but rather the desire to conserve ammunition, although US intelligence analysts believed that North Vietnamese had enough stockpiled supplies to sustain their campaigns throughout the autumn.

The intensity of the bombing campaign was reflected by a significant increase in the number of attack-and-support sorties in South-East Asia as a whole, this increase being from 4,237 for

of supply by destroying railroad bridges and rolling stock in and around Hanoi and north-east toward the Chinese frontier; the targeting of primary storage areas and marshalling yards; the destruction of storage and trans-shipment points; and finally the elimination or at least the severe damaging of North Vietnam's air defence system. With nearly 85 per cent of North Vietnam's supplies reaching the country by sea, and therefore checked by Pocket Money, the Nixon administration and the Department of

Defense believed the effort would result in the total severance of North Vietnam's lines of physical communication with its Communist allies. Communist China alone shipped an average of 22,000 tons of supplies per month along the two rail lines and eight major roads connecting the two countries.

Linebacker began on 10 May with major bombing attacks on North Vietnam by the tactical warplanes of the 7th Air Force and Task Force 77. The targets included the railroad switching

THE VIETNAM WAR

all services, including the South Vietnamese air force during the month before the North Vietnamese invasion, to 27,745 flown in support of the South Vietnamese forces from the beginning of April to the end of June. B-52 bombers provided an additional 1,000 sorties during the same period. North Vietnam was certainly feeling the pressure.

The Linebacker missions included the first large-scale use of precision-guided munitions. As well as its interdiction of the road and rail systems of North Vietnam, moreover, Linebacker also systematically attacked North Vietnam's air defence system. The North Vietnamese air force, with a strength of some 200 fighters, fought back tenaciously against these attacks, but US Navy pilots gained a 6/1 kill/loss ratio in May and June, following which North Vietnamese pilots tended to avoid naval aircraft. The USAF was opposed by MiG-21, MiG-17 and J-6 (Chinese version of the MiG-19) fighters, and experienced almost a 1/1 kill/loss ratio through the first two months of the campaign, as seven of its eventual 24 Linebacker air-to-air losses took place without any North Vietnamese losses in a 12-day period between 24 June and 5 July.

USAF pilots were hampered in their use of the outdated four-aircraft 'finger four' tactical formation, unlike the US Navy's more modern to-aircraft 'loose deuce', as mandated by service doctrine. Also contributing to the imparity was the USAF's lack of air combat training against dissimilar aircraft, a deficient early-warning system, and ECM pod formations that mandated strict adherence to formation flying. During August, however, the introduction of

A Sikorsky CH-53 Sea Stallion helicopter comes in to deliver a tractor to a US combat base.

real-time early warning systems increased aircrew combat experience, and degraded North Vietnamese ground control interception capabilities that reversed the trend to a more favourable 4/1 kill/loss ratio.

Linebacker was also notable for other first-time instances. On the initial

EXCURSIONS & THE FALL OF SOUTH VIETNAM

The fight for freedom in Laos. Laos played a critical role in the Vietnam War, especially since supplies from North Vietnam to its warring troops moved primarily along the Ho Chi Minh Trail that passed through Laos. Much fighting occurred along this trail and in Laos' surrounding regions while, at the same time, North Vietnam was actively helping the Pathet Lao take over the country. Thousands of poorly-equipped Hmong fought this war against terrible odds, many of them losing their lives in unpublicized battles in which much of Laos' limited infrastructure was destroyed, leaving its population to live in caves.

day of the operation, US Navy Lieutenant Randall H. Cunningham and his radar intercept officer, Lieutenant (JG) William P. Driscoll became the first US air aces of the Vietnam War when they shot down their fifth North Vietnamese fighter. On 28 August, the USAF also acquired its first ace when Captain Richard S. Ritchie downed his fifth North Vietnamese fighter. Twelve days later, Captain Charles B. DeBellevue (Ritchie's rear-seater during four of his five victories) downed two more North Vietnamese fighters, bringing his total to six. On 13 October another weapons officer, Captain Jeffrey S. Feinstein, was credited with his fifth Mikoyan-Guryevich fighter, making him the final USAF ace.

The checked offensive in South Vietnam and the devastation in North Vietnam had by now convinced the North Vietnamese to return to the bargaining table by early August. The meetings produced new North Vietnamese concessions, so helping to break the deadlock that had plagued negotiations since their start in 1968. North Vietnam no longer demanded the removal of President Nguyen Van Thieu in favour of a coalition government in which the National Liberation Front would participate. With the diplomatic impasse broken, Nixon ordered a halt to all bombing above the 20th parallel on 23 October, a change which meant that Hanoi and Haiphong were not longer targets, and halted the Linebacker campaign.

For several reasons Linebacker succeeded where Rolling Thunder had failed, the most important of which were President Nixon's decisiveness and the granting of greater latitude to the professionals in targeting the forceful and appropriately used weight of American air power, and the availability of new technology to make Linebacker truly effective.

During and immediately after the North Vietnamese ground offensive, the US air forces had flown 18,000 sorties in South Vietnam's four northern provinces and had delivered 40,000 tons of ordnance in the defence of An Loc. Between March and May, the sortie rate for the B-52 force had risen from 700 to 2,200 per month and the heavy bombers had dropped 57,000 tons of ordnance in Quang Tri province alone. During Freedom Train and Linebacker proper, the B-52 bombers had dropped 150,237 tons of bombs on the north, while USAF and US Navy tactical warplanes had flown 1,216 sorties and dropped another 5,000 tons of ordnance.

From the start of Freedom Train in April to the end of June 1972, some 52 US aircraft were lost over North Vietnam in the form of 17 to surface-to-air missiles, 11 to anti-aircraft artillery, three to small arms fire, 14 to fighters, and seven to unknown causes, the South Vietnamese and the North Vietnamese losing 10 and 63 aircraft respectively over the same period. North Vietnam claimed that it had shot down 651 aircraft and had sunk or set ablaze 80 US warships.

Linebacker had played a crucial role in blunting the northern offensive by drying up its vital sources of supply. By this time the North Vietnamese army

THE VIETNAM WAR

continued support for South Vietnam and to force North Vietnam back to the negotiating table, Nixon ordered the launch of Operation Linebacker II, a massive bombing of Hanoi and Haiphong, the offensive destroying much of the remaining economic and industrial capacity of North Vietnam. At the same time Nixon exerted pressure on Thieu to accept the terms of the agreement, threatening to conclude a bilateral peace deal and cut off US aid.

On 15 January 1973, Nixon announced the suspension of all offensive action against North Vietnam, and the so-called Paris Peace Accords on 'Ending the War and Restoring Peace in Vietnam' were signed on 27 January,

LEFT: Laos: An attack on the positions of members of General Vang Pao's band. During the 1960s and 1970s Vang, an ethnic Hmong, commanded the Secret Army, a highly-effective CIA-trained and supported force that fought against the Pathet Lao and People's Army of Vietnam (PAVN).

BELOW: A group of Pathet Lao soldiers eat their morning meal before accompanying visiting journalists deeper into their territory. Traditionally, the Laotians ate with their hands, but those who have been trained in Hanoi or who had been in contact with the North Vietnamese, used chopsticks. They are wearing Chinese-style caps, baggy green uniforms, and are armed with Russian or Chinese-made weapons.

had become a conventional military force, and as such became reliant on a formal logistical system which proved itself vulnerable to air attack. By September, North Vietnamese imports were something in the order of 35 to 50 per cent below the figure in May, indicating that air interdiction had clearly worked.

The war was the central issue of the 1972 presidential election. Nixon's opponent, George McGovern, campaigned on a platform of withdrawal from Vietnam, and during this period Kissinger continued secret negotiations with North Vietnam's Le Duc Tho. In October 1972, they reached an agreement, but President Thieu demanded enormous changes. When North Vietnam revealed the details of the agreement, the Nixon administration claimed that the North Vietnamese were seeking to embarrass the president, and the negotiations once again became deadlocked. North Vietnam demanded changes, and to demonstrate his

EXCURSIONS & THE FALL OF SOUTH VIETNAM

RIGHT: Members of the Laotian People's Liberation Army (Pathet Lao) attack an artillery position of Thai invasion troops at Ben Ton.

BELOW: Laotian freedom fighters attack a position held by members of the Laos Special Forces, a unit belonging to the American Secret Service. December 1971.

officially ending direct US involvement in the Vietnam War. A ceasefire was declared across South Vietnam, but North Vietnamese forces were allowed to remain on South Vietnamese territory; US prisoners-of-war were released; and the agreement guaranteed the territorial integrity of Vietnam and, like the Geneva Conference of 1954, called for national elections in the north and south. The Paris Peace Accords were based on a 60-day period for the total withdrawal of US forces.

The South Vietnamese were provided with massive quantities of new equipment, and their armed forces became the fourth largest in the world. Nixon promised Thieu that he would use US air power to support his government, but the scandals into which the Nixon administration had by now fallen combined with the war-weariness of the US people to make this impossible. Thus the balance of power swayed decisively from South Vietnam, supported by the USA, to North Vietnam.

In December 1974 the US Congress enacted the Foreign Assistance Act of 1974, which provided 'that after June 30, 1976, no military assistance shall be furnished to South Vietnam unless authorized under the Foreign Assistance Act of 1961 or the Foreign Military Sales Act'. The act fixed the numbers of US military personnel who could be stationed in South Vietnam as 4,000 within six months of enactment, reducing to 3,000 within one year. With Nixon's resignation as a result of the Watergate scandal, the newly installed President Gerald Ford signed the act into law. However, the act was not to come into force until 1976, and was thus

THE VIETNAM WAR

never implemented as South Vietnam had been defeated by this time.

By 1975 the army of South Vietnam was considerably larger than that of North Vietnam. This is a numerical tally, however, and in no way reflects the comparative combat capabilities of the two sides, for the North Vietnamese army was altogether better organized, more capably trained, highly determined, and well-supplied with the weapons it needed for its particular concept of conventional war. In South Vietnam, on the other hand, the training and discipline of the army saw the steady collapse of the country into chaos. This reflected the fact that the withdrawal of the US military had devastated an economy almost wholly reliant on US financial support and the presence within South Vietnam of very large numbers of US troops.

Between the signing of the Paris Peace Accords early in 1973 and a time late in 1974, both antagonists had been satisfied with small-scale operations. The North Vietnamese became ever more impatient with the Thieu regime during this time, however, for Thieu steadfastly refused to move toward the national elections demanded in the Peace Accords, and the North Vietnamese were worried that, in these circumstances, the USA might once again come to the aid of South Vietnam should North Vietnam begin a large-scale offensive.

Late in 1974 the politico-military leadership in Hanoi authorized a limited offensive from Cambodia into Phuoc Long province. This was intended to resolve local logistical problems, gauge the reaction of the South Vietnamese army and determine if the US would in fact return and intervene once more. Late in December 1974 and early in January 1975 the offensive quickly overran Phuoc Long province, and in North Vietnam there was great relief that US air power did not return, the speed of this success leading to a North Vietnamese reassessment of its strategy. The conduct of operations in the Central Highlands were allocated to General Van Tien Dung to take Pleiku.

On 10 March 1975 'Campaign 275' was initiated as a limited offensive into the Central Highlands, supported by tanks and heavy artillery. The target was Ban Me Thuot, in Daklak province. If the town could be taken, the provincial capital of Pleiku and the road to the coast would be exposed for a planned campaign in 1976. The South Vietnamese army was routed, yet again, its forces collapsing on 11 March. Van asked for authorization to take Pleiku immediately and then turn his attention to Kontum, arguing that with two months of good weather before the start of the monsoon it would be irresponsible to not take advantage of the situation.

President Thieu now committed a major strategic error: fearful that his forces would be cut off in the north by the Communist offensive, he ordered a retreat. But in what soon became a repeat of Lam Son 719, the withdrawal soon became a rout. Most South Vietnamese formations and units simply fled, but isolated units fought

Welcomed as liberators, units of the Pathet Lao armed forces arrive in a Laotian village after successfully overcoming opposing forces.

247

to Hue. Civilian refugees flooded the airport and the docks hoping to escape, and some swam out to sea to reach boats and barges anchored offshore. In the confusion, routed South Vietnamese soldiers fired on civilians to make way for their own retreat. On 31 March Hue fell, and even as this was happening the North Vietnamese rocketed Da Nang and its airport. By 28 March some 35,000 North Vietnamese soldiers were ready to attack Da Nang, but two days later 100,000 leaderless South Vietnamese troops surrendered. With the fall of Da Nang the defence of the Central Highlands and northern provinces came to an end.

With the northern half of the country under its control, the Politburo ordered General Van to launch the final offensive against Saigon. The operational plan for the Ho Chi Minh Campaign called for the capture of Saigon before 1 May. Hanoi wished to avoid the coming monsoon and prevent

ABOVE: Loc Ninh, Vietnam, the scene of the general POW release in February 1973. Here, Viet Cong prisoners-of-war are gathered together in a group prior to their release.

RIGHT: Loc Ninh, Vietnam: American POWs are briefed prior to their release.

desperately. Pleiku and Kontum were abandoned as the South Vietnamese forces in these areas pulled back to the coast, their columns interspersed and impeded by hordes of refugees. As the North Vietnamese forces approached, there was panic, and most officers deserted their men. The troops and civilians were shelled steadily by the North Vietnamese, and by 1 April the 'column of tears' had been destroyed.

On 20 March Thieu reversed his thinking and ordered that Hue must be held at all costs, but his orders were contradictory and confused. As the North Vietnamese launched their attack, panic once again ensued and the South Vietnamese resistance crumbled. On 22 March the North Vietnamese laid siege

THE VIETNAM WAR

any redeployment of South Vietnamese forces defending the capital. Northern forces, their morale boosted by their recent victories, rolled on, taking Nha Trang, Cam Ranh, and Da Lat.

On 7 April three North Vietnamese divisions attacked Xuan Loc, a mere 40 miles (64 km) to the east of Saigon, but met determined resistance from the South Vietnamese 18th Infantry Division. For two weeks, severe fighting raged as the South Vietnamese made a last-ditch effort to block the North Vietnamese advance on Saigon. On 21 April the exhausted garrison surrendered. Thieu resigned on the same day, declaring that the USA had betrayed South Vietnam. He departed for Taiwan on 25 April, leaving control of the South Vietnamese government, such as it was, in the hands of General Duong Van Minh.

At the same time, North Vietnamese tanks reached Bien Hoa and turned toward Saigon against only limited resistance. By the end of April, the South Vietnamese army had everywhere collapsed. Thousand of refugees streamed southward, ahead of the main Communist onslaught. On 27 April some 100,000 North Vietnamese troops encircled Saigon, defended by a mere 30,000 demoralized South Vietnamese soldiers. The North Vietnamese shelled the airport and forced its closure, and with the air exit closed, large numbers of civilians found they had no way out. There followed a total breakdown of order in Saigon as civilians, troops and government officials fought to leave the city as martial law was declared. US helicopters began to airlift US, South Vietnamese and foreign nationals from various parts of the city and also from the US Embassy compound.

Eventually launched on 29 April, Operation Frequent Wind had been delayed until the last, the US ambassador, Graham Martin, having felt that Saigon could be held as a political settlement was arranged. Within the higher levels of the US government, as among the American people, there was a general belief that South Vietnam was facing obliteration. On 23 President Ford gave a televised speech and announced the termination of all US aid as the Vietnam War was over. Frequent Wind continued on a 24-hour-a-day basis as North Vietnamese tanks broke through the city's outer defences. In the early hours of 30 April the last US Marines were lifted from the embassy by helicopter as civilians swamped the perimeter and poured into the grounds. Many of them had been employed by the Americans and were left to their fate.

Later that same day, North Vietnamese troops swept through the last of the defence to take key buildings and installations. Thieu's successor, President Duong Van Minh, attempted to surrender, but the local North Vietnamese commander told him he had nothing left to surrender and Minh issued his last command, ordering all South Vietnamese troops to lay down their arms.

Among the military forces involved, the Vietnam War had cost South Vietnam some 250,000 dead and 1.17 million wounded, the USA 58,209 dead, about 2,000 missing and some 305,000 wounded, South Korea 4,900 dead and 11,000 wounded, Australia 520 dead and 2,400 wounded, and New Zealand 37 dead and 187 wounded. North Vietnam and the NLF had lost about 1.1 million dead and more than 600,000 wounded.

Thus the allies had lost about 314,000 dead and about 1.49 million wounded, while the Communists had lost 1.1 million dead and more than 604,000 wounded. To these military casualties have to be added the civilians losses, which were in the order of 2 to 5.1 million Vietnamese, about 700,000 Cambodians and 50,000 Laotians.

Major Floyd J. Thompson is reunited with his wife Alyce after being held in POW captivity for nine years, the longest period endured by any American fighting man in Vietnam.

INDEX

A

AA (anti-aircraft) artillery 88, 90, 93
Abrams, General Creighton W. 113, 145, 152, 193, 224, 231, 237
Acheson, Dean 17
Agency for International Development (US AID) 54
Air Component Command 80
Allies' South-East Asia Command 16
An Khe 108, 115, 209
An Loc 228, 237, 244
Anti-war movement 10, 150, 151, 198, 221
Ap Bac, Battle of 43, 44, 45
Armed Services Committee of the US Senate 92
Army Airborne School, Fort Benning, Georgia 109, 110, 113, 114
Army Aviation School, Fort Rucker, Alabama 110
Asheville-class patrol gunboat 143
August Revolution (1945) 15

B

B-40 (RPG) grenade-launcher 204
Bao Dai, Emperor 15, 18, 21, 31, 33
Bell UH-1 Iroquois 'Huey' helicopter 111, 113, 134, 158, 167, 192
Bien Hoa airbase 102, 103, 157, 212, 249
Binh Gia, Battle of 60, 61, 62, 63, 64, 65
Binh Long 154, 173, 206, 236
Boeing B-52 Stratofortress 78, 83, 91, 99, 100, 101, 123, 124, 125, 130, 138, 139, 161, 168, 184, 219, 227, 237, 238, 239, 240, 243, 244
Boeing CH-46 Sea Knight 172
Boeing CH-47 Chinook 107, 111, 149, 227
Boeing KC-130 tanker 175
Boeing KC-135 Stratotanker 89, 221
Bon Homme Richard, USS 51
Border battles (1967) 153, 154, 206, 229
Brezhnev, Leonid 238, 240
British Indian 20th Infantry Division 16
Brown, Colonel T.W. 117, 121, 123, 124
Buddhists, suppression of 35, 36, 46, 58, 60, 203
Bundy, McGeorge 47, 66
Bundy, William P. 65
Bunker, Ellsworth 151, 152, 198

C

Cabildo, USS 106
Cambodia 8, 9, 12, 13, 18, 22, 32, 37, 88, 105, 114, 117, 129, 132, 133, 138, 141, 144, 145, 146, 151, 155, 166, 168, 171, 173, 194, 208, 224, 232, 233, 235, 236, 247, 249
Camp Holloway 66
'Campaign 275' 247
Cam Ranh Bay 144, 147, 249
CAP (Combat Air Patrol) 89
Castries, General Christian de C 29
Central Highlands, South Vietnam 97, 98, 100, 108, 130, 135, 138, 153, 156, 157, 168, 169, 225, 237, 247, 248
Central Intelligence Agency (CIA) 14, 46, 46, 47, 49, 79, 82, 93, 149, 182, 197
Central Office for South Vietnam (COSVN) 141, 201, 204, 229
Cessna A-37 Dragonfly 148, 157, 238
Cessna L-19 (later O-1) Bird Dog 109
Chaisson, Brigadier General John R. 168
Chapman Jr., General Leonard F. 183
Chicago, USS 241
Chemical warfare 12, 220
Cheu Hoi rehabilitation scheme 113
Chiang Kai-shek 16, 22
China 13, 15, 16, 18, 19, 22, 23, 32, 46, 68, 69, 70, 73, 75, 93, 133, 151, 201, 202, 203, 231, 240, 241, 242
Chu Lai 106, 136, 209
Chu Pong massif 116, 117, 118, 123, 124, 125
Civilian Irregular Defense Group (CIDG) 155, 158, 160, 161, 164, 172, 180, 186, 188, 225, 226, 227
Clear-and-secure missions 136, 137
Clifford, Clark 92
Cogny, General René 29
Cold War 69, 109
Constellation, USS 53, 68, 238
Con Thien 139, 153, 173, 206
Coral Sea, USS 156, 238

Corps Tactical Zones 99
Curtiss C-46 Commando twin-engined transport 34
Cushman, Jr., Lieutenant General Robert E. 139, 176, 177, 178, 188, 193, 218

D

Da Nang 50, 76, 94, 95, 96, 134, 136, 209, 212, 213, 228, 248
Dai Do, Battle of 225
Dak To, Battle of 146, 153, 155, 157, 158, 160, 161, 162, 163, 165, 168, 169, 173, 237
Davidson, Major General Phillip B. 194, 209
Deane, Brigadier General John R. 157, 159, 160
De Havilland Canada CV-2B Caribou 140, 172
De Lattre de Tassigny, General Jean-Marie 23, 24, 26
De Lattre Line 23, 25, 26, 27, 28
Department of Defense, US 46, 47, 49, 83, 93, 109, 113, 131, 134, 196, 205, 209, 224, 231, 237, 242
Department of State, US 45, 46, 54, 59, 82, 129
Diem, Ngo Dinh 31, 33, 34, 35, 36, 37, 38, 39, 41, 43, 44, 45, 46, 47, 48, 60, 61, 231
Dien Bien Phu, Battle of 28, 29, 31, 32, 139, 169, 182, 183, 223
DMZ (17th parallel De-Militarized Zone) 33, 37, 50, 66, 67, 83, 86, 92, 97, 99, 105, 139, 144, 153, 160, 172, 173, 177, 178, 206, 213, 224, 225, 230, 236, 238, 242
Douglas A-1 Skyraider 68, 77, 89, 111, 120, 128, 130, 156, 164
Douglas A-4 Skyhawk 66, 67, 90, 134, 163, 165, 189, 220, 222
Douglas AC-47 Dragon Ship (Spooky) 157, 166
Douglas B-26 Invader 68
Douglas B-66 Destroyer 74, 92
Douglas C-74 Globemaster 135
Drang river (see Ia Drang)
Duan, Le 36, 201, 202

E

Eisenhower, Dwight D. 33, 36, 38
English, Brigadier General Lowell 178
Enterprise, USS 67

F
Fairchild C-123 Provider 140, 226, 227
Felt, Admiral Harry D. 45
First Indo-China War (1946–54) 8, 10, 17, 20, 22, 23, 24, 25, 26, 27, 28, 29, 30, 31, 32, 202
First World War (1914–18) 13, 222
Ford, Gerald 246, 249
Foreign Assistance Act, 1974 246
Forward air control aircraft (FACS) 50, 51, 184
Forward Command Committee 62
'Freedom Train' 239, 244
French in Vietnam 10, 13, 15, 16, 17, 18, 20, 21, 22, 23, 24, 25, 29, 32, 169, 182, 183
French 1st and 2nd Parachute Battalions 28
French Far East Expeditionary Corps 18
French Foreign Legion 19, 22, 23
French Union 18, 19, 21, 22

G
Galveston, USS 106
Gavin, Lieutentant General James M. 110
Geneva Accords 31, 32, 33, 50
Germany 13, 69, 133, 222
Gia Long, Emperor 13
Giap, Vo Nguyen 14, 18, 20, 21, 22, 23, 24, 25, 26, 27, 28, 169, 201, 202, 203
Gracey, Major General D. 16
Greater East Asia Co-Prosperity Sphere, Japanese 15
Grumman A-6 Intruder 83, 241
Grumman F8F Bearcat 11
Gulf of Tonkin Resolution (South-East Asia Resolution) 48, 53, 70

H
H52 tank 136
Haiphong 16, 20, 72, 75, 79, 84, 91, 93, 237, 239, 241, 242, 244, 245
Hancock, USS 238
Hanoi 15, 16, 20, 23, 29, 66, 72, 79, 84, 91, 93, 130, 161, 199, 202, 212, 229, 230, 237, 239, 242, 244, 245, 247
Harkins, General Paul D. 44, 45, 58
'Hearts and minds' campaign 47, 113, 142, 175
High National Council (HNC), South Vietnam 57, 58, 59
Hill Fights 139, 158, 160, 162, 163, 164, 165, 166, 168, 176, 178, 179
Hobart, HMAS 98

Ho Chi Minh 13, 14, 15, 16, 17, 18, 20, 33, 37, 46, 92, 202, 212, 231
Ho Chi Minh Campaign 248
Ho Chi Minh Trail 37, 56, 75, 94, 97, 105, 117, 142, 144, 155, 169, 172, 177, 178, 182, 204, 205, 224, 225, 232, 233, 242
Hoa Binh, Battle of 26
House, Rear Admiral William Hiram 145
Howze Board 111, 113
Hue, Battle of 138, 203, 209, 212, 213, 214, 215, 217, 218, 219, 220, 221, 222, 223, 229, 248
Hughes OH-6 Cayuse helicopter 115, 118
Humphrey, Vice President Hubert H. 198, 231
Huong, Tran Van 58, 60
Hutton, Brigadier General Carl I. 110

I
Ia Drang, Battle of 117–129
Ia Drang river 108, 114, 116, 124, 136, 169
Information Agency Library, US 60
International Control Commission 49
'Iron Hand' defence-suppression role 88, 89
Iron Triangle 137, 140, 141
Iwo Jima, USS 107

J
Japan 13, 14, 15, 16, 28, 133
Jennings County, USS 134
Johnson, General Harold K. 183
Johnson, Lyndon B. 11, 38, 47, 48, 53, 54, 55, 56, 57, 59, 65, 66, 67, 70, 71, 73, 75, 79, 83, 89, 91, 92, 93, 96, 97, 98, 99, 100, 102, 103, 104, 132, 150, 151, 152, 153, 195, 196, 197, 199, 221, 222, 224, 225, 231, 236

K
Kalashnikov AK-47 assault rifle 204
Karsh, Brigadier General Frederick J. 96
Kennedy, John F. 11 38, 39, 46, 47, 48, 231
Kham Duc, Battle of 225, 226, 227
Khanh, Major General Nguyen 47, 56, 57, 58, 59, 60, 68
Khe Sanh, Battle of 138, 139, 169, 170–193, 194, 196, 203, 206, 207, 210, 223, 225
Khmer Rouge 233
Khrushchev, Nikita 38
Kinnard, Major General H.W.O 115
Kissinger, Dr. Henry 237, 239, 240, 241, 245
Kitty Hawk, USS 238
Korean War (1950–53) 32, 38, 93, 109, 122, 133, 139, 150, 202, 222

Kosygin, Alexei 66
Ky, Nguyen Cao 58, 59, 101, 153, 203, 231

L
Lang Son 22
Lanigan, Colonel John P. 176
Laos 8, 9, 10, 12, 13, 18, 22, 28, 31, 32, 37, 38, 46, 56, 57, 67, 73, 81, 88, 93, 94, 97, 98, 99, 105, 129, 132, 133, 144, 151, 155, 168, 169, 171, 172, 177, 178, 181, 182, 188, 190, 192, 205, 224, 232, 233, 237, 249
League for the Independence of Vietnam (see Viet Minh)
Leclerc de Hauteclocque, General Philippe 19, 20
Livsey, Colonel William J. 157, 159, 162
Loan, General Nguyen Ngoc 212
Loc Ninh 228, 237, 248
Lockheed AC-130 167
Lockheed C-130 Hercules 94, 162, 189, 163, 171, 184, 226, 227, 232
Lockheed P2V Neptune 144
Lockheed P-3A Orion 143
Lodge, Henry Cabot 47, 103
Long Beach, USS 241
LORAN (Long-range Air Navigation) system 184
Lownds, Colonel David E. 176, 178, 184, 187, 188, 190, 193
LZ (Landing Zones) Albany 124, 126, 128, 129
LZ Columbus 124, 128
LZ Crooks 129
LZ Victor 121, 123
LZ X-Ray 118, 120, 121,123, 124, 128, 129

M
M14 rifle 108
M16 rifle 122, 148
M18A1 Claymore anti-personnel mine 137
M48 tank 102
M50 Ontos light armoured vehicle 189
M50 Ontos self-propelled 106-mm recoilless rifle 140
M60 machine gun 118, 122, 142, 145, 159, 208
M79 grenade launcher 118
M101 howitzer 178
M110 howitzer 230
M113 armoured personnel carrier 57, 63, 152, 182
McChristian, Major General Joseph A. 197
McConnell, General John P. 83
McDade, Lieutenant Colonel Robert 124, 126, 128
McDonald, Admiral David 89
McDonnell Douglas F-4 Phantom II 83, 85, 90, 92, 137, 221, 238, 241, 242
McNamara, Robert S. 50, 53, 70, 71, 75, 89, 91, 92, 98, 103, 104, 111, 113, 151, 231
Maddox, USS 48, 50, 51, 53

INDEX

Malayan Emergency (1948–60) 38, 41
Man, General Chu Nuy 114, 117
Mao Khe, Battle of 24
Mao Zedong 22, 201
March North land campaign 56
Marm, Second Lieutenant Walter J. 119, 122
Martin B-57 twin-jet bomber 68
Martin P-5 Marlin 144
Martin, Graham 81, 249
Maxim machine gun 124
Media, effect of US (on war) 45, 54, 140, 150, 151, 152, 198, 222
Medical Civic Action Program (MEDCAP) 62
Mekong river 42, 47, 64, 99, 144, 145, 146
Mendès- France, Pierre 31
Midway, USS 238
Mikoyan-Guryevich 83, 91
  MiG-15 Fagot 76, 85
  MiG-17 Fresco 85, 242, 243
  MiG-19 Farmer 86, 90
  MiG-21 Fishbed 86, 90, 242, 243
MiGCAP role 89
Military Assistance and Advisory Group (MAAG), see Military Assistance Command Vietnam (MACV)
Military Assistance Command Vietnam (MACV) 32, 44, 49, 54, 58, 80, 81, 94, 97, 99, 129, 135, 144, 145, 153, 159, 160, 168, 170, 172, 174, 177, 182, 186, 187, 192, 193, 194, 197, 207, 208, 209, 210, 212, 214, 216, 217, 219, 229, 230, 231
Minh, Lieutenant General Duong Van 47, 249
Missiles
  AGM-45 Shrike anti-radiation missile 88, 89
  AIM-4 Falcon missile 83
  AIM-7 Sparrow medium-range missile 83
  AIM-9 Sidewinder short-range missile 83
  HAWK surface-to-air missile 95
  Katyusha surface-to-surface artillery rocket 29
  SA-2 SAM 'Guideline' missile 70, 78, 84, 88, 89, 90, 93
  Zuni air-to-surface unguided rockets 145
Momyer, General William 81, 139, 183
Montagnards 41, 53, 153, 155, 171, 179, 180, 186, 187, 188. 227
Moore, Lieutenant Colonel H.G. 117, 118, 119, 120, 121, 122, 123, 124
Morrison, Admiral George Stephen 51
Mountbatten, Admiral Lord Louis 16
My Lai massacre 233

N
Na San, Battle of 19
Nam Bo Regional Command 62
National Front for the Liberation of South Vietnam (NLF) see Viet Cong

National Security Agency/Central Security Service (NSA/CSS) 48
Navarre, General Henri 28
Nghia Lo 26, 27
Ngok Tavak 226
Nguyen Hue Offensive (Easter Offensive) 1972 235, 236
Nguyen Lords 13
Nhu, Ngo Dinh 36, 41, 46
Nixon, Richard M. 225, 231, 232, 233, 237, 238, 239, 240, 241, 242, 244, 245, 246
North American F-100 Super Sabre 85, 155
North American T-28 94
North American Rockford OV-10 Bronco 145, 223, 226
North Atlantic Treaty Organization (NATO) 17, 34
Northrop F-5A Freedom Fighter 166

O
Office of Strategic Services (OSS) 14, 15
Operations/Campaigns
  34A 48
  Attleboro 138
  Attleboro II 143
  Baker 145
  Barrel Roll 57, 67
  Barrier Reef 146
  Bolling 149
  Bolo 90
  Bullet Shot 238
  Castor 28
  Cedar Falls 96, 138, 140, 141, 197
  Constant Guard 238
  Crazy Horse 143
  Duck Hook 240
  Fairfax 139
  Flaming Dart 1 and 11 67, 70
  Francis Marion 156
  Frequent Wind 12, 249
  Game Warden 132, 146
  Giant Slingshot 146
  Greeley 155, 157, 160
  Helping Hand 58
  Igloo White 182, 184
  Irving 141
  Junction City 137, 138, 141, 197
  Lea 21
  Linebacker 235, 236, 241, 242, 243, 244
  Linebacker II 245
  Lorraine, 27
  MacArthur 155, 161, 162
  Market Time 143, 144, 146
  Masher (Operation White Wing) 140
  Menu 232

Muscle Shoals 182
Neutralize 173, 206
Niagara 171, 182
Niagara II 184, 185
No Name 133
Pegasus 171, 191, 192, 193
Pershing 145
Pocket Money 241, 242
Rolling Thunder 66–93, 94, 98, 133, 185, 200, 201, 204, 236, 240, 244
Scotland 170, 191
Sealords (South-East Asia Lake, Ocean, River and Delta Strategy) 143, 144, 145, 146
Starlite 106, 108
Tran Hung Dao I 146
White Wing 108
Workhorse 142

P
P-4-class torpedo boat 51
Paris Peace Accords, 1973 12, 245, 246, 247
Pathet Lao 38, 245, 247
Peers, Major General William R. 156, 157
Perth, HMAS 98
Phuoc Long 206, 247
Piasecki H-21 'Flying Banana' helicopter 32
Plei Me Special Forces Camp 115, 117, 118, 125
Pleiku 67, 70, 94, 108, 115, 126, 156, 161, 247, 248
Provincial Health Assistance Program (PHAP) 54
Pueblo, USS 224

Q
Quang Tri 138, 169, 170, 173, 177, 206, 225, 240
Quat, Phan Huy 68, 101
Qui Nhon 67, 70, 94, 194, 209

R
Ranger, USS 163
Red river 22, 23, 25, 27, 90
Republic F-105 Thunderchief (Wild Weasel) 72, 75, 78, 85, 88, 89, 90, 238
Riverine Assault Force 145 146
Roosevelt, Franklin D. 15, 17
Rosson, Major General William B. 138, 168
Route Package One 83, 93
Royal Australian Regiment 103, 113, 114, 115, 117, 152
Royal New Zealand Artillery 103, 114
Rural Community Development Program 39, 41
Rusk, Dean 59, 92, 151

S
Saigon 9, 12, 16, 21, 38, 47, 60, 66, 68, 99, 102, 103, 114, 137, 138, 139, 140, 144, 147, 156, 157, 160, 169,

170, 194, 196, 203, 208, 209, 210, 211, 212, 223, 224, 225, 228, 229, 231, 237, 248, 249
Salan, General Raoul 26, 27, 28
Saratoga, USS 23
Schumacher, Lieutenant Colonel David J. 162, 163, 164
Schweiter, Brigadier General Leo H. 160, 162, 166
Seaman, Lieutenant General Jonathan 138
Search-and-destroy missions 135, 136, 137, 138, 148, 149, 150, 155
Search-and-rescue (SAR) helicopters 89
Second World War (1939–45) 8, 9, 13, 17, 69, 93, 113, 132, 133, 139, 222
Sharp, Admiral Ulysses S. Grant 49, 95, 99, 183
Sihanouk, Norodom 129, 232
Sikorsky CH-34 179
Sikorsky CH-53 Sea Stallion 177
Sikorsky H-34 Choctaw helicopter 103
'Sky-Cavalry' platoon (see US Army 173rd Airborne Brigade)
South-East Asia Treaty Organization (SEATO) 34, 98
South Vietnamese Military Revolutionary Council 47
South Vietnamese Ranger Battalions 64
Strategic Air Command 83, 99
Strategic Arms Limitation Treaty 237
Strategic Hamlet Program 39, 41, 40, 42, 43
Sutherland, William H. 81
Suu, Phan Khac 58
Swift-type riverine patrol craft 143, 145, 146

T
Tan, Major General Le Trong 62
Tau Nguyen campaign 115
Taylor, Maxwell D. 54, 55, 56, 57, 58, 59, 65, 66, 95, 98, 103, 114
Tay Ninh 138, 141, 146, 228
Tet Offensive 91, 144, 168, 181, 186, 194–231
Tet Truce 66, 182, 194, 213
Thai air bases 73, 232
Thailand 81, 146, 232
Thanh, General Nguyen Chi 62, 161, 201, 202, 203, 204
Thi, Major General Nguyen Chanh 106
Thieu, General Nguyen Van 101, 153, 195, 203, 209, 212, 230, 231, 244, 245, 246, 247, 248, 249
Tho, Le Duc 201, 202, 240, 245
Throckmorton, General John 95
Ticonderoga, USS 51, 53
Tjeld-class fast-attack craft 49
Tolson, Colonel John J. 110, 114, 192, 218
Tonkin 18, 20, 23, 73, 74, 238
Tonkin Incident, Gulf of 48–65, 143
Tra, General Tran Van 204
Trinh, Nguyen Duy 202

Trinh Lords 13
Truman, Harry S. 17, 32, 38
Truong, Lieutenant General Ngo Quang 214
Tucumcari, USS 143
Tully, Lieutenant Colonel R.B. 123, 124
'Tunnel rats' 141
Turner Joy, USS 48, 51

U
United Nations Organization (UNO) 17
USAAF 69
USAF 12, 68, 69, 73, 74, 77, 78, 79, 80, 81, 82, 83, 88, 89, 90, 91, 93, 99, 109, 110, 118, 120, 128, 144, 146, 153, 183, 185, 189, 227, 238, 243, 244
  2nd Air Division (later the 7th Air Force) 68, 80, 81, 99
  7th Air Force 139, 182, 184, 236, 242
  13th Air Force 80
US Army 136, 153, 171
  8th Airborne Battalion 42
  173rd Airborne Brigade 102, 106, 110, 114, 120, 121, 138, 141, 146, 149, 155, 157, 159, 160, 161, 162, 168, 174, 207
  101st Airborne Division 114, 138
  20th Artillery 118
  21st Artillery 118, 120, 122
  1st Cavalry Division (Airmobile) 104, 108, 138, 139, 140, 141, 160, 162, 191, 192, 193, 218
  5th Cavalry 119, 120, 121, 122, 123, 124, 126, 127, 128
  7th Cavalry 117, 119, 120, 121, 122, 123, 124, 126, 128, 193, 218, 220
  9th Cavalry Regiment 116
  12th Cavalry Regiment 161, 218, 219, 220
  I Field Force 9
  II Field Force 9, 138, 194
  1st Infantry Division 138, 140, 154, 173, 206
  4th Infantry Division 117, 138, 155, 156, 157, 161, 162, 168, 174, 207
  8th Infantry Regiment 161, 163
  12th Infantry Regiment 168
  25th Infantry Division 138, 156
  26th Infantry Regiment 14
  42nd Infantry Regiment 165
  199th Light Infantry Brigade 138
  716th Military Police Battalion 211
  503rd Parachute Infantry Regiment 114, 157, 158, 159, 160, 161, 162, 163, 164, 166, 168
  Americal Division 138, 227
  Corps of Engineers 147
  Green Berets 38, 172, 186, 188
  Ordnance, Transportation and Signal Corps 110
  Special Forces Group 154, 155, 172, 188, 191, 228
US Coast Guard 100, 143

US Embassy, Saigon 45, 211, 212
USMC 73, 74, 76, 77, 83, 88, 91, 93, 95, 96, 98, 100, 106, 107, 108, 134, 135, 138, 139, 153, 167, 168, 169, 171, 172, 174, 176, 177, 180, 181, 182, 183, 184, 185, 187, 189, 190, 193, 206, 207, 208, 213, 215, 228
  11th Engineer Battalion 192
  III Marine Amphibious Force 96, 99, 106, 138, 139, 170
  9th Marine Amphibious Brigade 106
  9th Marine Expeditionary Brigade 96, 135
  1st Marine Regiment 192, 193, 200, 215, 216, 217
  3rd Marine Regiment 176, 178, 182, 192
  4th Marine Battalion 64, 130, 136
  5th Marine Regiment 133, 217, 219, 220
  9th Marine Regiment 176, 178, 181, 190
  26th Marine Regiment 176, 178, 180, 190, 191, 193
  Shu-Fly helicopter task unit 96
US Navy 12, 53, 66, 68, 73, 74, 77, 78, 83, 88, 89, 90, 91, 93, 99, 143, 144, 145, 153, 183, 213
  Cruiser-Destroyer Flotilla Seven 144
  Helicopter Attack (Light) Squadron Three (HAL-3) 134, 145
  Naval Forces, Vietnam 144
  Seabees (Construction Battalions) 147
  SEALs 145
  7th Fleet 99, 143, 238
  Task Force 77 74, 77, 80, 96, 236, 238, 242
  Task Force 115, Coastal Surveillance Force 143, 145, 146
  Task Force 116 (River Patrol Force) 145, 146
  Task Force 194 146
  Task Force 'Oregon' 138
USSR 9, 13, 15, 17, 23, 32, 38, 46, 68, 69, 70, 73, 75, 76, 82, 83, 85, 86, 88, 93, 133, 202, 231, 237, 240, 241

V
Vanderpool, Colonel Jay D. 110
Vernon County, USS 106
Vertol (Piasecki) H-21 Shawnee helicopter 42, 114
Vichy French 13, 15
Viet Cong (NLF) 31, 32, 36, 37, 39, 40, 42, 43, 44, 54, 59, 60, 61, 62, 63, 64, 65, 66, 67, 68, 76, 97, 100, 105, 106, 107, 108, 113, 114, 129, 130, 131, 132, 135, 136, 137, 138, 139, 140, 141, 144, 145, 146, 148, 154, 155, 157, 169, 173, 186, 196, 197, 198, 199, 201, 203, 204, 205, 208, 209, 211, 212, 213, 217, 220, 221, 225, 226, 227, 228, 229, 231, 232, 233, 244
Viet Minh 10, 13, 14, 15, 16, 17, 18, 19, 20, 21, 22, 23, 24, 25, 26, 27, 28, 29, 31, 33, 37, 169
Vietnam People's Army (VPA) 32
Vietnamese National Army (VNA) 18, 22
Vinh Yen, Battle of 23, 24
Vought A-7A Corsair II 87, 156
Vought F-8 Crusader 68, 83, 85

INDEX

W
Walt, General Lewis W. 135, 138, 139, 141, 174, 176
War Zone C Vietnam 138, 141
Ward, Rear Admiral Norvell G. 143
Western Highlands 172
Westmoreland, William C. 132, 134, 135, 136, 137,
 138, 139, 141, 142, 145, 146, 148, 151, 152, 153, 168,
 169, 173, 174, 176, 177, 178, 182, 183, 184, 185, 186,
 188, 192, 193, 194, 195, 196, 197, 198, 199, 206, 208,
 209, 210, 212, 222, 223, 224, 225, 226
Weyand, Lieutenant General Fred C. 194, 195, 208
Wheeler, General Earle G. 151, 195, 224

Z
Zumwalt, Jr., Rear Admiral Elmo R. 144, 145